ON JUSTICE

ON JUSTICE

ΠΕΡΙ ΔΙΚΑΙΟΥ

BY

J. R. LUCAS

Fellow of Merton College, Oxford

CLARENDON PRESS · OXFORD
1980

Oxford University Press, Walton Street, Oxford OX2 6DP

OXFORD   LONDON   GLASGOW
NEW YORK   TORONTO   MELBOURNE   WELLINGTON
NAIROBI   DAS ES SALAAM   CAPE TOWN
KUALA LUMPUR   SINGAPORE   JAKARTA   HONG KONG   TOKYO
DELHI   BOMBAY   CALCUTTA   MADRAS   KARACHI

Published in the United States
by Oxford University Press,
New York

British Library Cataloguing in Publication Data

Lucas, John Randolph
  On justice.
  1. Justice (Philosophy)
  I. Title
  179   B105.J/   79-41138

ISBN 0-19-824598-X

Filmset by Eta Services (Typesetters) Ltd., Beccles, Suffolk
Printed in Great Britain by Billings & Sons Ltd., Guildford, Worcester, London and Oxford

ΠΕΡΙ ΔΙΚΑΙΟΥ

to

R. H. P. and H. S. P.

CONTENTS

1

UNFAIR

Remota justitia, asked St. Augustine,[1] *quid sunt regna nisi magna latrocinia*? States without justice are but robber bands enlarged; and earlier Plato had taken it as the mark of the just society that it should be free from dissension. Justice is the bond of society, and without it, according to Hume,[2] no association of human individuals could subsist. Most thinkers, however, have sought the key to the concept of justice elsewhere, and have construed it in terms of rules or utility or equality; or, more recently, have been concerned simply to observe and record the different usages of the word 'just', without attempting to articulate an account of why the same word should be used in so many different contexts. Justice has in consequence been much misunderstood, and in practice much neglected. This is why our society has become increasingly divided, and why its members have become more and more alienated from its authority. Authority now is seen as something external, a force to be reckoned with, not a guidance to be reasoned with and accepted. It is a pity. We have been pursuing the wrong political goals—productivity, efficiency, equality—and have neglected the cardinal political virtue of justice, which, together with liberty, is the condition under which I and every man can identify with society, feel at one with it, and accept its rulings as my own. It is therefore justice that we must seek.

We can go some way by linguistic analysis. We use the word 'just' in many ways. In some the meaning is clearly different, as when I say 'I have just arrived' or 'he did not just borrow it, he stole it', or when printers talk of justified margins to a page. In many others, although we are aware of differences, and acknowledge that a just man, a just war, a just decision, a just price, a just law, a just apportionment, a just society and a just procedure are different, and do not simply share some simple unanalysable

---

[1] *City of God, IV*, iv.
[2] David Hume, *An Enquiry Concerning the Principles of Morals*, ed. L. A. Selby-Bigge, Oxford, 1902, §165, p. 206.

quality, we none the less reckon that the word 'just' is being used in the same sense. Although we distinguish different sorts of justice, they are different applications of the same underlying concept.[3] What exactly the important differences and similarities are is a difficult question, and we must be cautious in making too much of linguistic usage[4]—the English word 'just' does not have exactly the same use as the Greek word |δίκαιον|or the Hebrew *tsadiq*—and often in modern English the word 'fair' is more naturally used with a slightly less formal connotation: the word 'just' occurs more often in legal contexts and the courts of law, the word 'fair' in games and families and in other informal situations. But the uses shade into one another—we speak of a fair trial in the courts and of a father or a schoolmaster being just—and in this book, therefore, we shall not make any distinction between the pairs of words, 'just' and 'unjust', 'fair' and 'unfair'. If we start, then, by considering how these words are used, we can see that men, actions, decisions, laws, economic arrangements, legal procedures, games and social systems can be described as being just or unjust, and that justice is not the same as expediency, prudence, equality, liberty, generosity, friendliness, mercy or good will, and that since a decision can be said to be both just—in that it was reached by due process by an impartial judge who applied the relevant law—and unjust—in that the law itself was unjust or that the judge was precluded from taking certain relevant factors into consideration—justice itself must be a complicated concept.[5] But if we are to go further, and discover not only the uses of the word but the underlying resemblances in virtue of which the uses form a single family, we need to consider not merely the applications of the word but the arguments we use when issues of justice arise. We cannot know what justice is until we also know why it is a good thing, and by listening to its praises being sung can come to realise what it must be in order to be argued for in exactly those terms.

---

[3] Cf. J. Buridan, *Quaestiones super decem libros Ethicorum Aristotelis ad Nicomachum, V, Quaes. 7*, Paris, 1513, p. 98b. *Justitia distributiva et commutativa non sunt diversae species justitiae, sed sunt diversi modi ejusdem virtutis; Aristoteles autem aliquando solet modos tales diversos vocare species, utendo nomine speciei large.* Quoted by Giorgio del Vecchio, *Justice*, tr. Lady Guthrie, ed. A. H. Campbell, Edinburgh, 1952, p. 57.

[4] Renford Bambrough, *New Essays on Plato and Aristotle*, London, 1965, pp. 159 ff., draws attention to these pitfalls, but defends the programme of linguistic analysis.

[5] See further below, Ch. 8, pp. 168–9, and Ch. 5, p. 109.

According to the Greeks, justice was an ἀλλότριον ἀγαθόν, the other chap's good. Certainly, questions of justice do not arise except where other people are involved and except where some sorts of good, positive or negative, are in issue. Robinson Crusoe had no opportunity of practising justice or injustice until Man Friday came on the scene. He could be resourceful, brave and temperate on his own, but justice, like compassion and mercy, is an essentially other-regarding virtue. Only when two or more are gathered together, can either exercise justice towards the other, and only then can their arrangements and transactions be acknowledged as just or stigmatized as unjust. But justice is not the only other-regarding virtue. It differs from benevolence, generosity, gratitude, friendship and compassion. I can show forth benevolence by doing good to others without regard to what they have done or what they deserve, whereas an act of justice has to be justified by some argument bearing on the person to whom it is done. "I wanted to do him a good turn", "I wanted to make him happy", are reason enough for the benevolent man, but would not establish that his action was in any way just. Generosity is normally rather more specific in its object, but differs from justice in that if I chose not to be generous, you would not have any complaint, whereas if I were unjust you would. My reasons for being generous are less coercive than those requiring me to be just. Generosity is based on first-personal reasons—I have my reasons for being generous, and these make my actions intelligible, and so long as they move me, I shall be generous: but if they do not move me, if I choose not to adopt them or make them the basis of action, no further argument is in place; whereas arguments of justice, by contrast, can be put into every person, second and third as well as first, and urged unremittingly on me, however disinclined I am to heed them, and can be reinforced, if necessary, by the threat of sanctions, and the strong arm of the law.[6] Justice is what we can insist on. Unwilling justice is still justice, whereas unwilling generosity is scarcely a virtue at all. It is the same with gratitude. It is closer to justice in that the only reason for being grateful to a man is some good conferred by him on oneself or on someone with whom one identifies; but like generosity, it needs to be whole-hearted and autonomous, not constrained by force of argument or moral

[6] See further below, Ch. 3, pp. 37–8.

pressure. Justice is, contrary to Plato's account of it, a much less whole-heated and inward virtue. I can grudgingly concede that I ought to pay damages to some one or ought to remember a tiresome relative in my will, and although it might be better that I should do these things gladly, justice is satisfied if I do them at all.

Justice is also to be distinguished from other political ideals. It is not liberty, it is not equality, it is not fraternity. Justice is not liberty or freedom, because liberty and freedom are concerned with the question who shall take the decisions, whereas justice is concerned with how decisions shall be taken, in what frame of mind and with what result. Justice is not equality, because equality is concerned only with results, and not how they are arrived at, and equality is concerned only that people should be treated the same, whereas justice is concerned to consider each individual case on its own merits, treating, if necessary, different people differently, as when we punish the guilty and let the innocent go free. Justice is not fraternity, because fraternity is a warm virtue, concerned with fellow-feeling, whereas justice is a cold virtue which can be manifested without feeling, and is concerned to emphasize that the other chap is not merely a human being like myself, but a separate individual, with his own point of view and own interests that are distinct from mine.

The distinctness of the other chap becomes important when there is conflict, and one man can get his own way only at someone else's expense. It is only when somebody's rights and interests are in jeopardy that the unity and coherence of society is under strain, and it is only then that issues of justice arise. That is to say, it is when *in*justice is in danger of being done that we become agitated. Injustice wears the trousers. And therefore we should follow the example of Aristotle, and adopt a negative approach, discovering what justice is by considering on what occasions we protest at injustice or unfairness.[7] If we focus our attention only on the

---

[7] *Nicomachean Ethics*, V, 1, 5–12; 1129a 17–1129b 12. See also Edmund N. Kahn, *The Sense of Injustice*, New York, 1949, p. 13; A. M. Honoré, "Social Justice", *McGill Law Journal*, 78, 1962, p. 78; reprinted in R. S. Summers (ed.), *Essays in Legal Philosophy*, Oxford, 1968, p. 62; A. D. Woozley, "Injustice", *American Philosophical Quarterly*, Monograph No. 7, Oxford, 1973, pp. 109–10; J. S. Mill, *Utilitarianism*, Everyman edn., p. 39, "for justice, like many other moral attributes, is best defined by its opposites"; F. A. Hayek, *Law, Liberty and Legislation*, II, London, 1976, p. 36. In an extensive note (pp. 162–4) Hayek traces back the insight to Heraclitus, and cites many other thinkers. He says (p. 36) that it is "a feature that

positive virtue, we see it as something flat, without depth or dynamic vigour. We have already seen that justice is a cold virtue. But injustice is something we soon get steamed up about. Although it is not enough to be just or fair, and people and institutions need to be something more if they are to engage our allegiance and affection, nevertheless injustice or unfairness is a fundamental defect; a man who is unfair is one we want to have as little to do with as possible, and we have little loyalty to any institution or arrangement which we regard as basically unjust. Not only are our emotions a good guide to our intellectual discriminations, but they reveal in this case the underlying thrust of the concept. If I talk only about justice, I am in danger of relapsing into platitudes: it is when I get hot under the collar about some specific piece of unfairness, that my eloquence has an edge to it, and I really know what is getting my goat. And, as we are now beginning to see, the contrast between the mild favour I feel towards fairness and the intense fury unfairness arouses in my breast is symptomatic of a basic asymmetry between justice and injustice which, I shall argue, is crucial to the part they play in our conceptual structure.

'Unfair' is a word of protest. We use it to protest, either on our own behalf or on that of others, when someone has been *done down*. Both words 'done' and 'down' are important. We cannot entertain the complaint of unfairness, unless there was some agency involved, human or divine.[8] If the dice come down double one, and I have to move from Park Lane to Mayfair, I may complain of my hard luck but I cannot say that I have been treated unfairly. Equally with the changes and chances of our ordinary life, we cannot complain of unfairness, unless they are due to human actions or we attribute them to God's almighty hand. Moreover, it

---

has, again and again, as though it were a new discovery, been pointed out, but scarcely ever systematically investigated". It is the aim of this work to remedy that deficiency.

[8] F. A. Hayek, in *Law, Legislation and Liberty*, II, London, 1976, p. 31, says "Strictly speaking, only human conduct can be called just or unjust. If we apply the terms to a state of affairs, they have meaning only in so far as we hold someone responsible for bringing it about." This is a little too stringent. Even if nobody is responsible for bringing it about, we may hold some people responsible for not amending or ameliorating it. We cannot simply non-suit a complaint against a system—e.g. the market economy—as being simply a category mistake, since, although nobody brought it about, it is subject to human control. In *Anarchy, State and Utopia*, Oxford, 1974, p. 237, Robert Nozick seems to be making the same point, which fails for the same reason. See further, Ch. 12.

is not enough merely to be the result of some action or actions: the result must have been foreseen or at least foreseeable by some of the agents involved. The victim of an accident can bewail his misfortune, but not complain of having been unfairly treated, unless one of the agents was negligent and failed to discharge his duty of care towards him, that is, unless somebody failed to manifest sufficient consideration of his, the victim's, interests. We need to shift our attention from the bare consequences of actions to the actions themselves. It has been one of our main difficulties in reaching a proper understanding of justice that we are dominated by a wrong view of public life. We think of it as a course of events, not as a system of activities. We consider states of affairs, not actions. Hence we focus on the end-result of activities and processes, and ignore the procedures whereby these results were reached. But with actions, what is done depends partly on the doing of it. Different actions may end in the same state of affairs, but are different none the less, and have very different significance for agents and participants. Once we recognise the fact that human beings are primarily agents, not patients, our whole perspective alters. We are concerned as much with what people do as with what gets done, and will be concerned not only with whether the outcome is just, but with whether the agents acted justly in doing what they did. Although other things—laws, particular decisions, general economic arrangements and particular payments—can rightly be described as just or unjust, these are derivative uses, deriving from the man in a just frame of mind and the laws he would enact, the decisions he would take, the economic arrangements he would approve of and the particular payments he would make. Justinian and Aquinas were right in characterizing justice as a certain state of mind.

It follows that justice is concerned with procedures as well as with outcomes, and that the rules of natural justice are properly so called. Rules, such as *audi alteram partem*—hear the other side of the case before making up your mind—and that nobody shall be judge in his own cause, manifest to any potentially disappointed party our reluctance to decide against him, and our determination that any adverse decision shall be, and shall be seen by him to be, taken only for reasons which are relevant to his case and whose cogency he can appreciate. By keeping to those rules of procedure we show ourselves dispassionately tender-minded towards each and every one concerned, so that nobody can feel slighted or disregarded or believe that he and his interests are of no account.

It follows also that justice is concerned not only with the consequences of actions but with their significance. Although causality is important for evaluating actions, meaning is more important still, and many perplexing features of justice in general and of punishment in particular become intelligible only when actions are construed as a species of communication, like language, and not merely as events within the nexus of cause and effect.[9]

When we do a man an injustice we do not merely hurt him or harm his interests, but add insult to injury. We are angry when we are hurt, but indignant when treated unjustly. We can be angry with enemies or rivals, but scarcely indignant. Indignation, which is the conceptually appropriate response to injustice, expresses, as its etymology shows, a sense of not being regarded as worthy of consideration. Injustice betokens an absence of respect, and manifests a lack of concern. It is important, therefore, not simply on account of its undesirable outcome but as a manifestation of an uncaring and unfavourable attitude of mind; and to understand it properly we have to construe it as an affront which belittles the worth of the man who suffers it.[10]

Not every affront is an injustice. Insult without injury is rudeness, not injustice. Words by themselves break no bones, and a man has to be done down by deeds before he can complain of being unfairly treated (although, of course, in our society deeds can be constituted by words alone). We talk about actions constituting a language, but it is a natural language in which significance often depends on consequences. Issues of justice arise when the consequences of what is done affect a man in a fairly substantial way. In this justice differs from friendship and compassion. These, too, are concerned with the other chap, but the concerns they enter into are of an intensely personal and somewhat intangible kind. Justice, by contrast is concerned with a special sort of good, which I shall call assignable good, or interest. Thus I can show compassion

[9] See further below, Ch. 4, pp. 72–3, and Ch. 6, pp. 131–6.
[10] A. D. Woozley, "Injustice", *American Philosophical Quarterly*, Monograph No. 7, Oxford, 1973, p. 122. See also Edmund N. Kahn, *The Sense of Injustice*, New York, 1949, pp. 17–18; Giorgio del Vecchio, *Justice*, Edinburgh, 1952, p. 85, "... every subject shall be recognised (by others) for what he is worth ..."; and H. S. Pritchard, "Human Dignity and Justice," *Ethics*, **82**, 1972, pp. 299–313.

simply by extending sympathy, but that would not be an exercise of justice, because sympathy is not generally seen as an assignable good. Nor am I unjust if I am untruthful, unless I gain some advantage for myself, or put someone else to some disadvantage, thereby. It is only where some one has an *interest* in a matter that justice has any *locus standi*. Interests are not simply what I happen to be interested in, but are rather what other people can assume I am interested in. They are third-personal and vicarious—what he can and should impute to the other chap, and the other chap to him, in deciding to act considerately. They lack the absolute authenticity of values avowed in the first person, but for that very reason, can be understood and taken into consideration by third parties without their having to have first-hand knowledge of what each person actually aspires to, and hence enable us all to adduce arguments of justice in defence of the interests of each.[11]

The word 'down' is also significant. It indicates that justice is neither a mean nor a sort of equality, as Aristotle thought,[12] but is essentially one-way in its concern, and is focussed on the individual.[13] There is an essential asymmetry in justice. Good things and bad things are not on a par.[14] Instead of construing it as a concern for the other chap's faring well, the ἀλλότριον ἀγαθόν of the Greeks, we should understand it, rather, as an ἀλλότριον μὴ κακόν, a concern for the other chap's not faring ill.[15] Contrary to the opinion of many, it not inherently unfair if someone has more than anybody else, but only if others are done out of their due. If we

[11] See further below, Ch. 2; and Ch. 3, pp. 69–70.

[12] *Nicomachean Ethics*, V, 1, 1, 1129a 3–5.

[13] See further below, Ch. 6, p. 123, Ch. 8, p. 163, Ch. 14, p. 223.

[14] See further below, Ch. 14, p. 235.

[15] Compare J. S. Mill, *Utilitarianism*, Everyman edn., Ch. V, p. 46, "Whether the injustice consists in depriving a person of a possession, or in breaking faith with him, or in treating him worse than he deserves or worse than other people who have no greater claims, in each case the supposition implies two things—a wrong done, and some assignable person who is wronged." Also William K. Frankena, "The Concept of Social Justice", in R. B. Brandt (ed.), *Social Justice*, Englewood Cliffs, N.J., 1962, p. 14, "it is unjust for society or the state to injure a citizen, to withhold a good from him, or to interfere with his liberty (except to prevent him from committing a crime, to punish him for committing one, or to procure the money and other means of carrying out its just functions), and that this is unjust even if society or the state deals similarly with all of its citizens. It seems to me also that a society is unjust if, by its actions, laws, and mores, it unnecessarily impoverishes the lives of its members materially, aesthetically, or otherwise, by holding them to a level below that which some members at least might well attain by their own efforts."

have it in our power to confer some good, say honour, which does not have to be conferred at the expense of anybody else, and where there are no other cases calling for comparable consideration by us, we do not think it unfair if we give a man more than he deserves. A pacifist may not like it if a wartime leader has a statue erected in his honour in a park, and the military historian may say that in fact he was not a very good general and does not deserve to be remembered with respect, but neither of them can say that it is unfair or unjust that he should be thus favourably treated. Again, if there is a burden, say military service, which is not imposed on some, either because they would not be any use—cripples—or because they are more use elsewhere—miners or agricultural workers—we do not complain that it is unfair, so long as we can be sure that the exceptions are based on good reasons. Nobody during the war suggested that paralytics or miners should be made to sleep in big cities, so that they could be in as great a danger of death as their brothers on active service. Other sentiments and obligations could arise from the differential distribution of burdens: people knitted woolly scarves for our brave soldiers, sailors and airmen, but not our agricultural workers, and it was reckoned that those working in the safety of civilian employment were under a peculiar obligation not to strike while their fellow citizens were in jeopardy on the high seas or at the front. But the bare fact of someone's not being as badly off as others is not in itself unfair. Another example comes from the criminal law, where again the alleviation of one man's burdens does not necessitate a corresponding increase of some other men's, and we do not use the word 'unfair' in cases where less is demanded than might have been. A rational exercise of mercy is not unfair. If a judge passes a light sentence, on the grounds that the criminal is filled with remorse and that other potential criminals will not be the less deterred on account of his leniency, then his sentence is not unfair, although to pass too severe a sentence would be unfair. That is, leniency is unfair only if either the judge is failing in his duty towards society at large or is favouring with mercy one criminal, but not others similarly culpable and similarly penitent. Thus, whereas too heavy a sentence is inherently unfair, too light a sentence is unfair only under certain conditions where the interests of others are in consequence not being given proper consideration.[16] A similar argument can be extracted from the individual's

[16] See further below, Ch. 6, pp. 147–8.

discharge of the multifarious obligations of ordinary life. I am unfair if I pay too little, but if I pay more than I need, then, although I might be described as being generous rather than fair, I should not normally or naturally be described as unfair. It is only if there is but a limited amount of cake to be distributed, or if I should spoil the market for others, or if by paying more in this case I shall arouse false expectations in others, that my paying more than I need could be criticized as unfair. Generosity in itself is not unjust.[17] Finally, we should consider the bearing of Aristotle's dictum that a man cannot be unfairly treated with his own consent.[18] There are cases where a man may waive his rights, and may arrange or agree to something that gives him less than might reasonably have been expected, but for that very reason cannot be regarded as unfair. Yet whereas I can by my own waiver make fair an assignment that gives me too little, I cannot similarly legitimate an assignment that gives me too much. These two assignments are equally unequal, and if fairness were merely a matter of equality, both would be equally unfair. But fairness is not symmetrical, and is not an Aristotelian mean between favouring a man's interests too little and favouring them too much. To favour them too little is unfair; to favour them too much is not in itself unfair, but only when it would involve others being unfairly done by. Although often, in view of the limited amount of goods available, or the conflicting interests of the different parties involved, justice requires that our award should be just right, not too little nor too much, justice is essentially concerned that our award should not be too little. It is not a simple limit, dividing out the spoils exactly, but rather the result of the application of some maximum principle, giving to each the most we reasonably can, and being more immediately infringed if we err on the side of less than if we err on the side of more. It is bad if anyone is needlessly done down: it is not necessarily bad if someone is gratuitously done up.

Even where due consideration has been given to the interests of

[17] A. D. Woozley, "Injustice", *American Philosophical Quarterly*, Monograph No. 7, Oxford, 1973, p. 111, argues the contrary. "A father does not have the duty to meet the needs of his neighbor's children which he has to meet the needs of his own; but if he does respond to the former, discrimination, if it leaves the needs of some but not others inadequately met, is unjust." This would seem to imply that a just man, unable to rescue all the starving refugee children in the world, would not adopt any, rather than adopt one and not others.

[18] *Nicomachean Ethics*, V, 9; 1136a 10 ff. See below, Ch. 12, pp. 211–12.

those involved, it does not follow that an adverse decision can be avoided. To decide for the plaintiff is to decide against the defendant, and vice versa. Hard decisions have to be taken. We cannot ensure that nobody will ever be hardly done by, but only that those who are being hardly done by are being hardly done by for reasons which even they must acknowledge as weighty. Although a man may be disappointed at a just decision, he should not be angry or indignant. It may run against his interests, and he may wish that it could have been otherwise, but he has to acknowledge the justice of it, and cannot feel that he is being treated without due consideration, or that the decision shows that society has no concern for him, or that he is as nothing in its eyes. Not only was there a manifest reluctance to reach an adverse decision, but it was overborne by reasons into which he can enter as well as any other man. It is because there are reasons into which he can enter, that he can be reconciled to the decision, even though it was adverse; and, as Plato observed, his propensity to anger and righteous indignation is assuaged by the decision's being rational, rather than antagonized by its being adverse.[19] These reasons have to be of a special kind. Not every reason for an action will reconcile those who suffer in consequence. A government may act not only arbitrarily out of caprice, but for many reasons which will make the actions intelligible, but not just. Some people have opposed justice to arbitrariness,[20] but, although arbitrary decisions are likely to be unjust, not all non-arbitrary decisions are therefore just. A decision taken for fear or favour is intelligible, but not one whose cogency a disappointed litigant could be expected to accept. A government may be guided by *raison d'état*, and act entirely rationally, but quite unjustly. It may be highly expedient to hand me over to a neighbouring power, to destroy my house, seize my goods, arrest me, hold me as a hostage, or execute me as a grim warning to others, but none of these actions is just, although all are highly rational. These reasons will not reconcile unfortunate me to my hard fate, because, although they show why the government acted as it did, they do not show that it had to—that there was no reasonable alternative to coming down on just me alone, or that due weight had been given to my interest in escaping this fate.

---

[19] *Republic* IV, 440c.
[20] *Report of the Committee on Administrative Tribunals*, 1957, Cmnd. 218, §29, p. 6.

Sacrifices cannot be called for merely because they are expedient, from the government's point of view, but only if they are inevitable. And even if sacrifices must be made, the individual may still protest that they should not all fall on him. Justice argues against our picking on one man rather than another. Where there are burdens to be borne, they should be laid on everyone, or on everyone capable of bearing them, or at least on the relatively many shoulders of those best able to bear them. Reasons of state, that is, should not bear immediately on adverse decision-making, but only through the medium of general laws, applicable not to one individual alone, but to all those falling within some general category.[21] The fact that it would be expedient to deprive one man of his liberty is not warrant enough for doing so; but if it is not only expedient but necessary for the safety of the State that people be called up, and there are general laws governing conscription, and these for good reason make young men of good health liable for National Service for a limited period, subject to relatively few and reasonable exemptions, then a person called to the colours can no longer complain that he is being unjustly treated. Although the reasons for his loss of liberty are, basically, ones extraneous to his particular case, there are compelling reasons why the burden of National Service should be imposed in general, and why he should be one of those on whom it is imposed in particular. A person who none the less maintains that he ought not to be called up, is reduced to arguing either that the country should not be adequately defended, or that others, rather than he, should bear all the burden of defence. And, at that stage, he, as a member of the community, will acknowledge that these alternatives are not really available, and that, therefore, the arguments for calling him up are inescapable. And then, acknowledging the force of these arguments, he will accept the decision, even though adverse to his own interests, as fair and reasonable all the same.

Much follows. Only those reasons are just that are both inescapable and "individualised". They must show why the decision could not but be taken, and why it had to be that particular man who was decided against. It is because they have to be inescapable that we lay the burden of proof in the criminal law on the prosecution. Many of our other procedural rules, most notably the rule *audi alteram partem*, hear the other side, are consequences of our

---

[21] See, more fully, Ch. 14, pp. 235—7.

reluctance to take adverse decisions and the need to make that reluctance manifest.[22] Again, justice, in contrast to expediency, enlightened self-interest and utility, which look to the future, is backward-looking, partly on account of the inner logic of rationality,[23] but chiefly because only what a man has done or already is constitutes a firm fact about him. Although it may be rational, because effective, to "punish" him for what it is expected he will do, it is unjust because until he has done it, he may always change his mind and not do it. If I am to be just, I must concern myself with what a man really has done or really is, not with what he will do or might be. There are exceptions, but they are more apparent than real. There are criminal offences, such as loitering with intent, which have some sort of future reference: and in a university entrance examination I should be unfair if I did not look to a candidate's promise as much as to his actual performance. But the futurity in these cases is subordinate to the past or the present: the future is "already present in its causes"; the main reference is essentially past or present. Only past deeds or present facts are sufficiently actual and unquestionable to provide an adequate basis for an adverse decision.[24]

Good reasons must individuate. They must be based on the circumstances of the case, and a decision can be impugned as unfair if either it is based on some factor that is not relevant or it fails to take into account some factor that is. We have a fairly restricted criterion of what should count as relevant circumstances, and what are irrelevant so far as the particular case in issue is concerned. We have a distinction between the intrinsic merits of the case, which alone should weigh in the scales of justice, and extrinsic considerations, of expediency or public policy, which might guide a government's decision-making, but which would not assuage any feelings of unfairness on the part of those who suffered. It is a difficult distinction to draw, and no hard and fast line can be laid down for all cases. Although the reasons on which a just decision is based have to be individualised reasons, they do not therefore have to exclude all general considerations. General considerations, e.g. of expediency or utility, can justify there being one general rule rather than another: what justice requires is that any such general considerations shall issue in rules that apply generally, and that

[22] See, more fully, Ch. 4.   [23] See, more fully, Ch. 3, pp. 61–3.
[24] See further below, Ch. 3, pp. 62–4.

their application in the individual case must be justified by reference to the facts of that case.

Different sorts of justice raise different problems about the sort
of reason that can justify an adverse decision. When we do justice
between litigants—Aristotle's diorthotic, or corrective, justice—
there is no problem of determining which individuals are involved,
but only of deciding whether the reasons urged are individualised
reasons, and, if so, what weight should be given to them: in
adjudication of rights, the sort of cases that are decided by the civil
courts, the parties are involved because it is their claims that
conflict, and not anybody else's; in criminal cases the accused is
involved, because it is he who is alleged to have done wrong; and if
he can show that it was not he, but someone else, who did the
wrong, then he is free. What is at issue is not why this particular
man should be singled out for adverse treatment, but whether the
reasons for meting out such treatment are sufficiently compelling.
In the criminal case he can, according to English law, be punished
only if he is proved to have committed the crime beyond reasonable
doubt: in the civil case the burden of proof is not laid so heavily on
the plaintiff, because that would be unfair to him, and the case is
decided on a balance of probabilities: but in each case there have to
be reasons—good reasons—why our reasonable reluctance to decide against anyone had to be overridden.

In other sorts of justice, where we are concerned with the
distribution of benefits or the imposition of burdens, the emphasis
is reversed. Instead of starting with the individuals who are parties
to the case and having to decide what weight should be given to the
individualised reasons urged on their behalf, we start with a
discussion of individualised reasons, and, having decided that, we
thereby decide which individuals should have benefits or burdens
apportioned to them. In each case the basis of apportionment will
be relevant facts about the individual. Benefits are distributed
according to desert, merit, need, entitlement or status: contributions are called for on the basis of ability, demerit, expected
subsequent benefit, agreement or status. Each of these bases is an
individualised reason of the right logical type: the problem is to
determine which ought actually to be adopted in given circumstances. This done, we can tell which are the individuals involved,
and what their portion ought to be.

Not only are extraneous considerations to be excluded, but also some very intimate ones. Men should be punished for what they have done, not for what they think or have in mind to do, and should not be required to make utterly frank and embarrassing disclosures. The privacy of intentions, as well as their futurity, gives us qualms at making them relevant in law to any great extent or in the absence of some overt act creating a presumption of intent. There must be some definite action that establishes at least a *prima facie* case against the accused—*loitering*—which he may then rebut or excuse by reference to his own intentions—"I was waiting for my girl-friend." There is a certain veil of privacy which distinguishes justice from more personal relations and morality proper. In the confessional and between close friends, *uberrima fides* is expected, but in treating you justly I do not enter into all your concerns, and should not seek to take into consideration all the secrets of your heart. If I spoke French, I should not *tutoyer* you, but address you only as *vous*. Morally speaking, to lust after a woman is as bad as actually to commit adultery with her, but justice allows me to plead the Fifth Amendment. Justice may, indeed, require us to imagine ourselves in the other chap's shoes, but does not demand that we should get inside his skin.

We thus have an "anular" distribution of relevant considerations for a judicial decision: in saying that justice deals with cases, not persons, we lay down two limits, and exclude some considerations as lying outside the one and others as being inside the other. Several different arguments may be adduced in defence of the inner limit. It may be defended as a requirement not so much of justice as of liberty. A man should be free to think his own thoughts, and there should be a private sphere of his own into which the State should not trespass. If this is so, then the restriction is not really a requirement of justice, and should not be insisted on in adjudications by bodies other than the State. We may alternatively argue for the restriction on grounds of justice rather than liberty. In part it reflects the fact that arguments of justice are omni-personal rather than first-personal, coercive rather than spontaneous.[25] We may also argue that since justice is concerned only with what is actual, intentions and states of mind are, like the future, too tenuous to rest an adverse decision on. We may, finally, see the inner limit as a manifestation of respect for man's individuality. Justice is concerned with the balancing of one man's interests

[25] See, more fully, Ch. 3, pp. 37–9.

against others', and therefore presupposes that his scale of values will be in part divergent from the others, and that he will be in such matters differently minded, and therefore discounts differences of mental attitude *per se*, as to be expected and not to be regarded as morally relevant.

The last argument is of great importance. It is an argument for liberty, which, being an argument from justice, would carry weight even if we attached no independent value to liberty. We do injustice to a man if we do not ever let him make up his mind on his own, and if we are to be fair we must not only consider his interests but respect his rights. But once we recognise his right to make decisions for himself, we have to come to terms with the possibility of his deciding wrongly. Absolute justice becomes impossible. Either we respect his right to be wrong, and allow an unfair decision to stand, or we displace his decision by ours, ensuring that the interests of others are given due consideration but disregarding his right to have a say.[26] Besides obvious implications for the way we work out the bearing of justice on the law and on our economic life,[27] it raises the difficult question of what issues are, and are not, justiciable. Not every adverse decision can be complained about. If Amaryllis rejects my suit, the examiners find out how little I know, my boss promotes someone else, or the voters reject my candidature, I cannot on those grounds alone enter a protest. Only some sorts of interests, some sorts of rights, in some circumstances and subject to some conditions, ought to be cherished or tenderly treated.

The arguments of justice are essentially dialectical.[28] When a man complains of injustice, he is claiming that there is a reason *against*, and so, *per contra*, when a man maintains the justice of an action, he is claiming that there are other, adequate reasons *for*, which outweigh those against. What arguments may properly, on the score of justice, he adduced against or in favour of an action we have yet to determine. The action complained of should not be, or should not have been, done, on account of its adverse consequence for some individual or individuals. But not every ill consequence can be a conclusive reason against any action, or nothing could ever be done by anybody. The strength of the reason against will depend partly on the nature of the ill consequences and partly on the relationship with the agent. Certain interests, in particular those

---

[26] See, more fully, Ch. 11, pp. 197–9, and Ch. 12, p. 213. 8–9.
[27] See Chs. 5 and 13.　　　　　　[28] See, more fully, Ch. 3, pp. 39–42.

of life, limb and liberty, are particularly cherished, and in most countries chartered by law; a complaint on any of these scores is all but conclusive; with lesser interests, however, the agent may acknowledge the consequences but deny their relevance—"What is that to me?" If I decide not to leave my house to you in my will, you will be noticeably less well off than if I do; but that undeniable fact does not constitute by itself grounds for a valid complaint against my decision—why should I leave my house to you? Only certain people have a claim on me, and only on their behalf can the justice of my decisions be impugned. My wife, my children, my near relations, an adoptive heir, have some claim on me, and although it may not be a conclusive one, they still can question my decision, and I need to have some answer, if I am to avoid the charge of injustice; but for the rest, it is none of their business what I do with my own, and a complaint of injustice on their behalf is not so much to be answered as ignored. Again, if you are candidate for a job to which I am appointing, you have some claim on my consideration; it would be unfair of me to rule you out on manifestly untrue or irrelevant grounds—if you had got five O-levels, and I took no notice of your statement to that effect, and dismissed you from further consideration on the grounds that you had not got any O-levels; but if I entertain similarly untrue unbeliefs about Derek, who had not submitted an application, and did not think of offering him the job, I should not have done him any injustice. I had no duty towards him to apprise myself of relevant facts, or to be guided by them in reaching my decision; it depends both on the nature of the ill consequence and on the position of the man suffering it relative to the man bringing it about, whether his complaint can get off the ground. If it gets off the ground it may be outweighed by other arguments adequate to establish the justice of the action in question. These other arguments, if they are to succeed, must meet the arguments reasonably urged against the action, or be of sufficient strength clearly to override them. They must, therefore, depend on what arguments they have to counter or override, and therefore at a second remove on the untoward consequences of the action in question and the relationship of the agent to the victim.[29]

It is a complicated theory of justice. Most thinkers have elucidated justice in terms of some simple rule or symmetry. They see

[29] See further, Ch. 2.

that justice treats like cases alike, and is no respecter of persons, and is impartial as between all parties. But they fail to see that it is impartially partial to all parties, that justice favours each man as much as is possible to do without being unfair to others, that justice gives each man his due not merely reluctantly but of set purpose, and is reluctant only to have to disappoint the expectations of any may by arriving at a decision which is adverse to him. Instead of seeing justice as a simple static assignment of benefits, responsibilities and burdens, we should see it as a dynamic equilibrium under tension, wanting to treat the individual as tenderly as possible, yet being prepared, for sufficiently compelling reasons, to take a tough line. Although often, in view of the limited amount of goods available, or the conflicting interests of the different parties involved, justice requires that our award should be just right, and not too little or too much, justice is essentially concerned that our award should not be too little. It is not a simple limit, dividing out the spoils exactly, but rather the result of the application of a maximum principle, giving to each the most that we reasonably can, and being more immediately infringed if we err on the side of less than if we err on the side of more. Our rules of natural justice reveal a similar thrust. They are "process values"[30] showing our great concern for the individual and that he should not be needlessly done down.

And this is why justice is the bond of society. It enables the individual to identify with the actions of society, even those that are adverse to him or to someone else, because such actions are taken only if they are required by individualised reasons into which the individual can enter,[31] and whose force he cannot, if he is reasonable, help acknowledging. I can be happy to be one of We, if We are just, because then We will treat Me as well as reasonably possible; and We will be happy to have Me as one of Us, because We know that I, being just, will see things from Our point of view, and will not exclude wider considerations from My assessment of the situation, and will not construe everything in terms of My own exclusive self-interest. I can be sure that We will do well by Me, and We can count on My behaving as a member of the community should. There is no στάσις, no dissension, in the just society,

---

[30] R. S. Summers, "A Plea for Process Values", *Cornell Law Review*, 60, 1974–5, pp. 1–52.

[31] See further, Ch. 3, p. 42.

because it does not matter whether decisions are taken by me or by someone else—they will not conflict, because they are taken in the same frame of mind, whoever it is that takes them—and yet this absence of conflict is achieved not by some self-abnegation, some absorption in a higher whole, but by the acceptance on the part of each of the existence and legitimate interests of everybody else. If I am treating you justly, it will be all the same whether I am deciding what I should do to you, or you are deciding it, or somebody else is. It is not biased my way, so my decision will be the same as that of a third party; and above all, it is not biased *against* you, and so the decision of a third party will be no less favourable than what you would yourself decide, if you were deciding impartially and not unfairly in your own favour. And so you and I and all of us can live together in harmony and peace, each easily identifying with everyone else, because we all recognise the individuality of each, and respect his interests, and will cherish his interests as he would himself.

2

RIGHTS AND INTERESTS

Justice is concerned with not doing people down, and we therefore need to elucidate further what it is to do someone down. We have, first, the concept of an interest, and say that a person is being done down if his interests are being damaged. Since the seventeenth century we have also been developing the concept of a right, and injustice is done as much if a man's rights are overridden as if his interests are damaged.

Rights and interests are similar in being assignable; that is to say, we can always ask "whose right?" or "whose interest?", whereas these questions are not intelligible if asked of other values, such as truth. It is, as we shall shortly see, tempting to construe rights as being simply interests of a specially important sort, but that is too simple. Rights and interests can diverge: it may be in my interests to go into hospital and have an operation, but I have a right to refuse. More generally, rights make sense only within a complex web of social, moral or legal understanding, whereas interests can be ascribed apart from any special context; rights are essentially first-personal, whereas interests, although often ultimately appraised from a first-personal standpoint, are characteristically ascribed third-personally, and used in the context of vicarious decision-making.

Interests can be ascribed or imputed to third parties. I can look after or consider a man's interests in his absence, and often without consulting him. They should be contrasted with ideals, which can be ascribed only on the basis of some first-personal avowal. Interests are not simply what I happen to be interested in, but are rather what other people can assume I am interested in. They lack the authenticity of values avowed in the first person, but for that very reason can be understood and taken into consideration by third parties without their having to have first-hand knowledge of what each person actually aspires to. They are of many different kinds: some common to all men—life, health and liberty; some, like wealth, valuable not in themselves but on account of their facilitating whatever other ends may be sought; some more idealistic or idiosyncratic. Some are immediate, urgent and narrow; others long-term, flexible and pervasive. Some are much more important than others, and merit much greater consideration; life and liberty are more important than property and wealth, and usually it is worse to deprive a man of what he actually has than to disappoint his hopes of some future good.[1] Some interests are too trivial or peripheral to merit serious consideration. More often, the context in which the decision is made excludes certain sorts of interest from consideration altogether—it may be very much in my interest that I should win a prize, get a job or be elected to an office, but that is no reason to weigh with you in reaching your decision. A just man will give *due* consideration to the interests of those affected by his decision; but for some sorts of interest, when decisions of a certain type are in issue, due consideration is scant consideration or none at all. When someone complains of a decision of his, he may disallow the complaint, as well as acknowledge it but seek to justify his action as necessary none the less. We thus have to consider interests not only with respect to the person concerned—whether it is of great importance or only minor importance to him and whether it is a central or only a peripheral interest of his—but with respect to the decision-maker—whether it is an interest he ought to take into account or one he is bound to exclude from his consideration. Lawyers pose the question in terms of whether or not there is a duty of care owed to the person concerned: I have a duty to take care not to put your life or health in jeopardy, but not to protect you from the legal consequences of your crimes. But this is too rigid. Even when I do not have a duty of care to you, I might hesitate to do you down gratuitously, or say in answer to your protest that I am damaging your interests a brusque "What is that to me?" We should, I think, in most cases

---

[1] For a further account of the concept of interest see J. R. Lucas, *Democracy and Participation*, Penguin, 1976, Ch. VI, esp. pp. 87–94. See also, A. M. Honoré, "Social Justice", *McGill Law Journal*, 78, 1962, pp. 88–9, reprinted in R. S. Summers (ed.), *Essays in Legal Philosophy*, Oxford, 1968, p. 75, where he uses the word 'advantage' instead of 'interest', and says, "No rational distinction however can be drawn between the following categories of 'advantage', using that word in a wide sense: (A) material goods, (B) incorporeal things made as copyrights, contractual rights *etc.*, (C) interests which are not legally regarded as property but which are legally protected such as life, health, honour, reputation, and (D) opportunities or facilities such as the right to vote, to have free education, to leave property by will, travel *etc.*"

allow that if a decision would harm someone's interests, that fact constituted a *prima facie* objection. The objection then could be countered in two ways: it might be that I was bound or entitled to exclude such interests from consideration, as when I am a judge or an examiner, and am obliged to take only certain factors into account, or when I am choosing a present or going on holiday and am invited to consult only my own preferences; or it might be that I had indeed taken into consideration the interest in jeopardy, but found the countervailing arguments more weighty. In the former case the onus is not on the complainant to show that the decision-maker had some duty of care towards him, but on the decision-maker to show that for one reason or another the complainant's interest was excluded from the factors he ought to take into consideration. That claim may be rebutted by the complainant, and there may be further argument about whether or not the decision is justifiable or not. But in that case the argument is quite different from where the complainant's objection is overridden by counter-arguments of greater cogency.

Some decisions are not justiciable because of conceptual in-appropriateness, some because of the context within which the decisions are taken. All is fair in love and war—that is to say, nothing is unfair. If your heart proves fickle, or you fail to love me as I think you should, I may feel I am very hardly done by, but I cannot say you are being unfair. Fancy is free, and cannot be argued with. I can argue with you about specific action, but not about your emotional attitude in general. You are being unfair, if you refuse to come to a dance with me, after you had said you would and let me buy a ticket on that supposition; or again, if you betray confidences, and retail round Somerville all the secrets of my heart. But your feelings are not actions within the meaning of the act, and so are not justiciable; and if you no longer feel for me now as you did in yesterweek, my heart may be broken but my collar should remain cool. Again, not only in war but often in peace my situation is essentially a competitive one, and my aim can only be achieved at some rival's expense. In such cases I am not generally debarred from pursuing my own advantage on account of its being adverse to somebody else's interests. If I play a game or compete for a scholarship, I need have no reluctance in trying my hardest to do well. We distinguish trying to win within the rules from seeking an advantage by breaking the rules, and although it is unfair to break the rules of the game, no objection is made to doing an adversary down by fair means. Some decisions are to be taken without regard to the interests involved, because they are exercises either of liberty or discretion, and we do not want them to be hampered by overmuch considerateness. My choice of a holiday or a new hat is to be made on the grounds of what pleases me, not what would be profitable to travel agents or hat shops. It is important, if people are to fill out their personalities, that they should often have occasion to make up their minds for themselves, and therefore we confer on them a large measure of freedom, in order that many of their choices may be authentic, and that they may grow up into fully autonomous agents. There is a price to be paid for this freedom, that people will be able to abuse it, and that there will be no remedy for the adverse consequences of the wrong decisions they take. Freedom and justice are not always compatible, and sometimes we have to compromise justice in order to ensure freedom. It follows that some complaints of unfairness will be unheeded, not because no adverse consequences are suffered, but because we have structured the rights and responsibilities of the parties involved so as to confer the greatest possible freedom of action on the man making the decision. So, too, decisions may be taken without regard to the interests of the parties involved, in order to secure the effectiveness of a common enterprise. The criterion for deciding what post I shall get in the army is what the army needs, not what I would like. Although in employment generally some regard is sometimes given to the interests of employees, these cannot in general be the overriding concern, and must generally take second place to the needs and efficiency of the organisation. Often the interests of those concerned should be given some consideration, but should not be made a prime consideration. The interest of candidates for a job should be considered inasmuch as some attention should be given to their candidature and their merits and qualifications, but no more than that. If an employee is not up to this job, he should, in the absence of grave dereliction, be given notice, and perhaps the opportunity to pull up his socks, but not a right to retain his income indefinitely and irrespective of his performance. Although a prisoner found guilty may properly be sentenced, his interests should still be considered to the extent of hearing any plea, in mitigation or for clemency, that he may make.

Many decisions, especially those by public authorities, have great impact on individuals. To be deprived of a driving licence, a passport, a telephone or an electricity supply, is in the modern world a great deprivation. Even to be refused credit is in modern America to be cut off from a nearly essential facility. It is difficult to make out that all these interests are of central importance: but it is too easy to dismiss them as being of no consequence at all. There are gradations of interest, and the degree of consideration they ought to be given varies. It would be impracticable and wrong to give them all the protection the law gives to life, liberty and property. But often they should be given some protection all the same, and decisions which jeopardise them should not be taken lightly or casually, but only after due consideration for relevant reasons.

It is difficult to make any general statement about what questions are justiciable and what are not. There is a general presumption in favour of fair dealing whenever an individual's interests are involved, but that presumption can be rebutted. In some cases, as we have seen, it is on account of a conceptual inappropriateness. Where only actions issuing from first-personal reasons are desired it is incoherent to bring third-personal reasons to bear in order to elicit them. In other cases it is implicit in an activity that certain interests are being disclaimed, and sometimes the whole activity would be pointless unless this were so. In other cases again, interests are neglected in order to give untramelled discretion to the decision-maker. And there is a general tendency to replace in questions of justice the consideration of interests by the adjudication of rights.

The concept of interest, although of fundamental importance in deciding what is just, suffers from serious defects, especially from the practical point of view of potential litigants. It is fuzzy-edged, dependent on context, and always under strain between the actual concerns a man avows himself and those ascribed to him by others and taken into account on his behalf vicariously. Although a man may know what he wants, he cannot be sure exactly what interests will be imputed to him by others, nor what weight will be given them. Even if he could be sure of that, he still could not be confident of how his case would go if it came to court, because he would not know how the interests on the other side would be weighed against his. In most cases both parties have an interest involved which merits tender treatment. Justice will make the judge reluctant to decide against either party, but decide against one or the other of them he must, or he will be unable to decide at all. Someone is bound to be disappointed, and although under ideal conditions, a man should bear his disappointment bravely, comforted by the thought that justice had been done and the most deserving side had won, it will not always seem like that to the unsuccessful litigant. Although ideally the just decision is one that could have been reached, not only by the judge, but by any reasonable man, and therefore by the litigants themselves if only they were sufficiently reasonable and disinterested, under our actual conditions of imperfection, not every judge would reach the same decision, and therefore the judge's decision may be one which the litigants could not themselves enter into, however reasonable and disinterested they are. It is to them unpredictable and external. And even though they may be confident that the judge is reluctant to do them down, they will be diffident about the actual outcome of litigation, and will therefore feel insecure and inhibited in all their activities and arrangements. It is in order to obviate this that we need the concept of *right*. A right is stronger than an interest. If I have a right, it will not be overridden by the interests of others, unless their interests are also enshrined as rights. If we construe the trial of a case as a dialogue before the judge, we can see how my interests, if they are not chartered rights, may always be overridden by those of others. It is very much in my interests that I should keep my job, but it may be in the interests of everyone else that I should be replaced by Peter Smith, who would do the job much better and has greater need of the stipend. If, however, I have a right to keep my job, all such considerations are irrelevant. Only if I can be shown to have forfeited that right, for instance by failing to carry out my duties, can I be sacked. A right will trump an interest.

In some cases a right is simply an interest we think would be unfair to disregard or override, and then our determination of right should be seen not as an antecedent factor from which a decision of right consequently flows, but as a simple correlative of justice: in deciding what is fair, we are deciding what the rights of the various parties are. In most cases, however, a right is not merely a specially protected interest. Like interests, rights are assignable, but, unlike interests, rights are first-personal rather than third-personal and have a close connection with freedom. Like freedom, rights are systematically ambiguous: that is to say, we have moral, social, legal and natural rights, and I may have a legal right to do something that I have no moral right to do, or I may claim a natural right to something that I concede I have, at present, no legal right to. In much the same way I may be legally free to do something though morally bound not to; and what is logically possible is often physically impossible. Again like freedom, rights have more than one sense. Much as we distinguish *freedom to* from *freedom from*, we find that some rights are rights to do something while others are rights not to have something done. The relationship between these two sorts of right is, however, considerably more complicated than that between the different sorts of freedom, and rights to do one thing necessarily involve ancillary rights not to have other things done.[2]

Legal rights are in issue when there are legal disputes, but not all disputes involve rights. In the first place, we may differ about what a communal decision should be—for example, about who should have custody of some children or what education they should have—without anybody's having any rights in the matter. Only certain, highly individualised, disputes are resolved by a determination of right. It is usually when someone wants to do something and someone else objects to his doing it that a question of right arises. Nor is it just that. In the Rule of the Road, although we may say that one person is *in* the right and another *in* the wrong, we do not normally say that either of them *has* a right. This is because the Rule of the Road tells us exactly what each must do in given circumstances. Some philosophers—Stoics and Kantians—have thought that ideally the moral law should give us in all circumstances entirely specific guidance what to do; but, quite apart from the impracticality of this ideal, it is undesirable. Not only must we leave it very largely to each individual to decide what to do, but it is eminently desirable that we should, so as to enhance each man's individuality, and enable each to be an autonomous agent, and discover himself in his own authentic action. Hence, contrary to the Stoic ideal of a completely determinate law, we want the law not to lay down exactly what to do, but to take into account what people actually want or actually decide, and to tell us how to assess that. Essentially, it tells us not what is to be done in a

---

[2] See below, pp. 30–1, or more fully, J. R. Lucas, *The Principles of Politics*, Oxford, 1966, §36, pp. 155–60.

situation, but who is to decide what shall be done. And to have the say is to have a right.[3]

It is necessary, simply on the score of epistemological practicality, to decentralise decision-taking. By conferring a right on an individual, we enable him to know what he is going to do and what others are not going to do, because he knows what he is entitled to do and what others are not, at least without his consent, entitled to do. This knowledge gives him the liberty and security he needs, if he is to be his own master, and not subject to the possibly well-meaning, but none the less disrupting, interventions of others. He needs to know where he stands so as to be able to arrange his affairs himself. And, therefore, in order to guide his future actions and assuage his future fears, his rights need to be couched in fairly general terms, not specifying every detail of every situation, but telling him that in general he has got a right to travel, to speak his mind and to get married, and also a right not to be obstructed, not to be slandered and not to be assaulted. Granted this knowledge, he can act with reasonable confidence. If the question is whether to travel or not, whether to speak out or not, whether to get married or not, he need only consult himself in the first two cases, and in the third, only, should he wish to get married, persuade also his intended to say Yes. And whatever he decides to do, he can count on not being obstructed on the Queen's highway, not being slandered, not being assaulted. By establishing a system of rights, we enable a man to be a judge in his own cause. Instead of each case being decided impartially on its merits, we distribute the decision-making, so that different decisions are taken by different people—typically by the person most concerned. It may be in many men's interest that someone should not travel—nevertheless it is for him to decide: it may be in everyone's interest that I should marry Jane—but if she or I will have none of it, that is the end of the

[3] For a fuller elucidation see W. N. Hohfeld, "Some Fundamental Legal Conceptions", 23 *Yale Law Journal*, 1913, pp. 16–69; and "Fundamental Legal Conceptions as Applied in Judicial Reasoning", 26 *Yale Law Journal*, 1917, pp. 710–70; reprinted in W. N. Hohfeld; *Fundamental Legal Conceptions as Applied in Judicial Reasoning and other Legal Essays*, ed. W. W. Cook, New Haven, 1923, pp. 35 ff., Yale Paperbound, New Haven, 1964, pp. 35 ff. For an earlier statement, see Salmond, *Jurisprudence*, Section 77, pp. 269–70 in 11th edn. For subsequent development see H. L. A. Hart, "Are there any Natural Rights?", *Philosophical Review*, LXIV, 1955, pp. 175–91; reprinted in Frederick F. Olafson (ed.), *Society, Law and Morality*, Englewood Cliffs, N.J., 1961, pp. 173–85.

affair. By assigning rights, we enable people to know where they stand by limiting the factors to be taken into consideration. I characteristically am ill informed of other men's interests and am sometimes mistaken even about my own: but if it is for me to decide, then even though I am ignorant about where our interests lie, I still can know what my decision is. Facts I may not know, but I always can know my mind.

The epistemology of rights works being crude. If any specific action is in question, we have to see whose interests are affected, and then whether any affected interests are enshrined as rights. If so, the person who has a right has an effective say or an effective veto: if the right is a right *to*, then it is up to him whether to exercise his right or not; if the right is a right *not* to have something *done*, then, unless he waives his right, nobody else can do that something to him. Each person in knowing his own rights must recognise that every other person is a bearer of rights too, and therefore should guide his actions so as to respect the rights of others as well as of himself. And this he can do, up to a first level of approximation, by choosing ways of exercising his rights *to* so as not to trespass on the rights of others *not* to have things *done*: his right to wave his arms is to be exercised in such a manner as not to impinge on your right not to have your nose hit. He does not have to be clever or learned in the law to be able to see this. Beyond this, it is more difficult. Where rights conflict, and there is no way of exercising one right without infringing another, more careful consideration is needed, and the layman may need to turn to the lawyer for guidance. Nevertheless, he often will not have to have recourse to the expert. The language of rights enables a man in most of the ordinary business of life to know his own rights, and hence, very largely, those of others too, and thus to have available a workable outline guidance of what he may, or may not, do.

It is not merely a convenience to enhance liberties into rights, but a manifestation of a further facet of freedom. Freedom is not just the absence of rules or other conclusive reasons against something, important though that may be: it is also a matter of status, of being a full, enfranchised member of society—etymologically the word 'free' is connected with 'friend', and a free man is one who counts, one who is accepted as a fellow member of society. Although people may on occasion be glad not to be forbidden by law from doing what they want to do, it has been a common experience of recent centuries that this liberal concept of freedom—negative liberty as it is called[4]—does not satisfy men's deep desire for status, because it does not accord official recognition to their decisions. It is a freedom of indifference, whereas what men crave is the freedom of enfranchised respect. Not only do I want to be able to make up my own mind what I shall do, but I want it to matter what I decide. Rights minister to this need. I am allowed to choose not merely by oversight but of set purpose: and my decisions are treated with great respect, and actually determine the legal situation around me. Medieval man valued law, because it enabled him to be a citizen who knew what to do rather than a subject who had to be told:[5] modern man values his rights because it makes him not just a legal officer but in part a legislative one. In exercising my rights, I am investing my actions with the authority of law: while in recognising the rights of others I show myself to be no absolutist sovereign, but a responsible ruler abiding by the limitations inherent in any constitutional government.

Justice, we have already seen,[6] is to be construed as being in part a species of communication; and it is characteristic also of a legal system generally, that it depends essentially on communication— laws *tell* people what to do or what to expect, and are quite different from the manipulations psychologists perform on rats. Communication presupposes autonomy. I can only communicate with you, if you have a mind, and you have a mind of your own only if you can make it up for yourself. Only if you can differ from me are you someone other than me. And therefore it is implicit in a legal system that some regard should be paid to what each person thinks. Slavery is a legal anomaly, because slaves are being treated both as chattels and yet also as persons who can receive orders and give information; and so American law was involved in embarrassing inconsistency over the judicial process for deciding whether a runaway slave was in fact a slave or not, and Roman law over the testimony of slaves. A legal system which denies some people any autonomy is defective: and therefore we can argue that a legal system ought to accord some authority to the decisions of each individual—that is, ought to confer on him some rights. These are

---

[4] Isaiah Berlin, *Two Concepts of Liberty*, Oxford, 1958, pp. 6–16; reprinted in Isaiah Berlin, *Four Essays on Liberty*, Oxford, 1969, pp. 122–31.

[5] See below, Ch. 5, pp. 110–11.

[6] Ch. 1, p. 7.

grounded on the nature of man and the nature of law, and therefore can properly be termed natural rights, and can properly be claimed even if they are not granted by the particular legal system at present in force. It may be that under Russian law, having served my sentence in Siberia for publishing poetry illegally, I may be sent back to Siberia for a further fifteen years, should the Supreme Soviet fail to feel satisfied that I am sufficiently chastened. And if I have the misfortune to be in their clutches, there is nothing I can do to stop the Russians from incarcerating me in their prison camps for as long as they please. Nevertheless, I have a valid argument against them, in so far as their regime masquerades as a system of law. For it is part of the logic of punishment that penalties, like debts, can be paid, and once paid are paid and cannot be further exacted.[7] I may be imprisoned, but cannot be punished. A tyrant may tyrannize, but he cannot rule lawfully unless he himself observes the rules that the law, if it is to be accounted as such, requires of rulers. And of these the most fundamentally pervasive is that the rulers should manifest respect for the autonomy of each one of the ruled, not only by avoiding, if possible, decisions which would harm his interests, but by according to his actual decisions legal validity and consequence.

Rights may conflict. My right to freedom of speech may conflict with your right not to be slandered, your right to move your body as you please may conflict with my right not to be hit. There is thus a problem of demarcation. Often it is difficult to decide what the correct description of a particular action is, and whether it is to be characterized innocuously—waving one's hands about—or pejoratively—hitting someone. It depends very much on the purposes we ascribe to people and our normal expectations. If I open the door of my car and a cyclist runs into it, the fact that my car door is at rest and the cyclist is moving does not make him the cause of the collision: I have obstructed his free passage, because moving is just what people are expected to do on the highway. So, too, with rights, my right to speak my mind does not mean I am entitled to slander my neighbour or make untrue claims about my wares or bear false witness in court or incite racial hatred, and it may be difficult for a court to decide whether some particular action of mine falls under one of these descriptions. With rights, however, as opposed to liberties and duties, there is a further degree

[7] But see, more fully, Ch. 6, pp. 150-2.

of variability in the extent to which the law protects the right by means of ancillary rights and obligations. If I have a right, it means not simply that there is no law against my exercising it, but that if I do, my decision to do so is of some legal consequence, and that other people are not at liberty to frustrate me by every means possible. At the very least they are under some duty of non-interference. And in some cases the law goes to considerable lengths to ensure that my decision is effective. My right to urge my own views of what ought to be done does not carry with it any duty on the part of my fellows to listen to me. I am free to speak my mind at Hyde Park Corner, and if people try and suppress me they will themselves be restrained: but nobody need pay any attention to me. I am free to write letters to the papers, but the papers are not obliged to print them, and even if they do, nobody need read them, nor need anyone take up my points or act on them. These rights are little more than liberties. On the other hand, the right to marry and the right to vote are fairly fully protected by ancillary rights and duties. Various obstacles in the way of my getting married are circumvented—if I enter into a contract not to get married, I am not bound by it; if you leave me your money on condition I do not get married, the law will set that condition aside; if you try to get me to vote a particular way by bribes or threats, you are liable to heavy penalties; if I am blind or in the armed forces or away from home, special arrangements can be made for me to cast my vote all the same. Thus not all rights are equally important. Some are liberties with only minimal ancillary protection, others are easy to exercise effectively.

The possession of rights is no guarantee against some forms of injustice or disappointment. If we confer on individuals the decisive say about what shall happen, they may decide with scant regard for others. I have a right to leave my property as I think fit, and I may in virtue of that right disinherit my family unjustly: and if, as in Scotland, a man's wife and children have a right to his estate when he dies, it may prevent him doing justice to those with other, and in some circumstances greater, claims on him. Justice, as we have seen, is many-faceted, and we may not be able to do justice both to the testator, by respecting his disposition of his estate, and to his possible legatees, by ensuring that they receive legacies, in spite of his will. Moreover, however much authority is accorded to the individual's decision, it cannot be an absolute authority, nor can it be guaranteed always to be effective. The King of Scotland once decreed that in a leap year a woman could make a proposal of marriage which a man must accept on pain of a fine: even so, not every spinster that wanted to was able to exercise her right to get married. Often rights disappoint. They do not succeed in ensuring everyone is successful in implementing his wishes. And therefore often people feel done down on the score of their rights. They have been led to believe that in certain respects peculiar regard should be paid to their wishes; and find in the event that they have been frustrated in their heart's desires, and feel that they have been done out of their rights, and thus unjustly treated.

The sense of injustice arises most strongly not with legal rights but with natural rights. Natural rights are claimed rather than conferred, are independent of any particular system of duty and obligation, and, indeed, have only a tenuous connection with duty at all. I may claim a natural right to a full and happy life, but hesitate to maintain that it is your—or anyone else's—duty to slave away in order to provide me with the wherewithal. Natural rights are like natural law: they express certain canons and criteria for developing or assessing actual legal systems. A legal system must satisfy certain conditions if it is to count as a legal system at all: the laws must be generally known, and for the most part be of general application; there must be general agreement about what are to be accepted as laws, and a generally recognised way of adjudicating doubtful cases, with due regard for the arguments on either side. In addition we argue that the laws must work for the benefit, by and large, of the individual. Even Hobbes, the most ardent advocate of absolutism, allows that a sovereign's command to take one's own life cannot be a valid law. And this we may represent as reflecting a natural right to life.

Natural rights, like natural law generally, suffer from vagueness. They do not tell us where we stand, but only express a claim about where we ought to stand, and on this opinions may legitimately differ. As with all rights, there is a great problem of specification. Just as my right to wave my hands does not mean I may hit you, and my right to travel does not mean I can walk across your garden, so my right to life does not mean that I can annex your kidneys if I have need of them, nor that if I kill others I may not be killed in return: nor does my right to liberty mean that imprisonment or conscription is always wrong. Some people claim a natural right to three weeks' paid holiday annually, but even so would scarcely maintain that everyone, doctors and nurses included, was entitled to choose to take his holiday at the same time as everybody else. It is not feasible to make everybody's wishes entirely effective, and if we establish rules which give some weight to what each man might reasonably want, this is often the most that can be required of us.

But it is not the most that may be demanded. The language of natural rights suffers from a serious ambiguity between the minimum requirements which any legal system needs to meet and the maximum ones which some of us would like ours to satisfy. A legal system which allows men to be deprived of life, liberty or property without due process is unjust; and it is a reasonable extension of this principle to make some provision for legal aid. But it is barely intelligible to condemn a legal system as unjust if it does not provide me with a QC at public expense to defend me on a charge of not having a TV licence. Nor is it unjust if I am not given a job as a film star; nor if I am unable to find anyone to marry me. We need to insist upon the distinction between injustice and disappointment. It is part of the human condition that we shall sometimes be disappointed, but we should be careful against whom we lay our complaints at our ill fortune. Too many men in modern times have deified the State, and supposing the State to be omnipotent, have held it responsible for everything that happened or failed to happen; and then every adverse condition that may befall a man is seen as an adverse decision and therefore potentially unfair. But sins of omission should not be too readily imputed. The State is not omnipotent, and it is important that it should not be supposed to be omnipotent or assigned unlimited responsibility. Once it is conceded that not everything is possible to the State, it follows that not every undesirable situation is to be seen as the State's doing, either directly or through its failure to avert it. We may, of course, still wish that some undesirable situations should be prevented or remedied, and reckon that the State should undertake that responsibility. And then, if the State does take it on, but in some particular case fails to avert an untoward result, complaint can justly be made: if the State sets out to provide a medical service or old age pensions, and yet leaves me doctorless and in penury, I can complain that I have not had what I should have had by rights, and that this is unfair. But from the fact that I think the State ought to undertake to look after me in some way, it does not follow that the State has so undertaken, or that it is doing me an injustice if it fails to provide for me. We do ourselves a disservice if we claim a natural right whenever we want to put forward a programme for political action, because then we downgrade the peremptory language of natural rights into a wistful expression in the optative mood, and suggest that the right to a fair trial is of the same order of importance as a right to three weeks' holiday with pay.

Rights and interests are assignable to individuals, and therefore constitute individualised reasons of the correct logical shape to enter into disputes about what is fair or just. They are important for determining what issues are justiciable, and what weight should be given to different factors bearing on a decision. By conducting our deliberations in terms of rights rather than interests we make discussion cruder but easier for others to join in, and although it may lead to some people's interests being overridden, it also, and more importantly, manifests respect for people by investing their own actual decisions with legal significance.

3

RATIONALITY AND THE THEORY OF GAMES

Justice is reasonable. Some say it simply *is* embodied reason. Certainly, the word 'justify' in English simply means to give reasons. Yet despite a wide consensus among the many and the wise, not everyone agrees. Alf Ross, for example, maintains:

To invoke justice is the same thing as banging on the table: an emotional expression which turns one's demand into an absolute postulate. That is no proper way to mutual understanding. It is impossible to have a rational discussion with a man who mobilises "justice" because he says nothing that can be argued for or against. His words are persuasions, not arguments (§72). The ideology of justice leads to implacability and conflict, since on the one hand it incites to the belief that one's demand is not merely the expression of a certain interest in conflict with opposing interests, but that it possesses a higher, absolute validity; and on the other it precludes all rational argument and discussion of a settlement. The ideology of justice is a militant attitude of a biological-emotional kind, to which one incites oneself for the implacable and blind defence of certain interests.

Since the formal idea of equality or justice as a lodestar for social policy is devoid of all meaning, it is possible to advance every kind of postulate in the name of justice. This explains why all wars and social conflicts, as mentioned earlier, have been fought in the name of the exalted idea of justice. It is too much to hope that this will change in the future. The catchword of justice is far too effective and ideologically convenient a weapon for the hope that statesmen, politicians and agitators, even if they see the truth, would dare to agree on disarmament on this point. Besides, most of them are probably victims of the deception. It is so easy to believe in the illusions which excite the emotions by stimulating the suprarenal glands.[1]

These assertions carry little conviction except to those already imbued with positivist doctrines. Although people do get angry about injustice, they do not merely bang the table. They argue. The atmosphere of a lawcourt is very different from that of a battlefield, a tournament or a political campaign. Tables are seldom banged,

---

[1] Alf Ross, *On Law and Justice*, English tr., London, 1974, Ch. 12, pp. 274–5.

emotive rhetoric is at a discount, and the outward appearances are of intricate intellectual endeavour. If we understand the words 'reason', 'rational' and 'argument' in their ordinary senses, it is incontestable that justice has an intimate connection with reason and rational argument. The positivists, however, have their own special doctrine of the nature of reason, which they believe to be more in accord with the canons of scientific argument. And since, of course, arguments about justice are not scientific arguments, it follows that they are not rational arguments in their sense. But nothing follows from that. Unless it can be shown that the only respectable arguments are those of the natural sciences, and that there is no call for a reasonable man to be guided by any other sort of reasoning, we have no reason to suppose that reasonings about justice are, *eo ipso*, lacking in cogency. Indeed, we could not. For any such reasoning would be philosophical and not scientific, and therefore itself lacking in cogency. If all contentions about justice are emotional and irrational, then so are those of Alf Ross, and if his persuasions fail to persuade us, then they have failed and there is nothing more to be said. His irrationalism is self-defeating, as well as being false to the facts.

Nevertheless, Ross has a point. We have no satisfactory theory of reason. We have never succeeded in carrying out Descartes's programme of formulating complete and precise rules of correct reasoning, even in mathematics, and we know now, as a consequence of Gödel's theorem,[2] that we never shall. In the less precise realm of human affairs we cannot even begin to lay down necessary and sufficient conditions for an action or a decision being reasonable. This does not mean, as Alf Ross and the sceptics suppose, that actions and decisions cannot be reasonable. We are rational agents and can both ourselves act rationally and recognise rational action in others. But we are not very good at formulating our own reasons or assessing the reasons adduced by others. Often we act reasonably without being able to say exactly what our reasons are, and no set of reasons exhausts all the potentiality of rational action. We can characterize reason in broad and general terms, instancing marks or typical features of rationality; and sometimes we can lay down necessary, although not sufficient,

---

[2] See W. and M. Kneale, *The Development of Logic*, Oxford, 1962, Ch. XII, §4, esp. pp. 735–6 and also pp. 721–41; or J. Myhill, "Some Remarks on the Notion of Proof", *Journal of Philosophy*, LVII, 1960, p. 462.

conditions of rationality. It is this latter point that explains, in part, the dominance of injustice. Although we cannot in general specify what makes an action reasonable, we can sometimes say what makes it not reasonable, and hence not just. Often, therefore, our guidelines are rules, such as those of natural justice, which are intended to exclude certain forms of injustice, without being able to ensure that all decisions reached in accordance with them will be just.

There are many different sorts of reason. In contemporary English there is a slight difference in sense between the words 'reasonable' and 'rational', the former having a moral overtone, suggesting some degree of consideration for others, while the latter is austerely egoistical in connotation. The difference is important. Although social life would be impossible if we were not reasonable in the wider sense, and it is primarily in this sense that we require justice to be reasonable, justice is also concerned with rationality because it addresses itself to the individual, and needs to see things from his point of view and enter into his calculations of rationality. In the course of this chapter I shall argue that reasonableness and rationality, although distinct, are connected, and that the different strands of rationality are woven together to form a web of reasonableness. A policy of pure rationality which does not shade into reasonableness is incoherent, and therefore ultimately irrational, and a rational man will not confine himself to pure rationality, but come to see that reasonableness is the rationally best policy.[3]

A different distinction (or rather gradation, since there are many intermediate cases between the two extremes), which we already have had occasion to note[4] is that between first-personal and omni-personal reasons. First-personal reasons are those I give in explaining why I actually did what I did. They are often difficult to articulate precisely or fully, but are pervasive and, to me, persuasive. But although I can seek to explain them to you and invite you to share in them, I cannot insist that you accept them on pain of showing yourself unreasonable if you do not. Omni-personal reasons, by contrast, are those that lay claim on anyone and everyone. They are intended to be cogent, and to compel assent from every reasonable man. I can give you omni-personal reasons why you should pay your debts or keep your cattle from straying

[3] See below, pp. 48–58.   [4] Ch. 1, pp. 3, 8, 15; Ch. 2, pp. 20, 24, 25.

on my field, and could instruct my solicitor to bring these reasons to your notice, but not to tell you why you should marry me or be my friend. In being friends with someone, in choosing a career, in marrying, and throughout my personal life, I act on first-personal reasons, aspiring to some ideal, embracing some romantic image of myself, following some vocation or working out some pattern of self-realisation. Such reasons are of immense importance in life and literature, in love and religion, but do not enter into issues of justice. Justice is concerned with omni-personal reasons, which are universal rather than existential in import,[5] and tell people what they must do rather than articulate the intimate rationale of their own authentic actions. Justice is enforceable: it is what we can insist on. "When we think a person is bound in justice to do a thing, it is an ordinary form of language to say that he ought to be compelled to do it."[6] Although we prefer people to be just willingly, we are more concerned with the deed that the motive, and want it to manifest the right reason, not the authentic reasons of the agent. We would rather that they were just, unwillingly, unauthentically and for the wrong reasons, than that they were authentic in their actions but unjust. And we feel justified in substituting our judgement for theirs because we believe the reasons for acting justly are so compelling that no reasonable man should ignore them. But compelling reasons, simply because they are compelling, often seem external, legalistic and deadening. It is in authentically acting on our own reasons that our spirits revive and we really come alive. The best part of our lives is thus outside the purview of justice, and justice must limit itself if life is to be livable. We need liberty. We must reckon, therefore, to compromise justice on occasion for other goods, and acknowledge that there are whole areas of life—love, for example—where it would be conceptually

---

[5] See E. A. Gellner, "Ethics and Logic", *Proceedings of the Aristotelian Society*, LV, 1954–5, pp. 157–78.

[6] J. S. Mill, *Utilitarianism*, Ch. 5, in Everyman edn. p. 44. See also Adam Smith, *Theory of Moral Sentiments*, Part II, Sect. II, Ch. 1, vol. I, p. 165 of edn. of 1801: 'Mere justice is, upon most occasions, but a negative virtue, and only hinders us from hurting our neighbour. The man who barely abstains from violating either the person, or the estate, or the reputation of his neighbours, has surely little positive merit. He fulfils, however, all the rules of what is peculiarly called justice, and does *every thing which his equals can with propriety force him to do*, or which they can punish him for not doing. We may often fulfil all the rules of justice by sitting still and doing nothing' [my italics]; quoted by F. A. Hayek, *Law, Liberty and Legislation*, II, London, 1976, p. 162.

inappropriate to demand justice. It does not follow that it is always inappropriate to look for justice, or that fair dealing is not the essential background of communal life. Justice, based on compelling rather than authentic reasons, is not the whole of virtue, and cannot answer to all my first-personal aspirations in life: but is a necessary virtue none the less, and one I must practise if I am to live with others in society.

Reasoning about human affairs differs from reasoning in the mathematical disciplines in being characteristically *dialectical* in form. Its logic, instead of being a deductive logic, where premisses necessitate their conclusions, is a logic of one side of an argument and another, of pros and cons, of proposals and objections, of *prima facie* cases which may be countered, and presumptions which may be rebutted. We seldom establish sufficient conditions, as we do in mathematics, but often the premisses will be *adequate* to support a conclusion, and sometimes *conclusive*. Whereas in a mathematical argument, if we fail to show our premisses are a sufficient condition of the conclusion, we fail utterly, it is enough, when reasoning about human affairs, to produce an adequate reason, and then consider whether there are any counter-arguments, and if there appear to be none, draw the conclusion. A mathematical argument, if valid, rules out any possibility of the conclusions not being true provided the premisses are: arguments about human affairs, by contrast, characteristically contain a suppressed *ceteris paribus* clause, and hence are perpetually open to a further 'but'. In putting them forward we need to wait for an answer. We need to give our opponents, real or imaginary, time either to agree that they are convinced or to point out weaknesses in our own argument. An argument is not conclusive unless, although there are opportunities for countering it, no reasonable man feels himself able to do so.[7]

The dialectical structure of humane reasoning has great consequences for our intimations of justice. It makes it untidy. Mathematical reasoning, a few recherché Gödelian arguments excepted, is relatively clear-cut, inasmuch as the axioms of a theory,

[7] See, more fully, W. D. Ross, *The Right and the Good*, Oxford, 1930, pp. 19–20; *The Foundations of Ethics*, Oxford, 1939, pp. 83–6; H. L. A. Hart, "The Ascription of Rights and Responsibilities", *Proceedings of the Aristotelian Society*, 1948, pp. 171–94, reprinted in A. G. N. Flew (ed.), *Logic and Language*, vol. 1, Oxford, 1951, pp. 145–69; and J. R. Lucas, "The Philosophy of the Reasonable Man", *Philosophical Quarterly*, 1963, pp. 97–106.

together with the rules of inference, determine the theorems. In humane reasoning the conclusion depends not only on the initial premisses, but the moves made in response to them, the counters to them, and so on. At each stage there are many possible moves, and the cogency of each move depends on all those that have gone before. Quite apart from the fundamental unformulability of reason, therefore, there are also practical difficulties in laying down in advance what shall constitute good reasons. We can only assess them as they come, without there being any algorithm to guide us. The function of an adjudicator is, thus, essentially unlike that of an auditor. An auditor checks the books, and provided he is competent and honest, reaches the same result as any other auditor. Adjudicators, by contrast, can differ, without either being necessarily incompetent or dishonest. Although our concept of reason and our practice of adjudication would both collapse if wise men did not generally think alike, and although in some cases we can be mostly agreed and generally pretty sure that a given opinion is wrong or argument invalid, we have no generally applicable method or canon for deciding the rights and wrongs of every contention. We have to exercise judgement. One or more people have to deliberate, and decide where the balance of argument lies, and we have to be guided by the say-so of certain people, without being able always to reach the same result independently of them. That is, we accept their authority. Authority is much blown upon in the present age. It is often felt that an appeal to authority must be based on the assumption that the authority is infallible, and that once it is seen that the authorities can err, their pretensions to our allegiance must collapse. But that is a mistake. The appeal to authority is based not on their supposed perfection but on our undoubted imperfection. It is not because the authorities are always right that we have to have them, but because we are not always right. The concept of authority plays no part in our theory of mathematical knowledge, even though there are mathematical geniuses who are far, far better at mathematics than the rest of us, because a valid mathematical proof can, in principle, be followed and checked by anyone. The *esprit de géométrie* is a universal ordinary possessed by all men: whereas the *esprit de finesse*, just because it is subject to no algorithm, cannot be entirely independent of the judgement of particular men, and thus necessarily involves the concept of authority.

Judgement is essential, but it is also fallible. The very factors which make us have recourse to the judgement of men, make us unable to trust it absolutely. It is always possible that a judge—or an administrator, or a general, or an examiner, or a historian or a philosopher—however eminent, has got it wrong. Although we may, for good reason, make his say the final one, it remains intelligible to maintain that it is wrong, even though there is no way of putting it right. In this, reasoning about human affairs corresponds to the situation in which human agents find themselves generally, where they are constantly having to act under conditions of imperfect information, and make up their minds what to do as best they can, with a serious prospect of their decision turning out to be wrong. The fact that the authorities' decision may be wrong, although still authoritative, gives rise to many difficulties in elucidating justice. It leads the legal realists to take an entirely external view of the law. The law is, they hold, simply what the judges say it is. If the judges decide otherwise than we think they should, then since there is nothing we can do about it, there is, they argue, nothing more to be said at all. But the inference is invalid.

The dialectical and fallible nature of human reasoning bears also on our rules of natural justice. The rule *audi alteram partem*, hear the other side, reflects the dialectical structure of argument, and the rule that no man shall be judge in his own cause, reflects the fallible nature of judgement; but both run into difficulties due to our need for authoritative, and therefore definitive, procedures. It is not a problem peculiar to justice. In the war much friction was generated between British and American commanders because of different procedures for giving orders. In the British army commanding officers discussed with their subordinates the orders they were thinking of giving before actually doing so: in the American army the orders were issued first, and then modified in the face of expostulations from those receiving them. Legal procedures tend to follow British rather than American practice, and to elicit all considerations first before reaching a definitive decision: but often the logic of the situation makes the American practice more appropriate; often there is adequate, although not conclusive, reason for a decision, and it would be needlessly cumbersome not to take it on the spot; all that is required is that it should not be irrevocable, and that if objections are raised, they should be attended to.

Although we cannot formulate exact and exhaustive criteria for distinguishing good reasons from bad, and although we cannot count on always being able to recognise good reasons when we come across them, we can go some way towards characterizing them. Reasons are shareable. I can understand your reasons, and may adopt them as my own. Whereas your money cannot be my money, while still remaining yours, your reasons may be mine. This is why argument, as opposed to mere word-slinging, is possible; and also—of great importance to our understanding of justice— why I can identify with your actions and make them my own if I understand and accept the reasons behind them.[8] Not only can I understand your reasons, but, if I recognise them as reasons at all, I recognise some gerundive force in them. In being called reasons, there is an implied invitation to share in them. Many philosophers go much further, and assimilate all reasons to what I have characterized as omni-personal reasons, and hold that to recognise a reason at all is to commit oneself to acting on it as occasion arises. That is a mistake. For, as we now can appreciate, since reason is dialectical, besides reasons for an action there may be reasons against, and the reasons you act on may be outweighed in my judgement by other reasons you had not thought of or had discounted. In recognising your reason as a reason, I do not have to adopt it as mine, but only see that I could act on it in appropriate circumstances and in the absence of any considerations to the contrary. I can understand your ambition or avarice without having to endorse it, so long as I can see how under some conditions, granted that I should not be cutting anyone else out or compromising my own integrity, I should rather succeed than fail and should prefer having money to not having it.

Reason transcends tenses as well as persons. It is easy to misconstrue this, and make out reason to be entirely timeless, as Plato did with his world of forms. Reason is not totally timeless. There are important differences between the future, the present and the past, and we need to take account of them in our reasoning. Nevertheless, we cannot divorce the tenses. Every past was in its time a present and before that a future, and every future will come to be present and then past. We know it: it is fundamental to our view of ourselves and our own status as rational agents. And so,

[8] See, more fully, J. R. Lucas, *Democracy and Participation*, Penguin, 1976, Ch. 2, pp. 12–15.

though differences of time may well be relevant, as differences of person are, there is some pressure on the part of reason to transcend differences of time and to be omni-temporal in much the same way as it tends to be omni-personal.

The characteristics of omni-personality and omni-temporality are generalised into that of "universalisability". As Samuel Clarke put it, "Whatever I judge reasonable or unreasonable for *another* to do for Me: That by the same Judgement I declare reasonable or unreasonable that I *in the like case* should do for him"[9] or in Kant's more famous formulation, "Act only on that maxim through which you can at the same time will that it should become a universal law."[10] Nowell-Smith's formulation—that a man "is abusing language if he says it is a matter of moral principle with him to pay his debts and he pays Jones while refusing to pay Smith, without being able to give any reason for the discrepancy"[11] is significantly different, but the underlying rationale is the same. We must mete out the same treatment unless the cases are different, for reasons, λόγοι, apply analogously in analogous cases. Not only in moral argument, but in historical and scientific argument the same principle applies: a historical or a scientific explanation is covertly general, and applies not in one instance only but in others sufficiently similar; and where it is inapplicable we seek some differentiating factor to account for the difference. And hence it is a maxim of justice also, that we must treat like cases alike, for otherwise we shall be treating one of the parties worse than his case warrants. Only for very good reasons may we take an adverse decision, and good reasons have to be based on facts about him rather than any adventitious factors, and therefore if the cases are the same, must apply the same way in each case.

The principle of universalisability can be construed in two ways, a stronger, which underlies the principle of legality, and a weaker, which underlies the principle of equity. In the stronger form it is taken as requiring that the just or reasonable man should be able to specify on demand the relevant features of a particular case in virtue of which he reckoned his treatment of it appropriate, and

[9] Samuel Clarke, Boyle Lectures, 1705; in *Boyle Lectures*, II, London, 1739, p. 90; reprinted in *Works of Samuel Clarke*, II, London, 1738, p. 619; quoted by Henry Sidgwick, *The Methods of Ethics*, 7th edn., London, 1907, pp. 384–5.
[10] Kant, *Groundwork of the Metaphysic of Morals*, tr. H. J. Paton, pp. 52/88.
[11] P. H. Nowell-Smith, *Ethics*, Penguin, 1954, p. 309.

that he should then be committed to treating *every* other case with those features the same. This is the natural reading of Kant's formulation, and has been made the basis of Hare's system of ethics.[12] But although it adequately articulates an essential feature of our mathematical and scientific reasoning, it fits ill with the dialectical mode of reasoning about human affairs, according to which it is always open to an objector to interpose a 'but' and cite some further fact or adduce some fresh argument which alters the complexion of the case. We cannot lay down in advance an exact and exhaustive list of features which characterize those cases which are to be accounted like cases and treated alike. It is only when faced with new cases and having to decide about them that we come to realise the relevance of new factors. The principle of universalisability, regarded simply as a requirement of reason, should therefore be formulated in some weaker version, like that of Nowell-Smith, when it is to be applied to the humanities. Granted the infinite complexity of human affairs, we can never hope to specify all possibly relevant factors, but can expect a man who differentiates in his treatment or evaluation of two cases to say, at least approximately, wherein the difference lies. Whether it is actions, evaluations or judgements of cause and effect, I can always be asked 'Why the difference?', and although I sometimes may not be able to put my finger on it and say *exactly* why, I abandon all claims to rationality if I do not see the point of the question, and acknowledge no obligation to try and answer it.

Although the strong form of principle of universalisability is not in general a requirement of reason, and the claim that it is should be resisted as representing a misunderstanding of reason and an attempt to straitjacket it within the confines of mathematical and scientific reasoning, nevertheless the strong form is on other grounds quite properly required in some sorts of case, either on account of human finitude and the fact that we have to operate with relatively few and relatively crude categories,[13] or in virtue of the logic of certain games-theoretical situations,[14] and under these conditions gives rise to a requirement of equality.

Justice is not the same as reason. Although justice is reasonable,

---

[12] R. M. Hare, *The Language of Morals*, Oxford, 1952, and *Freedom and Reason*, Oxford, 1963.

[13] See below, Ch. 5, pp. 104–8 and Ch. 9, pp. 178–9.

[14] See below, pp. 55–8 and 14, pp. 235–7.

not all reasonable actions are just. Even actions undertaken for compelling omni-personal reasons, whose cogency all would acknowledge, such as *raisons d'état*, are still not just. Although the word 'judgement' and, as we noted at the outset of this chapter, the word 'justify' are used in a very broad sense, so much so that Frankena coins the word 'justicize' to have the more specific sense of making just,[15] the other cognate words are used in a much more limited sense, not at all coextensive with 'reason' and its cognates. "Can one not act reasonably without acting judicially?" asked Lord Radcliffe in *Nakkuda Ali*'s case,[16] and the answer is clearly "yes". There are many reasons which may guide my action but not make it just. In order to justicize an action, we must either establish that any complaint of injustice is itself unjustified—that the choice was an unfettered one, e.g. where to go for a holiday, or that it was one in which extraneous factors were supposed to be paramount, e.g. a service posting in the armed forces—or adduce for deciding against a potential complainant compelling reasons of a sort whose force even he cannot evade. We have to show not only that we had to bear hardly on someone but that it had to be him. Only then will he see that we were not acting with wanton disregard of his rights and interests, but, in spite of manifest reluctance to do him down, we still had no alternative but to decide as we did. For that to be the case our reasons have to be of a special kind. The must be, in a sense yet to be elucidated, *individualised* reasons. They must be based on facts about him, not exclusively but enough to justify, even to him if he is reasonable, not simply our reaching an adverse decision, but its being adverse *to him*. We have to structure the argument so that it can be seen from his point of view, as well as that of anybody else in danger of being done down. We therefore need to operate in terms of a rationality that sees things primarily from the agent's own point of view. For this purpose we shall use the Theory of Games, which will enable us both to elucidate the concept of rationality, showing how, in spite of its egocentric origin, it develops the same universal characteristics of omni-personal and omni-temporal concern as is manifested by reason itself, and to illuminate the rationale of political institutions,

---

[15] William K. Frankena, "The Concept of Social Justice", in R. B. Brandt (ed.), *Social Justice*, Englewood Cliffs, N.J., 1962, p. 16.

[16] 1951 A.C. 66: quoted by R. F. Heuston, *Essays in Constitutional Law*, 2nd edn., London, 1964, p. 188 n. 42.

showing the logic of laws, of political authority, of penalties, vengeance and the vendetta, and, in particular, revealing the distinctions between justice on the one hand and expediency, utility, and equality on the other, and revealing also our grounds for needing justice.

The Theory of Games is concerned with the results, called "outcomes", of the choices of a number of independent parties, called "players", who choose in the light of the value, called the "pay-off", each outcome has for each player. For many purposes, it is enough to consider two players, each making two choices, with therefore four possible outcomes, each giving two pay-offs. We give, as an example, which also will prove of fundamental importance, the Prisoners' Dilemma, first formulated in contemporary terms by A. W. Tucker. In this example two prisoners are each held by the police, who know that they have committed a serious crime, but cannot secure conviction against either unless at least one of them confesses. The police, however, have sufficient evidence to secure a conviction against each of them on a minor charge of income-tax evasion. The police offer to each prisoner separately the following deal: if that prisoner will confess while the other does not, the police will not press either the major or the minor charge, and he will go scot-free. If he does not confess, while the other prisoner does, the police will secure his conviction on both charges, and he will get ten years. If both prisoners confess, the court will give them five years each. If neither confesses, each will get one year for income-tax evasion. In the matrix below, we tabulate these alternatives and the corresponding outcome, giving the prison sentence on the bottom left for the prisoner who is represented as choosing between the rows, and on the top right for the prisoner who is represented as choosing between columns.

Prisoner B	keeps silent	confesses
Prisoner A		
keeps silent	1 Both jailed for tax 1	0 B let off: maximum jail for A 10
confesses	10 A let off: maximum jail for B 0	5 both jailed with reduced sentences 5

Prison sentences are clearly bad things. It might have been better to represent them with a minus sign in front of them. Hereafter we shall adopt the convention of representing pay-offs in a positive sense—the arithmetically larger one being the more desirable. Although in the case of the prisoners there is an obvious comparability between one man's prison sentence and another's, there is in general great difficulty in comparing one person's good with another's. Games-theorists have, like Welfare Economists, displayed great ingenuity in making do with only ordinal preferences, and a theory can be constructed which takes account of the scruples of the philosophical purist. But for our purposes we shall take the pay-offs as being given in ordinary numerical form, and assume we have been able to establish interpersonal cardinal utility-scales. It is an intelligible concept. Money posseses just the properties required, being assignable, measurable and transferable. There would be, of course, formidable objections to assuming that all values are like this. Many values are "invaluable"; often we can order them only lexically; even where one man can assess his values on a scale, we have no warrant for assuming that it will be the same for another. Nevertheless, it is illuminating to consider models with numerical pay-offs, and it is unobjectionable, so long as we remember that these are only models, and not to be applied insensitively to the moral problems of real life.

Each person has to decide what he is going to do. The standard assumption is that each is free to consult only his own interests, and will therefore choose to act so as to maximise his own pay-off. This is the principle of liberty as understood by *laissez-faire* economists, and is exemplified in the free market economy. It is important to realise, however, that this description is a mis-classification. The principle of liberty is concerned with *who* should make decisions, not with *what* decisions should be made. These are separate questions.[17] Although since men are somewhat selfish, each is likely to look after number one first, this does not have to be true, and sometimes is not true. Some people are very unselfish, and many people have some regard for other people. We therefore should distinguish the principle of liberty, which is generally taken for granted in the Theory of Games, from various principles, such as expediency or self-interest, which lay down how each person, or

[17] See further below, Ch. 11, pp. 197–9.

"player" in the terminology of the Theory of Games, should decide in the light of the pay-offs.

According to the principle of expediency, each person, or player, should act so as to maximise his own pay-off, without regard for the others. This principle is often commended as being the obvious rational one. It is easy to see why. Reason is, for the most part, gentle and sweet. I am led to see what is reasonable and right, not compelled to concede it. But economics generally, and the Theory of Games in particular, is largely concerned with conflict. Moreover, in an age of scepticism, the rhetorical question behind much philosophy is "Why should I?", and only very cogent arguments, whose strength we shall be forced to acknowledge, are countenanced. And, finally, it is implicit in the concept of justice that it is concerned with omni-personal, and therefore relatively cogent, arguments rather than the more intimate ones which may be equally appealing and effective as first-personal ones, but which cannot force acceptance or carry conviction when addressed to unwilling ears. Arguments of expediency make a minimal demand for commitment, and have a maximum range and effectiveness. I can address them to almost anyone, no matter how sceptical and tough-minded he is, for to his question "Why should I?", I have a sure-fire answer "Or else". If you will not believe me when I adduce arguments of expediency, say against smoking, or shooting traffic lights, I can prove beyond all reasonable doubt what the consequences will be, and you cannot make out that those consequences do not matter. In other cases, where my argument concerns other people or times past, you can cut them off with "Well, what is that to me?", but an autonomous agent can hardly be unconcerned with his own future concerns.

If we think further, the argument from expediency loses its appearance of paradigm cogency. After all, people do smoke. Although there is a conceptual argument for an autonomous agent's being concerned with his own future ability to carry out his intentions, it is not always effective in practice. People sometimes are misled by present pleasure into neglecting their own future interests, just as they are sometimes misled into ignoring other people or the past. In each case their actions are in some sense irrational and incoherent. Certainly, it is crucial to our concept of personal identity that one should be able to make up one's mind about what one is going to do, and therefore to make plans about, and hence be concerned about, the future, and especially one's future ability to implement one's intentions. But it is also essential to our concept of person that we have occasion to use the second and third persons, and not only the first person singular, and that we can remember the past as well as plan the future. These are all conceptual concomitants of our idea of ourselves as agents, and although each of them can be ignored in practice, the practice that ignores them will show itself one way or another as incoherent. Although in ordinary life we are all too familiar with the man who is heedless even of the most obvious counsels of expediency, and is "his own worst enemy", we tend to avert our eyes and theorize as though he did not exist. Economists often, and games-theorists always, make good their case by definition. Yet even so, too exclusive a concentration on one's own short-term interest can be self-defeating, as the Prisoners' Dilemma shows. To be really rational, we shall need to expand our concept of rationality, to take a wider perspective and a longer view.

Many thinkers suppose that the Prisoners' Dilemma arises from their selfishness rather than their too limited rationality. After all, the obvious alternative to complete selfishness is complete unselfishness, where one considers only the pay-off to others, and not that of oneself at all; and if each prisoner refused to confess, in order not to incriminate his confederate, then their joint unselfishness would be rewarded by the "best" outcome. But that fails to meet either the practicalities or the full logic of the situation: each would be so anxious to save the other by taking all the responsibility himself, that both would get a five-year sentence; the converse to the Prisoners' Dilemma is the Altruists' Dilemma, where the result of both being "beastly unselfish" is worse than if either had been willing to receive benefits at the other's

The Altruists' Dilemma (i)

He \ She	cooks	helps him mend the car
mends the car	good lunch followed by pleasant drive — **8** / **8**	record journey, with snack in Transport Cafe — **3** / **10**
helps her cook	super lunch but no drive — **10** / **3**	food ruined and car won't go — **0** / **0**

hands. Each altruist assumes that the other will act in accordance with his or her true preferences, and tries then to secure to the other an even better outcome.

Other variants can also be envisaged. If, for example, he were a passable cook and she a moderate mechanic, the outcome of his cooking and her mending might not be disastrous; the meal might be slightly less unappetising than the snack in the Transport Cafe, and the car might limp along lumpily at thirty-five. In that case the pay-off in the bottom right-hand box would be (4, 4) instead of (0, 0), and we get a second version, which will then constitute an exact inverse of the Prisoners' Dilemma, where, whether each

The Altruists' Dilemma (ii)

He \ She	cooks	helps him mend the car
mends the car	good lunch, followed by pleasant drive 8 / 8	record journey, with meal in Transport Cafe 3 / 10
helps her cook	super lunch, but no drive 10 / 3	mediocre lunch, followed by mediocre drive 4 / 4

assumes the other to act altruistically or selfishly, both will decide in what they take to be the other's interests, with the result that they both will be worse off than they need have been. From the formal point of view, it does not really matter whose pay-off each player is trying to maximise, so long as the different players are concentrating exlusively on different pay-offs. There will always be some assignments of pay-offs where the result of different people trying to maximise different pay-offs will demonstrate the irrationality of so limited a form of rationality.

The Prisoners' Dilemma arose in an artificial situation. It was an isolated occasion, and the prisoners were unable to communicate with each other. Normally things are different. We do not, in ordinary life, decide on a course of action independently of what other people do. We concert our actions. I will do this, *if* you will do that. I will keep silence, *if* you will keep silence too. We represent this, in the terminology of the Theory of Games, not as a strategy, but as a meta-strategy.[18] In formulating my meta-strategy, I need to consider every possible choice of other players, and decide on my response to it. Thus in the Prisoners' Dilemma I may decide on a meta-strategy of confessing if he confesses, and not confessing if he does not. Of course, in the original, once-only situation where neither prisoner could communicate to the other, neither prisoner could know what meta-strategy the other was adopting, nor which condition, in his own formulation of his own meta-strategy, had been fulfilled, or which conditional response was therefore called for. But in ordinary life we can communicate intentions, and can tell subsequently whether a man actually carried out the intentions he avowed. I can tell him what meta-strategy I intend to adopt: he can tell me in the light of that what actual strategy he will adopt; or by question and answer, considering various hypotheses in turn, I may elicit from him a complete meta-strategy—a compendious statement of what his response would be for each meta-strategy I might adopt. Once we see that parties are choosing meta-strategies or meta-meta-strategies, it becomes clear that if each says to the other, in effect, "I will keep mum, if you will; but if you confess, I will too", then both can agree not to confess, and suffer much lighter penalties than if both confessed. In the terminology of the Theory of Games, we form a "coalition". It is clearly a sensible policy. By not trying to snatch immediate advantage, both secure a better outcome than they could otherwise. In a once-only situation, each must rely on the other's altruism as well as self-interest not to go back on the agreement, but in real life I cannot go on lying successfully about my intentions, and once it is known, my protestations to the contrary notwithstanding, that I will go back on my agreement not to confess, the other chap will, in accordance with his avowed meta-strategy, confess too, with the result that I shall be worse off than if I had kept my word. In the long run honesty is the best policy, and enlightened self-interest should provide me with adequate motives, even if altruism will not.

The importance of the move from considering a strategy to considering a meta-strategy has long been sensed by moral philosophers. It is what gives force to the rhetorical question "What

[18] See Nigel Howard, *Paradoxes of Rationality: Theory of Metagames and Political Behaviour*, Cambridge, Mass., 1971, Chs. 3 and 4; or, more simply, Steven J. Brams, *Game Theory and Politics*, New York, 1975, Ch. 1, §1.8, pp. 30–9.

would happen if everybody else did the same?" In asking this question, we are not merely urging someone to entertain a false hypothesis, as C. D. Broad suggested.[19] Rather, we are urging the person to consider not just his strategy—a single decision in a once-only situation—but his meta-strategy, and the response that it would rationally provoke. In the long run, yielding to the temptation to maximise one's own pay-off without any consideration of others is an irrational meta-strategy. For everyone is tempted, just as I am, to do the same and to try and obtain greater short-term benefits for himself. The only way of avoiding this result is for us all to adopt the agreed meta-strategy, whereby we co-operate with one another on the condition that everyone does. If I go back on that agreement, the fact that someone has gone back will be known (even though it may not be known that it is I who am the culprit), and the whole practice will be jeopardised. If I take books out of the library without entering them in the register, other people will find books missing when they want them, and according to their meta-strategy of taking the trouble to enter books provided others do, but not otherwise, will also stop entering their books, and this will ultimately work out to my own disadvantage. Essentially, I had been too *simpliste* in my reading of the situation. I had construed other people as all acting on the unconditional meta-strategy of always keeping to the agreement, irrespective of what anybody else did. I had assumed that they were moral mugs; and if that assumption were right, then I should be very clever to take advantage of their naïvety. But if I analyse the situation from a games-theoretical point of view, I see that their rational strategy is not one of keeping to the agreement unconditionally, but only conditionally: and, therefore, in so far as I see them as being rational like myself, I shall see that the only solution that is satisfactory and stable over the long term is to be obtained by my responding to their conditional meta-strategy with a similar one on my part. The Prisoners' Dilemma is a paradigm because it reveals the conflict between short-term interest and long-term interest, and reveals an incoherence in the attempt to limit rationality to a simple principle of maximising one's own immediate interests. I am not the only pebble on the beach. There are other pebbles, not only with their own interests and own power of decision, but rational and

[19] C. D. Broad, "On the Function of False Hypotheses in Ethics", *International Journal of Ethics*, xxvi, 1916, pp. 377–97.

capable of rationally concerting their actions. And the only rational thing for me to do is to pursue a meta-strategy which takes account of that fact.

In order to establish an understanding which will enable us to break out of the Prisoners' Dilemma, we all need to see one another's point of view. "I won't split, if you won't" is not a sensible proposal on my part unless I can see the advantage from your point of view of my not confessing. The "rationality" of the solution of the Prisoners' Dilemma is its all-round advantages. I do not just see it from my point of view, and see my not splitting as the price I must pay to obtain your not splitting on me. I see, quite dispassionately, that it would be better for all of us if we all stuck to a common line of keeping silent. My enlightened self-interest is generalised from short-term expediency not only in being long-term, but also in being corporate. Not only is it not limited to the immediate future, but it is also not confined to the first person singular. I start using the first person plural: "Look here", I say, "let's both keep mum." I do not completely merge myself in the first person plural. I am not simply sacrificing my own interests for the benefit of all. I am to be advantaged along with every one else. But I do need to use other persons than the first person singular, and to make some sacrifices in consequence. Rationality may start with the first person singular, but needs to conjugate in other persons and other numbers too.

The Prisoners' Dilemma has long been known. According to Plato, Protagoras used it to account for the existence of political society, and Plato put substantially the same argument into the mouth of Glaucon in the *Republic*. Hobbes saw it as the fundamental problem of the human condition, for which the creation of the sovereign State was the only solution. Each man would naturally rob, and generally wrong, his neighbour, but would very much dislike being robbed or otherwise wronged. If we consider just me and the other chap, each of us can choose to wrong or not to wrong. Best of all, I should like to wrong my neighbour but not be wronged by him; failing that, it would be better neither to wrong him nor to be wronged by him than both to wrong him and to be wronged by him; and worst of all would be to be wronged by him although not enjoying any of the advantages of wronging him. And his preferences are similar, *mutatis mutandis*. We can express this in a table analogous to that of the Prisoners' Dilemma:

Other chap I	wrongs me	does not wrong me
wrong him	1 Life for both of us is nasty, brutish and short, but at least I occasionally get some of his goodies. 1	0 Life for me is lovely. I enjoy the security of not being wronged by him with the liberty of wronging him whenever convenient. Life for him is nasty, brutish and short, with no consolations whatever. 10
do not wrong him	10 Life for him is lovely. He enjoys the security of not being wronged by me combined with the liberty of wronging me whenever he feels like it. Life for me is nasty, brutish and short, and even when I get the opportunity of taking advantage of him, I don't take it 0	6 Life for us both is tolerable, but circumscribed. We both enjoy security from each other's depredations, but both are frustrated in the full exercise of our own personal potential. Life is comfortable, bourgeois and long, but lacking in authenticity; and we both suffer from *mauvaise foi.* 6

It is clear that if each of us is guided by the principle of simple expediency, then each will decide to wrong the other, since, if the other is going to commit any wrongdoing he can get away with, one would be a mug not do likewise, and if the other is a mug and is going to forbear from wrongdoing, one would be a fool to forgo the additional advantages that accrue from wrongdoing on one's own part. Arguing this way each will reckon that, whatever the other does, he will do better by wrongdoing than by abstaining from it. But the result of their both doing wrong is, from both of their points of view, worse than if they had both forborne. Enlightened self-interest indicates that everyone will be better off, if each abandons the path of simple expediency and all abstain from doing wrong to anyone. But there is a gap between refined rationality and action. We can see that the most rational, stable, and best all-round, meta-strategy for each is to abstain from wrong provided everybody else does, but it explicitly depends on this proviso. Meta-game analysis is constitutionally iffy. It shows that if others adopt such-and-such a strategy, it would be rational for me to make such-and-such a response. Actually to get anywhere, we need a coalition, which is, by contrast, constitutionally categorical. "Let's all agree to abstain from wrongdoing." Once agreed, we have made the necessary start, and satisfied the condition for every one's sticking to it. Hence the need for conventions.[20] They enable each to know what everyone else can be expected to do, and thus satisfy the condition for his doing the same. So long as we all agree, and all keep the agreement, we all shall be better off than if each acted on his own account so as to maximise his own pay-off regardless of others; and thus civil society, with all its artificial restrictions and conventions, makes sense.

But it is a big IF. Although we can all see that civilised society is better for all of us than the state of nature, each one of us can also see that he would be better off still if he did not keep to the agreement while the others did. It is easy to revert from the wider rationality of the meta-game analysis to the more limited rationality which does not enter into the reasoning of others, but, taking them for granted as given external entities, seeks simply to maximise one's own pay-off in the given situation. There is a standing temptation to cheat. And, men being frail, some will succumb. And once the condition of everyone else's keeping the agreement fails, it seems pointless to keep it oneself, and the whole agreement breaks down. Conventions are doubly vulnerable. Everyone is tempted, and once anyone yields to temptation, the rationale of others resisting is weakened, if not destroyed. An illuminating instance of the way in which our good behaviour is conditional on that of others is recounted by Mitchell:[21]

I have never forgotten an occasion shortly after the war when I was required to board the Rome-Paris express at Turin. We had chosen Turin because we were informed that three fresh coaches would be added to the train at that point. We could, therefore, go early, get into one of these coaches and secure seats without any trouble. But we had reckoned without the Italian railway authorities. Although the three coaches were clearly visible in a siding when we arrived on the platform, they were not moved until five minutes before the express was due, by which time about

---

[20] See further below, pp. 58-9.
[21] B. G. Mitchell, *Law, Morality and Religion*, Oxford, 1967, pp. 76-8.

twice as many people had gathered on the platform as could possibly secure seats. The subsequent struggle has provided a useful philosophical example ever since. It approximated closely to Hobbes' description of the State of Nature as "a war of every man against every man". What astonished me in particular was not the behaviour of the Italians, which to my insular eyes was only what was to be expected, but my own behaviour. I kicked, shoved, and elbowed, thrusting women and children from my path in a manner wholly out of keeping with the character of an English gentleman; and I secured two corner seats.

Reflecting afterwards on my conduct I realized for the first time how much of my normal good behaviour depended upon the conventions and the implicit sanctions of English life. To put it briefly: in England people queue. The queue is, in fact, a simple but by no means primitive institution. There is a tacit agreement among Englishmen that when waiting for anything people form themselves into a line and take their turn according to their position in the line. This principle defines the institution of 'the queue'. The institution has its associated morality; it is wrong to jump the queue. It is wrong even if the individual can get away with it. The institution can survive *some* parasites—habitual queue-jumpers who profit from the fact that others stay in their place. But if enough people jump the queue it will collapse into a free-for-all, which frustrates the purpose of the institution.

In this country queuing has become a settled disposition, People don't generally queue because they feel morally obliged to do so, though they would see the moral point if they reflected upon it, and feel morally indignant at people who jump the queue. They have got into the habit. If they were seriously tempted by examples of flagrant queue-jumping or lost confidence in the intention of other people to stay in the queue they would lose the habit. This is where an element of compulsion might help. The presence of a policeman ready and able to deter potential queue-jumpers would reinforce the disposition of the ordinary man—the man waiting for the Clapham omnibus—to keep his position in the queue.

Mitchell is willing to play the queuing game, but once he perceives that this is not the game that is being played, he would be a fool to exercise restraint. The advantages of queueing—freedom from jostling, orderly access to benefits—depend on everyone's taking his turn; and unless almost everyone does, there is no point in the practice at all. Granted the condition that others are forbearing to push too, gentlemanly second nature will suffice to prevent us from taking advantage of the forbearance of others: but as soon as we see that this condition is not fulfilled, the original Adam takes over.

Hobbes saw this. "Covenants, without the sword, are but words", he wrote.[22] Higher rationality is not enough to ensure that the agreement will be always observed, and therefore it must be enforced by force or the threat of force in the hands of a sovereign. Hobbes pushes the argument too far. He takes a very low view of human nature, and assumes that nobody would ever keep the law except under immediate threat of punishment, and therefore has to confer on the sovereign far greater power to coerce his subjects than is really needed. Hobbes's argument would go through, if men were all limited to acting only on the principle of expediency, so as to maximise their short-term interest. In that case they would be unable to resist the temptation to snatch advantage by breaking the agreement, unless the balance of advantage were immediately and evidently weighted the other way. But, fortunately, we are not all like that. Whether on account of social conditioning, as Glaucon assumed, or because we have an expanded idea of rationality, as I have argued, we are not all always guided by considerations of expediency alone. The problem, therefore, is not, as Hobbes supposed, that of establishing a system to coerce everyone into keeping the agreement, but only of deterring that smaller section of the population who would otherwise set a bad example to the rest; and this in turn can be achieved by the application of sanctions against that smaller section of those who need deterring, comprised of those for whom threats are not enough, and who persist in violating the agreement in spite of them; and this in turn can be achieved by the application of actual coercive force against that smaller section still of those subject to sanctions, comprised of those who will not submit to them if they can possibly help it, and for whom physical force is the only argument. We do not need nearly as many swords to make our covenants effective as Hobbes made out, and therefore do not need to have the sovereign as powerful as he concluded. Nevertheless, some power is sometimes needed. Although many people will keep to the agreement, provided others do, the whole logic of their doing so depends on the condition being satisfied, and hence they need to know for certain—at least reasonably for certain—that it will be satisfied, before it becomes rational for them to forgo the advantage of breaking the agreement. They need to be able to rely on other people keeping the agreement. And in many cases they cannot feel confident that others will do so merely on the

[22] Thomas Hobbes, *Leviathan*, Part II, Ch. XVII.

evidence that they have hitherto, because they impute rationality to others, and suppose them to be of like passions with themselves, and therefore assume them to be tempted and open to the argument of short-term expediency. Hence they distrust others, believing them to be as untrustworthy as they believe themselves to be. Only if it is evident to them that it must be evident to everyone, however much tempted and however much swayed by the argument of short-term expediency, that he cannot get away with breaking the agreement, and that however hard he tries to brazen it out, he will not succeed in outfacing the authorities and will ultimately be forced to ac-knowledge that crime does not pay, can the marginal man be assured that the condition is satisfied, and it really is reasonable for him to keep the agreement.

The Prisoners' Dilemma is not the only game to illuminate politics. "Zero-sum" games are important because they express the adversary aspect of social encounters. Some people construe every encounter as a confrontation because they suppose that every game must be zero-sum. A zero-sum game is one in which the total of the pay-offs for each outcome is zero, so that one player's winnings are achieved at the cost of the others' loss. If I play chess with you and win, you lose. If you win the tennis tournament, all the other competitors lose. A zero-sum game formalises the concept of a competitive enterprise, where one can succeed only by cutting other people out. Co-operative enterprises, by contrast, are non-zero-sum. Parties can all benefit by concerting their efforts, without anyone having to lose out. Besides the Prisoners' Dilemma, the Rule of the Road and the Battle of the Sexes also illuminate the logic of political situations. The Rule of the Road considers two motorists approaching each other from opposite directions in, say, the Channel Tunnel, where it is not clear whether British or French traffic laws apply. Each motorist has the choice of steering towards the right side of the road or the left. If both go right or both go left, they will avoid a collision, and can continue their journeys at speed: but if one goes right and the other left, there will be a collision, which will spoil their cars, and an altercation, which will spoil their tempers. We can tabulate the possible outcomes and their pay-offs like this:

Mr Knight	goes right	goes left
M. Chevalier *à droit*	5 each passes other safely 5	0 collision 0
à gauche	0 collision 0	5 each passes other safely 5

Here there is no conflict. Each is anxious to concert his action with the other so as to avoid a collision. The problem is simply that of knowing what the other will do. The will is free. Each person is free to make up his mind for himself what to do, and in this case there are no grounds for supposing that he will be led to choose one way rather than the other by considerations of expediency. But we need to know. And since there are no natural features of the situation, we shall be guided by any adventitious ones which we think will be taken as guides by the other man too. In particular, if anybody gives us a lead, we shall gladly follow his lead, and if any convention has grown up, we shall gladly follow its ruling. The importance of this type of social interaction is that it shows how authority can develop *without* needing to be backed by coercive sanctions, and how laws can grow up that are not subject to erosion by queue-jumpers. Authority does not just rest upon power, as Hobbes made out, but very largely itself creates power. Because we all often need to obey authority, we shall be disposed to obey it always: a word from authority will often, therefore, be enough to bring the incipient queue-jumper back into line; and if he should still be minded to be recalcitrant, authority can give the lead for considerable pressure to be exerted. Authority, therefore, is largely self-sustaining, and itself constitutes a form of power.

In the Rule of the Road, it would be enough for avoiding a collision if the drivers were to signal their intentions: we only need a rule because often there is not time for signalling. But once one driver has given an unambiguous lead, the other driver has no reasonable option but to follow suit. In Greek the word ἄρχειν, to rule, means also to lead off. So long as there is no latent conflict, there should be no objection to this: but often there is some conflict latent in the business of avoiding collisions. The Frenchman might not like driving on the left, whereas the Englishman is damned if he will move over for a Frog. The paradigm example is The Battle of the Sexes. He and She want to spend their holiday together, but he would prefer them both to go mountaineering in the Alps, whereas she would rather they both spent it sunbathing by the sea. The matrix is

He \ She	goes to Alps	goes to sea
goes to Alps	Lovely for him: good for her. 8 10	"wish you were here too". 4 4
goes to sea	beastly for him: beastly for her. 0 0	good for him; lovely for her. 10 8

Here it is clear that there is no one "best" solution; not because, as in The Rule of the Road, there were two equally good ones, and we just did not know which one to go for, but because of an irresoluble conflict between the two parties as to which is really the best outcome. But since the second best is so much better than the other two, it would pay either side to settle for that if the very best appeared unattainable. And therefore it would pay the other side to make it seem unattainable. If she can throw some hysterics and say she cannot abide the Alps, and will not go there at any price, then he, if he is reasonable, will abandon his hopes of an Alpine holiday, and settle for the sea, which he would like twice as much—8—as solitary mountaineering. But equally he may see that the moment has come to take a firm masculine line and let the little woman face up to the realities of the situation, and either come along with him or go her separate way. And if once it becomes clear that that is the choice, she will have no option but to cave in, and buy a rucksack instead of a new bikini. It is thus irrational to be commited to the principle of expediency, because that enables the other to manipulate one's choices. Threats, even if costly to oneself to carry out, can secure better terms. Better threaten, even if sometimes one has to cut off one's nose to spite one's face, than always seek to maximise one's immediate interests. This is the rationale of revenge and retaliation by the individual, and, in part, of the infliction of penalties and punishments by the State. It pays the State to commit itself beforehand to punish malefactors. If it is known that the State always exacts punishment as a matter of course, then actual criminals will be deterred; whereas, if the State is expected to be reasonable, and judge each case on its merits, and not to waste time punishing people unless some evident good will come of it, then crime will often pay, because it will not pay the State, once the crime has been done, to do anything about it. Thus, although punishing those who have committed crimes will usually be "irrational" in the limited sense of the word if we consider each individual case separately, the policy of always punishing criminals will pay off in the long run. The same holds good for retaliation and revenge. In any particular case it probably would be wise to let bygones be bygones: but a general policy of never letting anyone get away with it will pay better still. A man whose history and demeanour blazons forth to the whole world his motto *Nemo me impune lacessit* is evidently a man not to be trifled with, and therefore will seldom be troubled by triflers. But this general policy is itself not totally rational. It can lead to an endlessly escalating vendetta between two people both determined to pay back with interest any wrongs they have suffered. Granted the many accidental and unintended provocations of ordinary life, a too prickly determination to requite every wrong could well prove disastrous. There is wisdom, as well as Christian virtue, in turning the other cheek, at least at first.

The Battle of the Sexes thus reveals a new dimension of rationality. It shows that there is irrationality in restricting the range of rational calculation to the future alone. The man who is guided by short-term expediency or by any other consequentialist consideration exclusively lays himself open to being manipulated by others sufficiently determined who make their own choices in such a way as to make the action they want him to take more expedient from his point of view than any other. And once this point is taken, and it is realised that it can be in one's long-term interests to be "irrational", strategies diverge rather than converge, collaboration gives way to confrontation, and the separate parties, each seeking to maximise his own individual pay-off, mutually interact to bring about one of the worst possible outcomes. Only by not restricting rationality to the future can these consequences be avoided. We need to take into account not only future consequences but past actions and present commitments. Even if I thought that it were irrational to reward people for their past actions, and believed that the only good reason for conferring benefits was as an incentive to future action on their part, I should still want the future perfect tense to stipulate conditions and specify bargains. There are very few bargains in which the two sides are fulfilled simultaneously. I want to be able to commit myself to carrying out my side of the bargain, if you carry out yours, and that if it should be the case that you have already done your bit, I shall then regard this past action of yours as a good reason for my going on to fulfil my side; and, conversely, if I give you payment beforehand, I shall expect you to regard this, even though it will have been already accomplished, as an adequate reason for your being bound to carry on with what you had undertaken to do. If no past actions can, in principle, be reasons for any subsequent actions, then bargains are impossible, and not only rewards, but incentives, become conceptually incoherent. It also becomes impossible for an agent to form an adequate view of his own agency. By ignoring the past, he loses part of his roots, and ceases to be an independent originator of action, and becomes, as we have seen, manipulable, since anyone else, sufficiently determined and bloody-minded, can dictate to a consequentialist what he shall do, by rigging the situation so that the path it is desired he shall take is the most expedient of the available options. The sense that the past is not always to be immediately forgotten and that it is reasonable to remember what people have done, as well as calculate what they are going to do, in deciding how to act towards them, is, in part, an assertion of the independence of the agent. Agents are not to be trifled with, and cannot thereafter be bamboozled by offers of immediate carrots, because, like elephants, they never forget. A certain willingness to retaliate, and requite good for good and evil for evil, seems manly in addition to being, as we have shown, a meta-strategy which will work out well in the long run. This is not to say that it is wholly rational, nor that we should neglect the differences between present, past and future. Rather, we should recognise that the first person singular makes sense only on condition that we acknowledge also the validity of the first person plural and the second and third persons singular and plural, and only if we can take into account time past as well as time present and time to come.

Rationality, although centred on the agent who is having to decide what to do, leads him on to a consideration of all persons and all time which, we have already seen,[23] is the characteristic of reason. Decision-making, like other verbs, conjugates not only through the persons but through the tenses too.

The omnitemporality of reason makes it easier to accept the rationality of justice, and, together with its omni-personality, enables us to determine what lines of argument justice enjoins. It removes the reproach of backward-lookingness and reveals the difference between arguments of justice and those of expediency, enlightened self-interest and utility.

Justice, because it is concerned with the past, is often felt to be irrational, vindictive, superstitious and generally out of date, and is contrasted unfavourably with expediency, enlightened self-interest and utility, which are concerned only with what can be altered, reckoning that "bygones are forever bygones",[24] and not worth ratiocinating about. We now see that the case is very different. Far from making for rationality, the exclusion of the past makes for incoherence, and therefore it can be no criticism of justice that it takes cognisance of the past.

Justice is often taken to be not merely concerned with the past, but concerned exclusively with the past, as though it were a mirror image of expediency, enlightened self-interest and utility. That is a mistake. Although we discount purely consequentialist arguments, and sometimes say *Fiat justitia, et ruant caeli*, the concept of an action would be incoherent without some reckoning of consequences: I cannot say what you are doing without some reference

---

[23] pp. 42–3.
[24] W. S. Jevons, *The Theory of Political Economy*, London, 1871, p. 159: quoted by F. A. Hayek, *Law, Liberty and Legislation*, II, London, 1976, p. 121. Cf. Plato, *Protagoras*, 324a:

οὐδεὶς γὰρ κολάζει τοὺς ἀδικοῦντας πρὸς τούτῳ τὸν νοῦν ἔχων καὶ τούτου ἕνεκα, ὅτι ἠδίκησεν, ὅστις μὴ ὥσπερ θηρίον ἀλογίστως τιμωρεῖται· ὁ δὲ μετὰ λόγου ἐπιχειρῶν κολάζειν οὐ τοῦ παρεληλυθότος ἕνεκα ἀδικήματος τιμωρεῖται—οὐ γὰρ ἂν τό γε πραχθὲν ἀγένητον θείη—ἀλλὰ τοῦ μέλλοντος χάριν, ἵνα μὴ αὖθις ἀδικήσῃ μήτε αὐτὸς οὗτος μήτε ἄλλος ὁ τοῦτον ἰδὼν κολασθέντα.

Nobody with any sense punishes wrongdoers on account of the wrong done, unless he is taking revenge irrationally like an animal. The intelligent man punishes not to avenge past wrong—he can't undo what has been done—but for the sake of the future, in order that neither the offender nor anyone else who sees him being punished will offend again.

to what you will succeed in bringing about if all goes well. Hence the fact, as we noted in Chapter 1,[25] that there are some crimes, such as loitering with intent, which are defined with reference to the future, and that there are occasions when justice requires us to consider the candidate's promise as well as his performance, or to consider not only the criminal's misdeeds but the effect of different punishments on him and other people.[26] Thus justice is not exclusively concerned with the past. It is, nevertheless, much more concerned with the past than with the future. This is chiefly on account of the uncertainty of the future and the privacy of intention. Predictions are chancy and make for miscarriages of justice. Bad intentions may be repented of in time, and we can never be sure, in punishing a man for what he intended to do, that he actually would have done it. We do him wrong not only by invading his privacy but in denying his freedom, if we foreclose the possibility of his changing his mind and thinking better of what he had in mind to do. The future is not yet actual. What is in a man's mind is not yet public. Adverse decisions against an individual should not be based on anything except what are indeed facts, and facts in the public domain, not predictions which may yet prove false, or truths locked in somebody's breast, which cannot be surely known. The concern of justice with the past is, therefore, neither exclusive nor indicative of temporal bias, but is accounted for by the modal properties of time combined with the rational reluctance to decide against anyone except for unavoidable reason grounded on unalterable fact.

Justice then, is rational. But its rationality is of a special kind. Although it can take into consideration all times and all persons, it is not abstracted from them. It addresses itself to the individual, and seeks to show that the decision, even though in some ways adverse to him, is none the less undertaken for reasons which he, were he sufficiently rational, would himself accept. In addressing itself to the individual, it resembles expediency and enlightened self-interest, but its rationality is longer-term than that of expediency, which is concerned only with the immediate future, and wider than that of enlightened self-interest, which is concerned only with the interests of the agent. In taking into account the long-term interests of all, it resembles utility. Utility has the same attraction as expediency and enlightened self-interest, in being an entirely

---

[25] p. 13.   [26] See below, Ch. 6, pp. 148–50.

forward-looking principle, whose relevance, therefore, even the most sceptically inclined will find it difficult to deny. Unlike expediency, it enables the prisoners to escape from their dilemma. It evaluates each outcome by reference to the sum total of everybody's pay-offs. If the two prisoners are both utilitarians, each will consider the total prison sentence that would be imposed, and seek to minimise that. Clearly two years is less bad than ten, and therefore, each will not confess, reckoning that not confessing was most likely to promote the greatest happiness of the greatest number. Utilitarianism thus captures the logic of the coalition, in which you and I and other players each abandons his entirely self-interested strategy, and we merge ourselves in a collective first person plural. It thus not only proves a more expedient policy than expediency, but seems more enlightened than enlightened self-interest. In avoiding the obvious selfishness of expediency and enlightened self-interest, it has strong moral appeal, and is widely regarded as the one theory which is both rational and moral. Many attempts have been made to establish all our moral principles, and in particular those of justice, on utilitarian foundations,[27] but they have failed, partly because of the difficulty of accommodating a predominantly backward-looking concept within an exlusively forward-looking theory, partly because justice is concerned with distribution, whereas utilitarianism, notoriously, is not. It is all one to the utilitarian whether the prisoners get five years each, or whether one gets ten years and the other gets off altogether. These two considerations disqualify utilitarianism as providing a rational reconstruction of justice, and reveal fundamental defects in the whole theory. The utilitarian, like any other consequentialist, lays himself open to being manipulated by any other party, as we have seen in the Battle of the Sexes,[28] and thus fails to maintain his own independence and integrity as a rational agent: and although he takes account of the *interests* of other people, he fails, in simply summing their pay-offs, to treat them as fellow rational agents at all. He does not address himself to them, or concert a plan of action with them, but only decides on his own what had best be done with, as well as for, them. From the games-theoretical point of view,

---

[27] Most notably by J. S. Mill, *Utilitarianism*, Ch. V, "On the connection between Justice and Utility".

[28] See above, pp. 60–1; see also J. J. C. Smart and B. A. O. Williams, *Utilitarianism: For and Against*, Cambridge, 1973, pp. 138–40.

utilitarianism collapses the *n*-person game into a one-person game. Although there may, as it happens, be more than one person making decisions, each is to ignore completely the difference between different persons and their different pay-offs. Utilitarianism, as Rawls complains, does not take seriously the distinction between persons.[29] It treats people as units, not individuals. It is, fundamentally, *simpliste*, and loses all the fine structure of the Theory of Games.

Another approach we can conveniently formulate in games-theoretical terms is that of the egalitarian. Its most sophisticated exponent is Rawls.[30] Rawls enjoins each player to adopt a "maximin" strategy; players are to consider who comes worst off under each outcome, and then to choose that course of action which will result in the least bad outcome—they should seek to maximise the minimum pay-off. This approach is free from several of the grosser injustices that can be brought about by a straight utilitarian approach, but is still over-simplified, and open to objection on the score of fairness. In its concern for the underdog, it neglects all the other dogs. If we evaluate every outcome only by reference to the minimum pay-off, we neglect many factors which might make a considerable difference to our view of what would be a fair thing to do. Certainly, it is possible for someone to feel unfairly treated, even though he has not got less than anybody else.

Other principles are possible, but need not detain us long. A Renaissance ideal of individualism would be expressed by a "maximax" policy—one should try and maximise the success of the most successful individual, regarding successful individuals as works of art, and hoping that one's own age would be remembered for its production of great men. In the Age of the Common Man two principles of Mediocrity are often acted on: one the principle of envy, a "minimax" principle, which seeks to cut great men down to size by minimising the maximum pay-off; the other concerned to maximise the median pay-off, the one of the man who has as many people better off as he has worse off than he is himself. Other egalitarian principles seek to minimise the gap between the richest and the poorest, or the standard deviation of the distribution of

[29] John Rawls, *A Theory of Justice*, Oxford, 1972, p. 27.
[30] "Justice as Fairness", *The Philosophical Review*, LXVII, 1958, pp. 169–94, reprinted in many anthologies. *A Theory of Justice*, Oxford, 1972. For a fuller discussion see Ch. 10.

wealth. These have the disadvantages, which Rawls's principle is free from, of leading us to prefer a state in which we were all equally poor over one in which we were unequally rich. We can in addition obtain a further set of principles by inverting the ones we have already articulated. The masochist seeks to minimise his own pay-off, the sadist to minimise that of others, and the Satanist seeks to promote the greatest misery of the greatest number, while it is an all-too-human characteristic to adopt the "minimin" principle, and to kick the man who is at the bottom of the heap.

The principle of justice cannot be given any such neat formulation. It depends on reason, and reason cannot be confined within the abstract features characterized in the Theory of Games. The principle that approximates to it most clearly is that of Rawls; but whereas Rawls is concerned only with the underdog, justice is concerned with everybody and seeks to maximise not only the minimum pay-off, but every pay-off; that is to say, a just distribution would be one in which nobody was getting less than they should, that is, less than he otherwise would were it not for good reason. The reasons which can justify a person's not getting more depend on factors outside the formal approach of the Theory of Games, and, in particular, on the nature of the interaction, the substantive actions of each of the parties and their contribution to the over-all result, and the background of agreement and understanding on the basis of which joint action was concerted. These we shall return to in due course. For the moment we are concerned only with the general strategy of argument. It is to take every player's point of view seriously, and consider how the outcome appears to him, and whether it can be justified to him. The dialogue which Rawls conducts with the worst off, seeking to reconcile him with his lot, needs to be conducted with each person, seeking to reconcile him with the outcome, looking at the pay-off that he receives, considering whether any other outcome, with a larger pay-off for him, would be better, and if not why not. Of course, the player may be unreasonable, and refuse to acknowledge the cogency of arguments for not giving him more—much as a Rawlsian underdog may "irrationally" refuse to accept a system under which he gets less than other people even though more than he otherwise would have done, and insist on cutting off his own prudential nose in order to cut down to egalitarian size other people's greater pay-offs. We are not concerned with such irrational vetoes. Although we look at things from each man's point of view, we impute a reasonableness to him that may be belied by the facts. We cannot avoid some people being disappointed at the outcome, some being angry at it: the most we can hope to achieve is that, even though disappointed, they *ought* not to be angry, because they *should* recognise the cogency of the reasons behind the decision, and realise that it was, in that sense, an unavoidable one, and that therefore it betokened no unconcern for their interests or disrespect for their persons.

It is not simply niceness that leads us to consider things from each person's individual point of view, manifesting a general philanthropy, which we may welcome in others but do not really expect. It is not a grace note, but a requirement of reason. We want the individual to accept our reasons and be able to identify with the decision, but we cannot expect him to enter into our reasons if they manifest scant regard for his individuality. This is what vitiated utilitarianism. It made no concessions to the individual, treating him only as a unit; and in submerging his pay-off in an anonymous sum total, it was, in effect, inviting him to merge his individuality in a collective whole; and much though an individual may be inclined to identify with his fellows, he does not want to do so entirely, and needs to retain a sense of his separate identity and to have it recognised by others. And so we need to consider his pay-off. It is not enough simply to show that it would be greater if he co-operated than otherwise. We need to show that we have considered it, and have ourselves had regard to it in our own deliberations, else he will see us as an external factor in his calculations, and will not enter into our reasonings or see the validity of our point of view. The importance of each person's having some regard for others is shown by what can happen in the Battle of the Sexes if He perceives Her as cutting off her nose to spite his face, or vice versa. Their feelings begin to change. They both feel that the other should give way, and start getting cross with each other, and saying things like "I'll see you in hell first" or "over my dead body".[31] This "preference deterioration", as it is called, is illuminating. It shows how we resent being manipulated by others. We are prepared to do business with them. We do not expect them to be altogether altruistic or to be unconcerned with their own advantage. But we do expect them to move some way towards taking a more general

[31] See Nigel Howard, *Paradoxes of Rationality*, Cambridge, Mass., 1971, p. 199.

view, and to make some concessions to the interests of others. A person who will not make the slightest sacrifice for the sake of considerable benefits to others, and who will try and squeeze the greatest possible advantage, thereby reveals himself as not being one of Us, but an alien instead, a potential enemy to be frustrated, circumvented, exploited or manipulated, not a fellow worker with whom we can make common cause.

Justice is, thus, the condition of our being able to enter into the reasoning behind decisions and accept them, even though adverse, as our own. Besides this internal aspect, it also, especially in large, imperfect societies, has an external aspect. It not only enables us to identify with adverse decisions, but arises from our identifying with the victims of adverse decisions. It is in part simply a matter of sympathy: if my neighbour is struck down by drought, pestilence or misfortune, I am sorry for him, as he might be sorry for himself; and if he is struck down by violence, deceit or policy of State, I am indignant on his behalf. But it goes further than that. I perceive that the structure of civil society is, in games-theoretical terms, a coalition, a coalition of all against each. The logic of the situation demands that everyone, but everyone, must keep in line, or the coalition will collapse, and this generates strong feelings of hostility against potential law-breakers and a great emphasis on solidarity. But we need then to redress the balance, and take the part of the individual as against the community. And this gives the external rationale of justice. Justice is needed to offset the inevitable tough-mindedness of society towards the individual. The rationality of the solution to the Prisoners' Dilemma is compelling, and could easily become too compelling. We could easily sacrifice every individual interest on the altar of the collective good, and reckon my concerns, your concerns and his concerns of little account as compared with the public interest. Public policy could easily be like Tennyson's Nature

> So careful of the type she seems,
> So careless of the single life;[32]

and this we cannot stomach. The logic of Leviathan appals us. And therefore, like Locke, we seek terms on which we shall not be led like sheep to the slaughter, but may, vulnerable lambs that we are, lie down with Leviathan in peace. As a counterweight to the

[32] *In Memoriam*, LV.

coalition of all against each, we set up also a coalition of each against all, or rather of all for each. Although many of your concerns are not naturally my concerns, and I may not care very much if you are killed or maimed, imprisoned or expropriated, I have good reason, based on simple considerations of expediency, for caring none the less: for as you go off to the scaffold unjustly condemned by an unjust State, I can soon figure out that there, but for the luck of the draw, go I. And although, of course, there never was an original contract, and I never was in an original position engaging in a Rawlsian dialogue with my peers, I do reason within myself, and construe injustice to others as a threat to me. And thus our sense of it denotes, as Kahn says,[33]

that sympathetic reaction of outrage, horror, shock, resentment and anger, those affections of the viscera and abnormal secretions of the adrenals that prepare the human animal to resist attack. Through a mysterious and magical *empathy* or imaginative interchange, each projects himself into the shoes of the other, not in pity or compassion merely, but in the vigour of self-defense. Injustice is transmuted into assault; the sense of injustice is the implement by which assault is discerned and defense is prepared.[34]

Justice, then, is rational in a deeper sense than short-term expediency, enlightened self-interest or utilitarianism, in that it provides a meta-strategy or meta-meta-strategy, which we each can endorse in the reasonable expectation that everybody else will endorse it too, since it takes into consideration each and every man's point of view, and will not allow their significance to be eroded with the passage of time. It is thus all-ways and always symmetrical and therefore stable, and hence not only is rational but constitutes that meta-strategy which can attract the greatest measure of agreement because it does not impose avoidable sacrifice on anyone. So justice *is* rational. It is not the whole of rationality nor are all questions justiciable: in many cases a more limited view is appropriate—after all, now is the time I have to decide, just as I am the person in whom the decision is vested, and these are both

---

[33] Edward N. Kahn, *The Sense of Injustice*, New York, 1949, p. 24.

[34] G. del Vecchio (*Justice*, ed. A. H. Campbell, tr. Lady Guthrie, Edinburgh, 1952, pp. 173–4) quotes Janvier (*La Justice et le droit*, Paris, 1918, p. 15) to much the same effect. "La justice est essentiellement *altruiste*. Par la justice, nous sortons de nous-mêmes, nous brisons avec le souci de notre étroite personne pour nous occuper de nos semblables. La justice est en chacun de nous le défenseur des êtres distincts de nous; elle est dans l'individu le défenseur des autres individus."

important facts, and may justify my being guided by considerations of expediency or generosity or some other principle of reasoning. Justice is not, *au fond*, an alternative strategy displacing every other one based on other principles (although in particular cases justice and some other principle of reasoning may be mutually exclusive) but is an overarching principle directing us generally to see things from the point of view of each individual man, and to frame our decisions accordingly, a *constans et perpetua voluntas*, as Justinian says, *jus suum cuique tribuere*.[35] Of course, overarching principles are general, and thought to be vague; it is often complained against Justinian's formulation that it is vacuous—how are we to decide what each man's *jus* is? That is, indeed, a real question, but a subsequent one. In this chapter we have seen how justice is rational, and what that implies, and how the rationality of justice turns upon its concern for the individual—Justinian's *cuique*, which Aquinas rendered *unicuique* for added emphasis.[36] It is in virtue of this that we are able to specify justice further. Adverse decisions may be justly taken against individuals only for good reasons that are also individualised reasons. What count as individualised reasons will become clearer as we consider different aspects of justice, first the procedural requirements of natural justice, then the substantive requirements of the law, and finally the issues of distributive justice that are much contested in our time.

---

[35] *Inst.* Bk. I, Ch. 1.   [36] *S.T.*, *q.* LVIII.

4

NATURAL JUSTICE AND PROCESS VALUES[1]

Our concern for natural justice arises from the fact that we are dealing with human actions rather than states of affairs.[2] So far as end-states are concerned, it is all the same if I am hanged for a murder I committed, whether my trial was fair or not. But if the execution is construed as society's action against me, it makes all the difference. If after due process I am proved guilty beyond all reasonable doubt, society has little option but to punish me, or it will be condoning the crime and taking the blood of my victims on its own hands. Its action against me, although undoubtedly adverse, can be seen as unavoidable, granted its commitment to uphold the law and to vindicate the sanctity of innocent life. If I am executed without due process, the case is very different. It is no longer the case of society being reluctantly compelled to take action against me, on pain of otherwise compounding a worse evil, but of their getting rid of me gratuitously, or at least without great reluctance and without trying their reasonable utmost to avoid sending me to my death. I am being wantonly sacrificed, only, so far as society has tested the truth of the matter, on suspicion. It merely thinks that it would be expedient that I should die: and in acting on that supposition it shows how little it cares for me or takes my interests into account.

Actions are not to be identified with their consequences. I may suffer much more pain at the hands of a dentist or a doctor than I do from a bully or a bandit, but the actions of the former are welcomed, or at least put up with, whereas those of the latter, because they manifest ill will or reckless unconcern, fill me with furious resentment. I can partially identify with what the dentist or doctor is doing, and co-operate and open my mouth or swallow pills as I am told: we entirely repudiate the beatings of the bully,

[1] For a much fuller discussion see R. S. Summers, "A Plea for Process Values", *Cornell Law Review*, 60, 1974–5, pp. 1–52.

[2] Ch. 1, pp. 5–7.

and regard them as alien intrusions to be resisted by whatever means available. The spirit in which an action is done is as constitutive of what was done as the states of affairs that ensue. And, therefore, when we are dealing with the collective actions of corporate bodies, the procedure by which they were decided on is of paramount importance in manifesting their rationale and spirit, and hence in determining whether they have taken the rights and interests of the individual sufficiently into account, and thus whether they are actions which the individual could, rationally, be willing to accept as his own. The rules of natural justice thus are rules of procedure manifesting our concern for the individual, and our rational reluctance to do him down except for good cause, which shall show not only that the action should be done but that the individual concerned is the one who should bear the brunt.

It is impossible to spell out the requirements of justice precisely, or to say exactly what reasoning or what conclusions are right. Instead, we characterize what they are *not* like.[3] If a judge decides against a party without having heard his side of the case, or if the judge's own interests would lead him to decide against him, or if he was known to be partial to the other side, or if he took no account of the arguments adduced, his decision would be one that the disappointed party could hardly be expected to acknowledge or own. The rules of natural justice are thus necessary, rather than sufficient, conditions. Even if all procedural requirements are observed, it is still possible for the wrong decision to be reached, one that not merely disappoints a man's hopes, but is so far from being reasonable that he cannot be expected to accept it. But justice is something we cannot guarantee in this imperfect world. The best we can do is to provide some guarantees against some sorts of injustice. And the rules of natural justice, although they cannot protect us against all wrong decisions, can guarantee that decisions shall not be unacceptable on certain counts.

The rules of natural justice have been articulated by lawyers concerned with parties litigating about their legal rights, and therefore have been specified in precise form to fit adjudications of that sort. They tend to be quoted in Latin as self-evident truths, whose application, however, often turns out to be restricted by other considerations. We need, therefore, to go behind the Latin,

---

[3] Compare Ch. 3, pp. 36–7.

and work out the underlying arguments, and how they may be applied in deciding other sorts of question. Does the rule *audi alteram partem* mean that every candidate in an examination should be subjected to a viva? Does the principle that no man shall be judge in his own cause preclude the same man being both an executor and a beneficiary under a will? We need also to consider the counter-arguments. Our decisions would be less well grounded, and therefore less just, if no information could be given in confidence. Procedural requirements can obstruct, as well as protect, the course of decision-making, and may prevent the right decisions being made as well as wrong ones. Justice is affronted if the guilty cannot be brought to book on account of some procedural technicality. Sometimes we accept it as the lesser of two evils—better have rules that let some guilty men escape than might allow any innocent man to be wrongly convicted—but it is an evil and one we should seek to obviate as much as possible. Outside the restricted range of the criminal process, the dangers of procedural formalism are much greater, as a failure to reach a decision adverse to one party is likely itself to be adverse to some one else. The Protection of Employment Act has produced ludicrous results of employees winning cases for unfair dismissal when they had been stealing from their employers, sleeping on duty, or assaulting their work-mates, because the wrong person told them to leave, or because a wrong reason was given, or because no opportunity of explaining their actions was afforded even though the case was already clear beyond reasonable doubt. Results such as these bring the procedures of natural justice into disrepute, and lead men to make out that their decisions are not justiciable at all in order not to be caught up in the inappropriate and often unworkable complexity of the judicial process. For many years English law has distinguished administrative from judicial decisions, and has allowed administrative decisions to be free of any restraint on the score of justice. But this is monstrous. In the modern world decisions taken by administrators often bear far more heavily on the individual than those taken by judges. The decision of a fire officer or public health officer may impose great costs on an individual or even deprive him of his livelihood, and should certainly be governed by the canons of justice. We must therefore articulate the underlying procedural requirements of justice in such a way that they can be applied to different sorts of decision appropriately, rather than formulate a rigid code of procedural requirements which often will be inappropriate, and in practice, therefore, ignored altogether.

A decision fails to be just if it is taken in a way that precludes its being reasonable. Suppose a judge decides a case, after hearing all the evidence and submissions, by tossing a coin. He had no personal interest, he had listened to both parties, his decision-procedure was of necessity impartial, but his decision is unacceptable, because irrational. Equally if it were avowedly an arbitrary decision. Monarchs sometimes in the past have been misled by flatterers into believing that they could dispense justice according to the Royal Pleasure. But then it is not justice. It is a conceptual truth that a judgement cannot be capricious. We may, for the sake of peace and public order, accept the arbitration of arbitrators, even if altogether arbitrary: but if the decisions are to be judgements, so that all can accept them as just and identify with them, they must be guided by reason, not whim. And hence we lay it down as a necessary, but not a sufficient, condition of justice that like cases be treated alike.[4]

Even if decisions are non-arbitrary and guided by reason, they may be unacceptable none the less. A decision-maker may have his reasons all right, but the wrong reasons. His discretion is not absolute, unconditional. If I decide where to go for a holiday or what car to buy, I am not acting irrationally if I am guided by my disapproval of the regime or my views about foreign car manufacturers. Other people may not share these reasons, but they are possible reasons, and I am entitled to act on them. But if I am to decide justly, the range of possible reasons is restricted.[5] When a Californian judge gave us his reason "Waal, I can't let all that money go outa the State", his decision was quite rational, but unjust. Reasons of State, reasons of political expediency, reasons of party advantage, are all reasons, but not ones on which a just decision may be based, any more than a decision can be just that is arrived at by chance or caprice; "for bias and ignorance alike preclude fair judgement on the merits of a case".[6] Other reasons too, although not corrupt, are none the less bad. Improper purpose,

----

[4] See above, Ch. 3, pp. 43–4.

[5] Ch. 1, pp. 11–12.

[6] *R*. v. *Halifax City Council Committee of Works, ex parte* Johnston (1962) 34 D.C.R. (2d) 45, 57, *per* Macdonald J.; quoted S. A. de Smith, *Judicial Review of Administrative Action*, 3rd edn., London, 1973, p. 193.

bad faith and acting under dictation have all been struck down by the courts.[7] Together with these exclusions is an insistence that certain sorts of reason be attended to. A decision is bad not only if it is taken on irrelevant grounds but if it is taken without regard to relevant considerations,[8] and "in one case a requirement that a statutory tribunal base its decision on evidence having some probative value was said to be a principle of natural justice."[9] For similar reasons failure to exercise discretion, undertaking not to exercise discretion, or fettering discretion by self-created rules of policy will vitiate a decision reached thereby.[10] We do not do justice to the individual's case if we do not allow ourselves, or even through the fault of others fail, to take into account all the relevant facts and arguments.[11] We do him injustice if we exclude proper reasons in reaching our decision, as we do if we admit improper ones. The distinction, however, between proper and improper reasons is difficult to draw. Although we disallow reasons of state as grounds for judgement, we allow public policy. Although it is not right or just that one man should die for the sake of the people, it is just, if he has broken a law, itself enacted on grounds of expediency. And more generally, as we have seen,[12] extraneous considerations can enter in, as long as they do so in the form of rules or policies that apply generally, and whose application to the case in question is justified by its particular circumstances. Reasons, if they are to be reasons of justice, must be individualised; but what individual circumstances can count as a reason may well depend on general considerations.

Two principles of justice arise from the need to exclude all improper considerations and include all proper ones, the principles of legality and equity. The principle of legality requires us to formalise the sort of reasons which can lead to an adverse decision, and require a decision-maker to have regard only to these. It is a

---

[7] S. A. de Smith, op. cit., pp. 283–93, 293–7, 273–4.

[8] S. A. de Smith, op. cit., pp. 297–303.

[9] S. A. de Smith, op. cit., p. 134, quoting *R.* v. *Deputy Industrial Injuries Commissioner, ex parte* Moore (1965) 1QB, 456, 488–9.

[10] S. A. de Smith, op. cit., pp. 263–72, 277–9, 374–7.

[11] *Regina* v. *Leyland Justices, ex parte* Hawthorn, Queen's Bench, July 24, 1978; a conviction for careless driving was quashed because the prosecution failed to notify the defendant of the existence of witnesses which the prosecution knew about but did not intend to call.

[12] Ch. 1, pp. 13–14.

safeguard against the judge being moved by other reasons of an inappropriate kind, and can invest his decision with an authority which stems not from his personal qualities of mind or official position but from the laws he cites in justifying his decision. Legality is also a concomitant of the principle of treating like cases alike, which, as we shall see in the next chapter,[13] gives rise to the rule of precedents. And finally, we require legality for the sake of formality. "Who made you a judge over us?" springs readily to the lips of the man in danger of being decided against, and although often the situation itself affords an adequate answer—as when a testator is deciding to whom to leave his money or an employer whom to employ—there are other cases where the legal rights, chartered interests, or legitimate expectations, of one of the parties will be disappointed by an adverse decision. The decision, therefore, cannot be a completely extraneous one, or it will not be identifiable with: it must be taken by someone acting in a representative capacity, and hence must be subject to certain rules of recognition. A certain degree of formality is required, in order that the parties may be able to identify the occasion on which an adverse decision may be taken against them as a piece of decision-making which none the less calls for their allegiance. We do not need all the paraphernalia of an English court—the judge in his wig, the royal arms, the strict rules of procedure—but we need to know that this is no kangaroo court, and that our rights, interests and legitimate expectations are not being illegally infringed, but are being duly considered by those properly entitled to determine them. We must therefore be brought into the picture, and be informed what sort of occasion it is, and what its *locus standi* is. And that requirement of information imputes a necessary formality to the proceedings.[14] And the formalities, in turn, constitute a certain degree of legality.

Legality, whether substantive or procedural, can supplement justice, but can supplant it, or even run counter to it. The judge may be forced to give a judgement that seems to him harsh or unconscionable, saying, *Durum, sed ita scriptum est*. The established and promulgated conventions may be inadequate to accommodate all the complexities of an actual case, and may oblige us, if we are bound by the principle of legality, to ignore factors which clearly are relevant, or treat as conclusive factors whose relevance is

---

[13] Ch. 5, pp. 104–6.
[14] See J. R. Lucas, *The Principles of Politics*, Oxford, 1960, §4, pp. 14–16.

merely marginal. If there are rules and conventions of procedure, which are constitutive of the due process of some community, a person who does not know the ropes may be disadvantaged thereby. Many a widow has appealed to the king for justice, and he has been unable to give her justice because he was the wrong person to hear her case. Few of us, without benefit of professional advice, know where to turn to obtain our just dues or remedies for our wrongs. It is arcane knowledge, not evident by the light of nature, because it depends essentially on conventions required to establish rules of recognition of communal decision-making, and these conventions could have been otherwise. The general knowledge of conventions possessed by every member of the community is very low—we all can recognise the Queen, but very few a High Court judge—but the level required to secure complete identification of a legal process is very high, and in between lurk many possibilities of injustice.

Against the principle of legality we set that of equity, Aristotle's ἐπιείκεια. For the most part, it is defined negatively. It points out the defects of legality, and to need to remedy them. It stresses the particularity of the individual case. Justice is not comprised by conformity to rules, which, being general, cannot accommodate the circumstances of every case. Whereas a decision in accordance with legality is bound by the rules, equity appeals from the rules to the principles behind them, and seeks that decision which the rule-giver would himself have given, had he been available and apprised of the particular case.[15] Ideally, a just decision should be based on all and only those factors relevant to the particular case. Any attempt to lay down in advance and in general terms what factors shall be accounted relevant may, if it seeks to ensure that *only* relevant factors be considered, exclude other factors which also should be considered, and, if it seeks to ensure that *all* relevant factors be considered, include others which ought properly to be excluded. Rather, therefore, than lay down general rules, we appeal to the discernment of the ideally just man, vesting in him unfettered discretion to decide each particular case on its merits. As a critique of the principle of legality and the worship of rules, arguments of equity have their point: but as a positive principle, it is vague, often to the point of incoherence, and attempts to give it practical expression are always going awry. In England the Court of Equity

[15] *Nicomachean Ethics*, V, 10, 5; 1137b 19–24.

was established to redress the injustices of the precedent-bound decision of the Common Law, but over the centuries Equity developed into as technical a branch of the law as what it was intended to correct. This was not due to the wickedness of lawyers. The pressure towards legality is generated by thrusts that are integral to the dynamic of justice. But although integral they can also subvert it. There will always be cases where conventions and formalities, although stemming from justice, obstruct its course. The principle of equity then allows us to formulate criticisms and look for remedies, but cannot itself constitute a code of remedial practice. It is complementary to legality, not co-ordinate with it. We may on occasion cut through red tape, but cannot cut it out altogether.

These guidelines, together with that of due deliberation, to which we shall return later,[16] are designed to secure that the reasoning leading up to a decision shall be right, or at least free from avoidable error. But even if a decision is right, we shall not acknowledge it unless we know that it is right, and can feel sure that due weight was given to the interests of those decided against. We need, that is, to bring into the picture all those who may be disappointed, so that in spite of their disappointment they may be reconciled to the decision as being not only right but manifestly concerned for them. It was, we have already seen, one of the arguments for legality that it enabled the parties to identify the process as a properly accredited one of their community. And many other rules of natural justice arise from our need to ensure not only that just decisions are reached but that they can be seen to have been reached justly.

If people are to be convinced that decisions are just, they must be able to know the reasons on which they are based. Although many of us often are willing to accept the judgement of a man we respect, that acceptance depends on our sometimes knowing and approving his reasons. It is inherent in the concept of judgement that it is based on reasons, and only if the reasons are sometimes available for independent criticism and assessment, can we ever come to trust a man's judgement at all. Reasons must sometimes be available, or decisions will seem arbitrary, and will not enjoy public confidence. The requirement that reasons should always be available goes further. It recognises a party's right to be disappointed by an

[16] See below, p. 95.

adverse decision, and the need to assuage it. Instead of demanding
simply that he trust the judge, it allows that the judge could
conceivably be wrong, and that the disappointed party could,
without irrationality, attribute the adverse decision to an error of
judgement on the judge's part, and therefore goes some way to
allay this suspicion by èxposing the reasons to scrutiny, and
enabling everybody concerned to assess them and feel their force
for themselves. The Donoughmore-Scott Commission rightly saw it
as a principle of natural justice "that a party is entitled to know the
reason for a decision . . ."[17]

Reasons, however, are difficult to formulate, and may sometimes
be tactless to tell. Even if we give our reasons, they are unlikely to
be so complete as to express all we had in mind or so conclusive as
to compel consent from those unwilling to be convinced. In the end
there will be still some appeal to the authority of the judge, not
merely by reference to his position as official arbitrator but in virtue
of his qualities of mind : and in some cases it seems appropriate to
lay much more stress on the latter. Examiners do not normally give
reasons for their decisions. Although in some cases it would in
principle be possible to itemise errors and defects, often they are
guided by general impressions that are not readily amenable to
further discussion. Equally in a beauty contest an eye for feminine
beauty is what is required, and is not easily reduced to words. In
musical competitions the examiners assess performances under
different heads, and say how candidates fared on accuracy, rhythm,
expression, etc., but cannot go much further. An employer would
normally, and is now legally obliged to, give reasons for dismissing
an employee, but although gross lapses are easily itemised, often all
they can really say is "not up to the job". Candidates for a job,
however, are not entitled to be told why they were unsuccessful,
and normally it would be needlessly unkind to do so. Similarly,
judges at a Gymkhana are well advised not to say, even when they
very easily can, exactly why Fiona on Blackboy failed to qualify for
the under-elevens. We have to weigh the fundamental desirability
of giving reasons against the difficulty, and sometimes the unde-
sirability, of doing so. Decisions taken by the State need to have

[17] *Report on Ministers' Powers*, 1932, Cmd. 4060, Section III §§3, 13, pp. 80, 100.
In the Franks Commission, *Report on Administrative Tribunals and Enquiries*, 1957,
Cmnd. 218, §§23, 24, p. 5, openness is taken as one of the characteristics required of
acceptable decision-making.

their reasons fairly fully formulated: for the State possesses coercive power, and its decisions may affect the rights and chartered interests of citizens. Decisions taken by voluntary associations can rely more on authority, because merely by belonging to them members have accepted their authority, and an adverse decision impinges less forcefully on their rights and chartered interests. If I enter for a beauty contest I thereby submit myself to the judges' verdict, and if it goes against me, my vanity may be wounded, but my life, liberty and property will remain intact.

In so far as disappointed parties are expected to accept the say-so of an authority, we owe it to them that the authority should be competent and impartial. Justice is affronted if judges are incompetent. It was a blot on the polity of ancient Athens that cases were tried by huge, uninstructed juries, who often were swayed by prejudice and rhetoric and were unlikely to concentrate on the relevant considerations of the case. Our juries are small enough to address themselves properly to the case and reach a common mind on the questions that the judge, himself a man of long experience and great clarity of mind, puts to them. This works well enough in most criminal cases where the issues are within the understanding of the average juror, but is open to criticism when sophisticated crimes, involving subtle matters of science or accountancy come before the courts. A man is not justly condemned if the verdict is given by people who do not understand what is in issue. His right is to be tried by his peers, that is to say people who, coming from the same walk of life as he, can easily and adequately put themselves in his position and see whether what he did and the explanations he offers could be reasonable and acceptable, or whether anyone who in his position did that must have been doing wrong. Unless we ensure this, and more generally unless we ensure that decisions against people are taken only by those competent to understand and assess the reasons on either side, we cannot expect people to accept adverse decisions as being rationally unavoidable.[18] Although authority is required, as we have seen,[19] by reason of our own inability all to agree on the reasons bearing on a particular decision, authority requires itself as high a degree of rational ability

---

[18] See R. S. Summers, "A Plea for 'Process Values'", *Cornell Law Review*, 60, 1974–5, p. 51, item 7.

[19] Ch. 3, p. 40.

as is available if its word is to be accepted in the absence of universally agreed reasons.

Besides competence, we need impartiality in order to assure the authority of the judge, and for that reason lay down the principle that no man be judge in his own cause. Once again, if reasons could be formulated fully and were utterly compelling, we should have no need of judges being debarred by interest—there is no objection to a treasurer having a private interest, for we can audit his accounts for ourselves. A judge's decision cannot be checked up on in that way. Although he may give his reasons, they are not foolproof. He could be wrong—judgements are often reversed on appeal—and even if right he could be thought to be wrong. There is, therefore, an ineliminable appeal to authority, and hence a need to secure it against abuse and calumny. If a man has an interest in the outcome of a dispute, he may be tempted to decide in his own favour, and that reason is not one whose cogency the disappointed party can be expected to acknowledge. But though some are tempted, not all are; some lean over backwards not to favour themselves unduly. In particular, our judges in Britain are exceptionally good at putting aside improper considerations, and reaching a decision in a purely judicial frame of mind. It would, on the evidence, be unreasonable to suspect them of partiality even if they were parties to the case. Nevertheless the rule still stands. The reason now is not that we actually suspect the judges of partiality, but that we recognise that somebody could, without irrationality, so suspect them, and that therefore the disappointed party might. The rationale is the same as for giving reasons. We owe it to him to recognise the legitimacy, if not the truth, of his suspicions, and our consequent duty to assuage them. Not only must he not be done down needlessly, but he must be able to know that he is not being done down needlessly, for only then can he be reconciled to an adverse decision. We owe it to thim to try all we can to reconcile him, if the decision be adverse, just as we owe it to him in the first place to try all we can to avoid having to reach an adverse decision at all. Otherwise we show we do not really care for what he thinks any more than we care for his substantial interests, and are, in effect, extruding him from our community of action. Justice must not only be done, but be seen to be done, because only so can it be effective in enabling even the disappointed party to identify with the decision. And from this it follows that a man should not be judge in his own cause, because, no matter how honest or unselfish he is, other people cannot be absolutely sure about it, and the disappointed party might be prey to a sneaking suspicion that the case went against him not on its merits but by reason of the judge's private interest.[20]

There is some question of how far the principle should extend. Its traditional *locus* is legal adjudication, where one party's rights are set against the other's, and one can prevail only at the expense of the other. We do not feel so strongly in distributing benefits or burdens, where often one man may be allocating them to himself among others. If he is giving himself an unfair share, we may protest, and appoint someone else. But we do not feel obliged to guard against the mere suspicion of partiality. Again, where the decision-maker's interest is of a different sort from the other party's, the rule is not wholly appropriate. An employer, deciding whether to dismiss an employee, ought in justice to consider what justification or excuse or mitigation the employee can bring forward in his defence: but is not debarred from deciding the case on the grounds of having an interest in the success of the business. A judge, committing a recalcitrant party for contempt of court, has an interest in the case. A minister deciding a planning case after a public inquiry is often deciding between his own department and the objectors. These cases show the awkwardness of the position. Although the official does not have a personal or pecuniary interest, he may come to be so much identified with the official cause, or have his own *amour propre* so much involved that he cannot give due weight to the interests of others.[21] And then we

---

[20] See, more fully, Torstein Eckhoff, "Impartiality, Separation of Powers, and Judicial Independence", *Scandinavian Studies in Law*, 9, 1965, esp. §II, pp. 12–22.

[21] See especially the discussion in the Donoughmore-Scott *Report on Ministers' Powers,* 1932, Cmd. 4060, Section III, §3, pp. 78–9. "Indeed we think it is clear that bias from strong and sincere conviction as to public policy may operate as a more serious disqualification than pecuniary interest. No honest man acting in a judicial capacity allows himself to be influenced by pecuniary interest: if anything, the danger is likely to be that through fear of yielding to motives of self-interest he may unconsciously do an injustice to the party with which his pecuniary interest may appear to others to identify him. But the bias to which a public-spirited man is subjected if he adjudicates in any case in which he is interested on public grounds is more subtle and less easy for him to detect and resist.

We are here considering questions of public policy and from the public point of view it is important to remember that the principle underlying all the decisions in regard to disqualification by reason of bias is that the mind of the judge ought to be free to decide on purely judicial grounds and should not be directly or indirectly

begin to be uneasy, and to demand independent adjudication, just as we deny to the police, although free of personal or pecuniary interest in the punishment of crime, authority to inflict punishments on their own. In all, the rule that no man be judge in his own cause is a derivative, not a fundamental, rule. A man can decide justly even when his own interests are involved, and often we have to rely on his doing so. But where the conflict of interest is obvious and unavoidable, or where there are good reasons why the disappointed party might impute partiality, we allay his suspicions by separating functions, and reserving the decision to a different person who cannot have acquired even a representative or corporate interest in the decision going one way rather than the other.

The rule about hearing both sides of the case goes back to the ancient world. Aristophanes referred to it:[22] Nicodemus appealed to it:[23] Zeno argued against it:[24] The actual phrase *audi alteram partem* was first formulated by St. Augustine.[25] It was thought of in two ways, as a rule of wisdom and as a rule of justice.[26] On both counts it is very largely to be seen as a safeguard against some piece

---

influenced by, or exposed to the influence of, either motives of self-interest or opinions about policy or any other considerations not relevant to the issue.

We are of the opinion that in considering the assignment of judicial functions to Ministers Parliament should keep clearly in view the maxim that no man is to be judge in a cause in which he has an interest. We think that in any case in which the Minister's Department would naturally approach the issue to be determined with a desire that the decision should go one way rather than another, the Minister should be regarded as having an interest in the cause. Parliament would do well in such a case to provide that the Minister himself should not be the judge, but that the case should be decided by an independent tribunal.

It is unfair to impose on a practical administrator the duty of adjudicating in any matter in which it could fairly be argued that his impartiality would be in inverse ratio to his strength and ability as a Minister. An easy-going and cynical Minister, rather bored with his office and sceptical of the value of his Department, would find it far easier to apply a judicial mind to purely judicial problems connected with the Department's administration than a Minister whose head and heart were in his work. It is for these reasons and not because we entertain the slightest suspicion of the good faith or the intellectual honesty of Ministers and their advisers that we are of opinion that Parliament should be chary of imposing on Ministers the ungrateful task of giving judicial decisions in matters in which their very zeal for the public service can scarcely fail to bias them unconsciously."

[22] *Wasps* 725—6, πρὶν ἂν ἀμφοῖν μῦθον ἀκούσῃς, οὐκ ἂν δικάσαις.

[23] John 7:51.

[24] Plutarch, *Mor.* 1034E.

[25] *De Duabus Animabus*, XIV, 22, J.-P. Migne, *PL*, 42, 110.

[26] John M. Kelly, "*Audi Alteram Partem*", *Natural Law Forum*, 9, 1944, p. 103.

of information not being made available or some relevant consideration not being thought of. Although often we may be able to give due weight to the interests of all those affected by a proposed course of action, we may sometimes overlook something. By giving a right of audience to those who stand to lose if we decide in one way or another, we can hope that their concern with their own interests will remedy any lack on our disinterested part. We are imperfect. But they have every incentive to remedy some of our imperfections. We shall be less imperfect if we let them.

Thus far the argument manifests more a desire to include all proper reasons than to exclude improper ones. To this extent it is akin to the principle of equity, and is to be contrasted with the principles of legality and impartiality, which are concerned only to exclude improper considerations. In legal contexts, however, the right of audience goes further, and includes a right of cross-examination. A party is entitled not only to bring to the attention of the court all those reasons he thinks proper but to challenge and seek to exclude from their consideration any he thinks improper, and to counter a *prima facie* case by citing further facts or deploying fresh arguments to rebut it. Again, it is wise to submit one's ratiocinations to critical scrutiny. Some facts on which one was relying may be unreliable: some arguments invalid. In excluding considerations, however, our appeal will often be not to wisdom but to justice. It may be wise to be guided by counsels of expediency, but a man may properly protest that it would be unfair to be guided by these in deciding against him, and by being present when all the arguments for an adverse decision are being adduced can secure that no improper ones are among them, and that only individualised reasons of the proper kind are being urged against him.

The right of being heard is pre-eminently important in the criminal law. The Athenian juror promised "I will listen alike to both accuser and defendant."[27] Menander said "Do not punish anyone unexamined."[28] It was when action against Jesus was mooted that Nicodemus asked the chief priests and Pharisees "Does our law judge a man before it hear him and know what he

---

[27] Demosthenes, *In Timocr.* 149–51, καὶ ἀκροάσομαι τοῦ τε κατηγόρου καὶ τοῦ ἀπολογουμένου ὁμοίως ἀμφοῖν. Cf. fn. 1 on p. 90 below.

[28] Menander, Fr. 17, ἀνεξέταστον μὴ κολάζε μηδένα.

doeth?"[29] An accusation in such cases seeks to ascribe an action to the accused, and an adverse verdict not merely brings on him untoward consequences, but announces that he did in fact do the deed alleged. It pins it on him. But actions, as we have seen,[30] are not merely patterns of bodily behaviour: some element of intention, *mens rea*, is essential. Although later, with the development of the civil law of tort, men can be held liable for consequences they neither intended nor even foresaw, in the simple, primitive case 'I didn't mean to' 'I didn't realise' or 'I couldn't help it' is an adequate exculpation. And, as we have seen, many patterns of behaviour are susceptible of different interpretations.[31] There is a logical gap between the overt behaviour that others can witness and the actual action the agent would, if honest, acknowledge, and before proceeding to a definite conclusion we need to pause and give him the opportunity of interposing a 'but' and showing our ascription to be mistaken.[32] Hence, when we are judging deeds, and may find that a man did wrong, there is a requirement of logic that we should allow the putative agent to correct misinterpretations or disavow the intention imputed to him or otherwise disown the action. God needed to ask Adam 'Hast thou eaten of the tree whereof I commanded thee that thou shouldest not eat?'[33] because it was essential that Adam should not be blamed or punished unless he had done exactly that deed. If the serpent had planted the evidence, or if he had beguiled Adam into eating it under the misapprehension that it came from another, non-forbidden tree, then Adam had not sinned and should not have been expelled from Eden. Only if the accused admits the charge, or, faced with the accusation, cannot explain his behaviour convincingly in any other way, are we logically entitled to conclude that he did indeed do it.

---

[29] John 7:51. μὴ ὁ νόμος ἡμῶν κρίνει τὸν ἄνθρωπον, ἐὰν μὴ ἀκούσῃ πρῶτον παρ' αὐτοῦ, καὶ γνῷ τί ποιεῖ;

The New English Bible renders this less directly; "Does our law permit us to pass judgement on a man unless we have first given him a hearing and learned the facts?" which fits the general run of cases but lacks the special emphasis on what the man has *done*.

[30] Ch. 1, p. 6.

[31] Ch. 1, p. 15.

[32] Ch. 3, p. 39.

[33] Genesis 3:11; see also Lucifer of Cagliari, *pro S. Athan.* 1.1, J.-P. Migne, *PL*, vol. 13, col. 817 ff.; and *The King* v. *The Chancellor, Masters and Scholars of the University of Cambridge*, 1 Str. 557, 567, 83 Eng. Rep. 693, 704 (1723), quoted R. F. Heuston, *Essays in Constitutional Law*, 2nd edn., London, 1964, p. 185.

The need to hear the accused can be seen in another light. If we dispense with it, we either are guilty of a logical error, or if not, must be working on the assumption that the accused is not an agent. Only if we are dealing not with a person but with a mere thing, are we logically entitled to count behaviour as altogether conclusive. And therefore if we are not guilty of a logical error it is because we are regarding him as a mere thing, a body to be bundled about, not a person to be communicated with. Not to hear him is implicitly to deny his status as a person, his human worth.[34] There is a perpetual danger of this in the criminal law, since criminals, when sentenced, are to some extent treated as objects not persons, and there is a propensity on the part of officialdom to anticipate the sentence and treat him already as an object, a stray bull or a dangerous dog, whose fate is to be decided impersonally by the court. Against this, we insist that he is still a person, to be talked to and not just talked about. We owe it to the prisoner as a human being to include him in when we are discussing what should be done with him.

The right to be heard is a requirement of justice in legal adjudications outside the criminal law and where there is no imputation of wrongdoing. It stems from the need to include the parties in the process of decision-making, and in large measure is meant to compensate for the necessarily non-consensual aspect of legal adjudication. Since I cannot be judge in my own cause, I should at least be allowed to be its advocate. I am guaranteed a voice in order to make up for not having a vote. Deprived of both, I should have little reason to regard the result as in any way my own. We do not need to be so scrupulous in other sorts of decision-making, because parties are not so rigidly excluded from a vote or comparable consideration. The mere fact that I want, or do not want, something is, in many situations and with many people, sufficient reason for deciding the way I want. If in my absence my colleagues or my family take a decision that is adverse to my interests, I can be fairly sure of their reluctance to do so, and can assume that there must have been overwhelming arguments in favour, or they would not have done so; and that they would have considered all the arguments against, and have given them due weight. Of course, they might have overlooked some vital point—the argument from fullest information still has force. But

[34] Cf. Lactantius, *De Justitia*, J.-P. Migne, *PL*, vol. 6, col. 546 f.

there is no reason to assume any such negligence, and good reason to suppose my colleagues and kinsmen were as anxious to avoid it as I should have been. In the case of legal adjudication, however, I cannot suppose it so easily. The judge is not partial to me, as my friends and family are. He is supposed to be impartial, and therefore reasonably reluctant to decide against me, but against that I must set his equal reluctance to decide against the other party, and the fact that he cannot avoid deciding against one of us. Although he ought to exert himself to find out every fact in my favour, and consider every argument for not deciding against me, I find it difficult to believe it unless I have urged them all on him myself. It may be that he would anyhow have reached the right decision on his own: but only if he has made manifest his concern for me and his desire not to find against me needlessly by listening to all the points I make, can I be sure that he is deciding in a just frame of mind. So Seneca:

> Qui statuit aliquid parte inaudita altera
> Aequum licet statuerit, haud aequus fuit.[35]

There is also an argument from political liberty. Our ideal of society is one in which people do things rather than have things done to them, and are the initiators of action rather than merely the beneficiaries of other men's concerns. People therefore should be free to take steps to further or protect their own interests, and officials should have some duty—details depending on circumstances—to listen to their suggestions and complaints. Although in legal adjudications it is primarily a question of their being done down or not, and not of their doing anything themselves, nevertheless there are things they can do—namely arguing on their own behalf—and these they should be entitled to do.[36]

To set against these arguments for the rule *audi alteram partem* there are some arguments against. It gums up decision-making. It causes damaging delays. It may introduce a needless degree of formality into what can better be settled informally. By stressing the adversarial processes of the law courts it engenders conflict. It may preclude confidentiality. It may result in the wrong decision being

---

[35] *Medea*, ll. 199–200, He who decides anything with the other side unheard, may have reached a just decision, but is not himself just.

[36] Compare R. S. Summers, "A Plea for 'Process Values'", *Cornell Law Review*, 60, 1974–5, pp. 16–17.

made. It sometimes is not possible, and often not necessary, since the good to be secured can be better secured in other ways. The arguments on either side apply differently in different circumstances, and we cannot give a complete account.

The Judicial Committee of the Privy Council has suggested[37] three matters to be taken into account when considering whether an implied duty to observe the *audi alteram partem* rule ought to arise: first, the nature of the complainant's interest; secondly, the conditions under which the administrative authority is entitled to overreach on these interests (e.g. where misconduct is proved); and thirdly, the severity of the sanction that it can impose.[38]

It is also helpful to consider what sort of decision is being taken, and what the rationale for the rule in that particular case is.

In so far as the rule is a rule of wisdom, it offers one way of securing that our decisions are adequately informed and properly thought out, but not always the only way. Sometimes we might already have adequate information to justify a decision—in a very straightforward case, say of an employee seen filching goods from the company store—and often this information is available anyhow, and does not need to be elicited by sworn testimony. We do not always need to subject either the evidence or the argumentation to a full judicial trial in order to test whether they are strong enough to support the conclusion; although in many cases this may be the most practicable way to ensure that result. In other cases it is not only impracticable but counter-productive. Confidentiality is essential when choosing people for appointment or promotion, because otherwise referees will not speak frankly, and the decision will have to be made on needlessly inadequate information.

Particular difficulty arises over the clear case, where we already have adequate information to justify a decision. Although logically speaking there is always room for a further 'but',[39] practically speaking there is often no room for doubt, and life would be impossible if we could not often reach firm decisions on the strength of the immediately available evidence. Our judgement is fallible, true: but it is not that bad. Often we can reach a firm conclusion

---

[37] *Durayappa* v. *Fernando* (1967) 2 A.C. 337, 349.
[38] S. A. de Smith, *Judicial Review of Administrative Action*, 3rd edn., London, 1973, p. 156.
[39] Ch. 3, p. 39.

which will not be upset by any further considerations. It would seem absurdly hidebound to lay down a hard and fast rule that we must always stop and listen even when it is plain that there is nothing to be said.[40]

In so far as the rule *audi alteram partem* is a rule of wisdom, it can be dispensed with in clear cases: and even on the score of justice, it is possible, as Seneca allows, to reach just decisions on occasion in spite of not having heard the other side. Many adverse decisions are reached for reasons I could not possibly controvert or impugn; I know all too well why I am passed over for promotion, why I am not awarded the Nobel Prize, why I am not invited to take the lead role in the village play, why nobody gets up a testimonial to me on account of my beauty of face or of character. These decisions may disappoint me, but they are eminently just, and I cannot but acknowledge them as ones I ought to identify with. Although consultation is generally a good thing, its absence does not betoken a disrespect except in decisions which are in some way focussed on me more than on others—in particular an accusation of a crime, but also any adjudication of my rights. When these are in issue, even though the case is clear, to prejudge it without reference to the individual concerned is to manifest an adverse assumption, a belief that he is of no consequence and nothing that he says could matter. But even prejudgement might be differently construed if there was need for speed or great difficulty in securing representations from the individual concerned. Even the logical requirement that an agent should have the opportunity of rebutting accusations and explaining his behaviour is attenuated when he has openly avowed his actions and made them a matter of common knowledge. If a man makes himself a public enemy and the public take action against him on the basis of what he has done, it is hardly unjust that he was not brought to trial first. We might perhaps construe

---

[40] Compare Aristophanes, *Wasps*, 919 ff.

ΒΔΕΛΥΚΛΕΩΝ	πρὸς τῶν θεῶν μὴ προκαταγίγνωσκ᾽, ὦ πάτερ, πρὶν ἄν γ᾽ ἀκούσῃς ἀμφοτέρων.
ΦΙΛΟΚΛΕΩΝ	ἀλλ᾽ ὦγαθὲ τὸ πρᾶγμα φανερόν ἐστιν· αὐτὸ γὰρ βοᾷ.
Bdelycleon	For goodness sake, don't condemn, father, until you have heard both sides.
Philocleon	But, good chap, the case is clear: it speaks for itself.

his actions as a declaration of war and the subsequent actions of society as hostilities rather than punishments. But we should be chary of extending the concept of war. In most cases punishment can hardly be exacted unless the alleged wrongdoer is in the power of the authorities, and if he is they can afford to listen to his representations. But this need not necessarily be a condition precedent for the rest of the judicial process. Although in practice there are often grave objections to a trial *in absentia*, the logical requirement would be satisfied if there were provision that before sentence was irrevocably carried out the man convicted could make representations and these representations would be duly considered. Although in the great preponderance of cases our present procedures are practicable and desirable, it is possible to envisage cases—where a notorious criminal flees to another country—in which justice would be thwarted if his deliberate absence prevented any other steps being taken. It would be fair for his property to be forfeit, so that recompense could be made to his victims. It might be important for the sake of justice to hold the trial quickly while evidence was fresh, rather than run the risk of the procedure being defective at some future date through effluxion of time. And in so far as it is one of the functions of justice to vindicate the right and condemn wrong, it would again be important to do this and pass sentence promptly, even though it could not then be carried out, and some reconsideration would be necessary before it was carried out.

In a very different context, we also dispense with prior notice and formal hearings for simple domestic misdemeanours, when the child's naughtiness is met by an instant slap. Delay, as we shall see, is often undesirable. If there can be no question but that the deed was done by the agent and done deliberately, it is pointless to pause: sufficient to allow subsequent expostulation, and apologies and recompense in the unlikely event of the situation having been misjudged. Legal procedures are not a perfect guide to our intimations of justice, because they need also to satisfy the requirement of definitiveness. For good reason, although not reason of justice, we need to be able to rely on the results of legal processes without fear of their being consequently upset. We therefore import into the law a conclusiveness that does not naturally accord with the dialectic of reason and our intimations of justice. In order to secure justice none the less in legal procedures, we sometimes have to distort the natural order of argument, and make the right expostulation into a right to be heard, as a condition precedent of due process.

The arguments from human worth and from consensus apply far more widely, but less insistently. It is good to consult people, but not always practicable, and where the adverse consequences do not reflect upon their status as human beings, not so necessary. If I turn down an applicant for a job, I am not treating him as a mere body. It is courteous to write and tell him of my decision, but if I did not take up his references or did not short-list him for an interview, I am not manifesting disrespect for his personality or bundling him about as though he were a sack of potatoes. Saying No is not the same as sentencing a man to prison, and where the grounds for an adverse decision are not some alleged action of the agent but a whole complex of personal qualities, qualifications and performances, we are not denying his status as an agent if we do not give him the opportunity of rebutting an accusation that has not been made. The rationale of the argument from consensus is like that of the principle of impartiality, and they apply under similar conditions. If a man is included in the decision-making, he will more readily identify with it, even if it is against his interests. But sometimes his identification is secured by other means. I do not argue with the umpire or the referee because although they may be wrong, and I may know that the ball did not hit my bat or that I was still holding it when I touched down for a try, in playing the game at all I accept his word, even though mistaken. In matters of worth and of identification much depends on context and convention; so that adverse decisions need not be construed as slights, and may be identified with by virtue of some prior understanding rather than the way in which they are reached. Thus in sending goods on approval or submitting estimates free, I court rejection in the hope of sometimes securing a sale or a contract. Many commercial activities are undertaken on such terms, and many jobs were. R. F. Heuston, after quoting Fortescue J. in Bentley's case,[41] with its appeal to God's giving Adam the opportunity of defending himself, adds, as an aside,

It has, however, been noticed that the biblical precedents on the point are conflicting, for at the lugubrious dinner party recorded in Daniel V, at which the moving finger interrupted the proceedings by writing on the wall

---

[41] See above, p. 86.

"mene, mene, tekel, upharsim" (you have been weighed in the balance and found wanting), the prophet does not indicate that Belshazzar was given any summons, information of the nature of the complaint, or opportunity to answer.[42]

But this is standard form. If I were Chancellor of the Exchequer, and the Prime Minister decided to get rid of me, I would have no right to argue with him, and would have to content myself with writing in my memoirs an explanation of how well I had done and how unfairly I had been misunderstood. Although some—many, now—jobs have tenure, and their holders hold them during good behaviour, or can be dismissed only for certain sorts of dereliction of duty, subject to some formal process, other jobs are held only 'at pleasure', and no reason need be given, nor any process gone through for terminating them. This is not to say that it would be right to dismiss a man merely for fun. Nor was Belshazzar. But the reasons do not have to be individualised reasons—the Prime Minister may be reconstructing his Cabinet, and axing me to make room for a younger man—and even if they are—you have been weighed in the balance and found wanting—the man being dismissed does not have to be included in the decision-making process, because in accepting the job in the first place he had accepted the right of the authority to make a decision without reference to him. Much of our thinking about justice is structured by conventions which determine what is to be expected in various situations and what is to be construed as an affront: and although on the one hand the application of the rule *audi alteram partem* is governed by whether or not the decision impinges on the individual's rights,[43] on the other hand the exact determination of the individual's rights is often itself governed by whether or not we think it is a decision on which he should have some special *locus standi*.[44] Justice, being concerned with the significance of actions and regarding them therefore as a species of communication, is in part constituted by conventions, like language: but only in part, since the language of actions is a natural language, whose significance cannot be entirely separated from the consequences of what is done;[45] and therefore

---

[42] *Essays in Constitutional Law*, 2nd edn., London, 1964, p. 185. See further below, Ch. 6, p. 126.

[43] See above, p. 89.

[44] See above, Ch. 2, p. 25.

[45] See above, Ch. 1, pp. 7–8.

the rules of natural justice, although often influenced by convention, cannot be altogether altered or abridged by the understandings current in any particular society.

We may summarise, at the risk of over-simplification, by saying that the rule *audi alteram partem* stems from a number of different arguments, some insistent and stringent, but applying to only a few sorts of decision, others applying to a wider range of decisions but capable of being satisfied in a wider variety of ways. Decisions, like a finding of guilt, which pin blame on an individual, require that he should have a proper opportunity of disowning responsibility and exculpating himself, and although in theory the American practice of subsequent expostulation might sometimes be acceptable, there are good legal reasons for making the British practice of prior protestation a rigid rule.[46] Other decisions impinging on the rights and central interests of the individual require great procedural protection, and the rule *audi alteram partem* is usually if not invariably the best protection available. Many other interests ought to be protected, and the rule *audi alteram partem* is often the best means of ensuring that proper regard is had to them; but other means are available or can be devised, and may, in view of counter-considerations, be preferable.

The rule *audi alteram partem* applies in very many cases, but often is in danger of not being effectively observed. Only the expert can make himself heard. If the ordinary man is to be heard, he must be professionally represented. The right to be represented by an advocate has long been recognised: in recent years we have increasingly come to realise that many people cannot afford to hire an advocate, and that justice requires that they should have some legal aid. Such rights of representation are subordinate maxims, intended to secure that the principle of legality does not occlude that of *audi alteram partem*. They are not absolute maxims, and the way they are to be specified in practice depends on the sort of issue being decided and is subject to the overarching aim that justice shall be done. In some cases the effect of providing legal aid is the opposite of that intended. The law becomes more legalistic, as defence counsel seek to exploit technicalities for the benefit of their clients, and courts, under social pressure to punish wrongdoers and to maintain law and order, become more mechanical in their procedures and less ready to take account of the circumstances of the

[46] See above, Ch. 3, p. 41.

individual's case. Sometimes tribunals have for this reason sought to exclude professional advocates altogether. There are grave objections to that. But often we need to restrict the professionalism of advocates, or we lose sight of justice in a maze of legal technicality.[47] It is for this reason that prosecuting counsel are instructed not to seek to secure a conviction by every means at their disposal, but only to do what is needed to enable the court to dispense justice. Barristers generally are in theory officers of the court, and subject to a professional etiquette intended to avoid the worst excesses of unscruplous presentation of a client's case. But it is a difficult attitude to enforce, and more needs to be said and done on the rights and duties of advocates.

Timeliness is a process value intimately bound up with justice. It is often laid down that judges shall decide only after due deliberation. Due deliberation is intended to secure ratiocination and hence rationality. But besides not being sufficient, the condition is not even necessary. We can, on occasion, size up a situation at a glance, check quickly whether there is anything else to be said on either side, and see what ought to be done in a flash. Absence of lengthy deliberation does not betoken irrationality in the way tossing a coin does. Nevertheless, it does remove one safeguard. Hasty decisions may be ill considered. The requirement of due deliberation should be seen therefore, as a subordinate maxim of natural justice. It is a good rule to adopt to secure against the imperfection of decision-makers, and by adopting it we demonstrate to those who are disappointed with our decisions our determination not to decide against them easily or casually. We should give time for thought, even though thought does not always take time.

Much more often, however, our complaint is with the law's delays. There are many general grounds for regarding the dilatoriness of the law as inefficient and contrary to the public interest, but it is not immediately evident that justice delayed is justice denied. In the case of distributive justice it is not always true: when burdens are being allocated, e.g. conscripted service in a jury or the armed forces, I may well be glad to have my burden deferred to some later date. It is much more in cases of crime and tort—Aristotle's rectificatory justice—that we sense injustice in delay. In these cases the legal process is being invoked to put to rights some wrong done, and the point of the legal action is largely lost if it takes place so

[47] H. J. Elcock, *Administrative Justice*, London, 1969, Ch. IV.

long after the original misdeed that it no longer seems to alter its significance. If a punishment comes quickly, while the action is still fresh in the agent's mind, it can signal to him as well as to bystanders, that one cannot get away with that sort of misdoing, and the action is registered as a mistake at once, and then passes into the past. The more time that elapses between the wrongdoing and its penal consequences, the more separate the two appear, and the more gratuitous the imposition of penal sanctions seems. It is not only hard to keep a court case hanging over a man, but it is counter-productive. Far better, from his point of view as well as that of the community as a whole, to get on with it and get it over. Similarly speed is important from the point of view of those who have been wronged. If wronged they have been, the sooner things are put to rights the better, because then they will no longer have to live with a sense of injury. Not to take prompt steps to redress wrongs is to show lack of concern for the plaintiff. He is ceasing to be a person, and is become merely a case, to be kept waiting at other people's convenience. English legal practice is grossly defective on both these counts. It is common for petty crimes to take up to eight months before coming to a magistrates' court; and the county courts are equally dilatory. It is seldom that there is any justification for the delay. Almost always it is because the courts are overloaded and solicitors incompetent. But promptness is important, and we should take steps to secure it, sometimes even at the cost of other legal goods.

Definitiveness is a process value in as much as it is a corollary of timeliness,[48] but it is also to be argued for on grounds of liberty and security. It is important that people can know where they stand without being forever liable to the authorities' having fresh thoughts. Hence, although there needs to be some provision of reconsideration—some procedure of appeal—there needs also to be an end of rethinking and a stage after which a question is closed and known to be no longer openable. Like legality, definitiveness is needed by reason of the imperfection of our understanding—if we all could be sure of agreeing on the right answer, there would be no argument, save that of avoiding tedium, for preventing a question being reopened, and the same answer being given, as often as anyone liked—and like legality it introduces further imperfections

---

[48] See R. S. Summers, "A Plea for 'Process Values'", *Cornell Law Feview*, 60, 1974–5, p. 27.

all of its own into the law. Bad decisions sometimes have to stand even though they are admitted to be bad, and, injustices once committed, justice requires us to uphold them, on pain of creating even further injustice. Once again, we have to recognise that absolute justice is unattainable, and all we can hope is that by a system of appeals we may eliminate the worst injustices.

These rules of procedure do not guarantee that decisions will be just. Rather they constitute necessary, or near necessary, conditions of the decision-making being a process with which a man could be expected to identify. Decision-making which lacks these characteristics is wide open to repudiation, and a man disappointed at its outcome can find fault with it and plenty of reason to reject it. Even if it satisfies all these requirements, he may find fault with it on other grounds, and even if there are no reasonable grounds for impugning it, he may still reject it simply because he does not like the result. But then at least we can reckon that he ought to accept it, and insist that he shall. By observing the rules of natural justice in reaching decisions we make it less easy to take exception to them, and make it manifest to anyone disappointed at the outcome that we were solicitous of his interests and did not reach an adverse decision lightly or wantonly, but only for good reason and with evident reluctance.

Often the rules of justice are not observed, sometimes in respect to only a minor provision, sometimes in some very important respect, and the question then arises "What is to be done?". The courts have been unclear in their rulings, and seem to some to be securing the shadow rather than the substance of natural justice.[49] It is a mistake to be over-legalistic, for most decisions are not taken by lawyers and will not come up to lawyers' standards of formality, and the courts will be faced with the alternatives of either invalidating non-legal decisions wholesale, or declining to review many of them for the wrong reasons. In assessing breaches of natural justice we need to go behind technicalities, and look at the underlying principles. The result of not observing these is to make a decision *impugnable*. Normally even wrong decisions stand provided they are taken by the proper authorities. If, however, the man taking the decision had an interest of his own, or failed to hear the other side of the case, or was too hasty or too dilatory in reaching a decision,

[49] D. H. Clark, "Natural Justice: Substance and Shadow", *Public Law*, 1975, pp. 27–63.

then the decision lays itself open to question. If, furthermore, it seems to be a wrong decision, it evidently should be invalidated—quashed—and either reversed by the court or sent back to be reversed by the relevant authority. Difficulty arises where it is obviously right or not obviously wrong. In the former case it would be wrong to reverse the decision: to replace a right decision by a wrong one does not advance the cause of justice. The complaint is that the decision-maker failed to manifest sufficient respect to the person decided against. Occasionally, in serious criminal cases, the only way to show the very great reluctance we should all feel about condemning a man is to order a new trial. In other cases this is of no benefit to the man concerned, and often the best the court can do is to reconsider the case itself, and having observed all the niceties of procedural justice, come to the same conclusion as the original authority. Where the case is doubtful, the courts are properly reluctant to substitute their judgement for that of those with whom the decision normally rests. Sometimes the case can be sent back for a fresh hearing; but some bureaucrats are bad at reconsidering properly, and do not bring a fresh mind to the case but merely are more careful about procedural niceties as they come to the conclusion they had already decided on. Where feasible, the case may be sent to a different, but comparable, authority to be heard afresh without their minds being predisposed to reaffirm the original decision. But often this is not feasible, and the courts can do nothing but substitute, although reluctantly, their own decision for that impugned.

5

JUSTICE AND THE LAW

Justice is commonly supposed to be exemplified in the law, but the relationship is more complicated than at first sight appears. The courts of justice are the law courts, and it is the function of the law to uphold justice, so much so that it is a very serious criticism indeed of a legal official that he has acted unjustly, or of a law or legal system that it is unjust. Yet this criticism can be made without its conclusively impugning the authority of the official or the validity of the law. Often we draw a contrast between the positive law, which can indeed be unjust while still remaining valid, and the law of nature which perfectly exemplifies our ideal of justice. Even if, as often in modern times, we are unhappy at the idea of a law of nature, we still contrast the legal pettifogging procedures and precedents of positive law with the ideal requirements of justice. Justice cannot be defined as what the law lays down: there are many uses of the word 'just' which cannot be explicated in terms of law—an examiner's mark, for example—and the fact that laws often *are* said to be unjust is further evidence against the adequacy of any such definition. We cannot merely identify law and justice: yet we cannot, if we are honest, simply divorce them as the positivists sought to do.

The positivist analysis of law was simple but wrong. Laws were construed simply as the edicts of an external authority enforced by sanctions. It was based partly on the assumption, false as we have seen,[1] that reason had no force in itself, so that only physical force, or the fear of it, would be of any avail in influencing conduct. It was also a conclusion, easily drawn by a practical man, from the fact that there is no remedy, within our legal system at least, for an unjust law. But the conclusion does not follow, as can be seen from a comparison with particular adjudications and allocations; these also may be unjust, but, if they are decisions of the highest court of appeal, there is nothing to be done about them. But that does not make them any the less wrong. Although a bad decision may have

[1] Ch. 3, pp. 35–6.

to stand, it still is a bad decision, and can be stigmatized as such. For the whole point of the legal action was to find a just decision, and since at the outset the different parties maintained their different views of what would be a just decision, it would still be intelligible afterwards to maintain that the decision actually given was unjust. The judge tries to reach a just decision: but as with all the things we try to do, he may not succeed. The possibility of failure is inherent in the aim for success. And therefore a judge may get it wrong. Thus, an authoritative decision can be unjust, even though it cannot be upset. And so, equally, a law can be unjust, even though validly enacted and authoritative.

The positivist analysis fails to do justice to the phenomena. It fails to account for the fact that we, most of us, most of the time, think we *ought* to obey the law, quite apart from the possibility of our suffering ill consequences if we are caught breaking it. It fails to account for the fact that we often think it is unfair of someone to break the law, but sometimes hesitate to condemn it as unfair, although still thinking it wrong. It does not fit the way that the law has grown up and continues to develop, and cannot convincingly accommodate the role of judicial discretion and, hence, judicial innovation. And it gives us no basis for assessing laws on the score of justice, for determining the status of iniquitous laws, or for deciding when the obligation to obey no longer holds. These failures stem from a misapprehension of the nature of law and, in particular, a neglect of the internal aspect of law.[2] The law cannot be understood entirely from an external standpoint. At least for the officials who administer it, the internal aspect must be dominant. They look to the law for guidance not because they are anxious to avoid incurring penalties, but because the law is constitutive of their activity. In much the same way as chess-players must be guided by the rules of chess, or their activity becomes pointless, so legal officials must refer to the law in undertaking their activities, if they are to have any significance. We need, however, to go much further than Hart, and say that the same holds good to a very large extent for ordinary non-official members of the public too. The crucial characteristic of law is that it is to a very large extent internalised. If I accept that something is the law, then I accept also that, in the absence of weighty countervailing considerations, I ought to do it. In this laws resemble moral principles, social conventions and the

[2] H. L. A. Hart, *The Concept of Law*, Oxford, 1961, pp. 86 ff.

laudable customs of institutions we are members of. Within this genus, laws and moral principles are differentiated from the others by being much more important, and laws are distinguished from moral principles in their being enforced on the recalcitrant by the threat of sanctions. This was the kernel of truth in the positivist analysis. But the specific difference had obscured the generic similarity. Laws differ from moral principles in that if a man is not convinced he ought to obey them, we do not leave him to act autonomously according to his own lights, but add external persuasions to ensure that, convinced or no, he does what the law lays down. Most people, however, obey the law not just because they are afraid that they will cop it if they are caught breaking it, but because it is the law and they think they ought to keep it. Nor is this just an accident. Not only is it integral to the concept of law that some people should some of the time think themselves under an obligation to obey it, but it is a necessary condition of its efficacy that most people should do so most of the time. This internal aspect is thus the dominant one. The laws and *mores* of a society are what guide its members in their dealings with one another, without their normally having to have recourse to the law courts for adjudication or enforcement. Although in modern, highly sophisticated societies we do not know all the details of contemporary legislation, we have an outline knowledge of the rules relevant to our normal spheres of activity. It still makes sense to lay down the principle that "Ignorance of the law is no excuse", because we know in most of our transactions who is entitled to do what, and not only can settle almost all disputes out of court, but can nearly always avoid even getting involved in a real dispute. Law is not simply something the sovereign tells his subjects to do, but is rather something that the subjects themselves work out in their daily lives. It is a social phenomenon, part of their way of life. It is not the whole of social life, which includes many customs and conventions which could not be dignified with the name of law, but it consists of those rules which we not only expect every member of society to be guided by, but insist that he shall conform to, even if he does not want to, even if we have to do violence to his conscience, and apply sanctions to secure compliance. The law is what, if need be, will be enforced. Hence the need, on occasion, for superior power, and thus the involvement of the sovereign or the State. The law thus differs from other social patterns of behaviour in that it has an external aspect too, in that it will be enforced on those who are otherwise recalcitrant, but is nevertheless primarily regarded from the internal point of view. The positivists have been so much concerned with its external aspect that they have ignored the internal aspect altogether, and thus have misdescribed the phenomenon of law.

The enforcement of the law is through the courts, and it is in the decisions of the courts that we discover what is to count as law and distinguish it from what is merely customary and from those moral principles which, although important, are of value only if they are acted on freely and not from fear of legal sanctions. Aristotle distinguished the justice of the courts, what he called corrective justice, from distributive justice, and it is an important distinction, although his own account is a muddle, partly because he is trying to represent justice, like all the other moral virtues, as a mean, partly because he is trying to give an account of both corrective and distributive and commutative justice in quasi-egalitarian terms.[3] He takes over from Plato[4] a confusion between torts and crimes, and tries to make the legal process both compensate the victim—as is done in a successful civil suit for tort—and ensure that crime does not pay—as is to some extent done by the punishment of the accused at the conclusion of a criminal case in which the prosecution is successful. But these aims are not always compatible. The focus of attention is different. In a civil case it is on the plaintiff, the man who was wronged. If the court finds that he was indeed wronged, then its concern is to restore the *status quo* from *his* point of view. If he has suffered a lot of damage, then the damages will be great, even though the defendant's fault was venial: and no matter how badly the defendant misbehaved, the damages will not reflect that fact, but will only be enough to restore the plaintiff to his previous position. In the criminal case attention is focussed on the accused. The question is whether he did wrong or not. The victim does not come into it, except as evidence of wrongdoing on the part of the accused. It is no defence to a criminal charge, as it would be to a civil suit, to show that nobody suffered any harm: and, *per contra*, a man may be acquitted of a crime, even though much damage resulted from his actions. What is important is not how much damage was done but whether the deed was contrary to the law. It is an adequate defence, save in special cases, such as where

---

[3] *Nicomachean Ethics*, V, 4; 1131b 25–1132b 20.
[4] *Laws*, IX, 860 ff.

strict liability is imposed by statute, to show that one had no *mens rea*, no intention of doing wrong; "I could not help it" or "I did not know that it would have that effect" are valid pleas in a criminal court. Moreover, if a criminal charge is proved, it is not very helpful to see the sentence as an attempt to restore the *status quo* by taking from the criminal the unfair advantage gained by the crime. Although in a metaphorical sense the sentence is an attempt to cut the criminal down to size, it is not governed by any strict canons of equality. It is no reason for reducing a sentence that a criminal had not, in fact, gained by his crime: if a rapist says that it had not been much fun, the judge is unlikely to be lenient in consequence. From a practical point of view, sentences would fail of their effect if they were uniformly too light. It is important that crime should not pay, and therefore sentences need to be sufficiently severe to act as an effective deterrent. But, provided they are heavy enough to deter, there is no objection, from the deterrent theory, if they are somewhat heavier still. If they are very heavy, then there may be objections on the score of justice. But the range between a sentence's being too light and its being too heavy is considerable, and certainly too large for us to be able to construe sentencing as being in any sense a sort of equality.

We defer until the next chapter further elucidation of the rationale of criminal trials and punishment. Although it is a mistake to suppose that the law of tort comprises the whole of the civil law, it is typical of civil suits that there is a conflict of interest or right between the two parties, and that both are in danger of being done down. Since the court cannot find in favour of one without finding against the other, it must inevitably find against one or the other for good reasons. The problem, as we noted in Chapter One,[5] is to determine which reasons are individualised reasons, and what weight should be given them. In non-legal contexts—domestic disputes arising within the family or some small community—and in primitive legal systems, it is left to the judge to decide the relative weight of the reasons on either side. It is not always an impossible task. But it is sometimes difficult; that is why we need to choose men of wisdom to be judges.[6] Moreover, we cannot be sure that their decisions are right—that is why we need to invest them with authority[7]—nor, indeed, in all cases that it is even possible in

[5] p. 14.   [6] See above, Ch. 4, pp. 81–2.
[7] See above, Ch. 4, pp. 80–1.

principle to reach a right decision. Solomons are seldom come by. Ordinary men, even wise men, find it difficult to decide where the right lies. Often there seems to be right on both sides. Often what should be accounted right depends on the legitimate expectations of the parties, and these in turn depend on the conventions current among them. Justice, at least in the understanding of ordinary fallible man, is not sufficiently finely grained to discriminate between all cases, and needs, if it is to be applied by ordinary men, to be filled out by rules of thumb and accepted standards. In medieval theory, it was only a failure of human understanding, and it was felt that in principle justice operated in a plenum of possible cases, giving an exact division among them. It is an attractive theory, but it is difficult to state in satisfactory form, and it may not be true. It may be the case that not only are human beings inadequate judges, but justice itself is indeterminate. Not all cases admit of a definitive decision which is just, but in some a decision either way involves injustice and in others both sides lack merit. Whether the inadequacy lies solely in the human understanding, or whether there is also some measure of indeterminacy in the concept of justice itself, the result is the same: justice by itself is an incomplete guide to decision-making, and needs to be eked out by other principles. If a man dies intestate, it stands to reason that his estate should go to his next of kin. But whether is should all go to his widow, or half to his widow and half to his children, or a third to his widow, a third to his children, and a third to his parents, brothers and sisters, is a question to which reason, unaided by custom, convention or precedent, returns no definite answer. But a definite answer is needed: and different definite answers are developed by different systems of positive law. And although they are different it does not follow that only one can be just and the others must be unjust. For justice, since it is concerned with the significance of actions, is, in part (though only in part) conventional. In the same way as there can be different languages, each capable of expressing truth, so there can be different positive laws, each capable of doing justice.

We need some measure of conventionality because of the inadequacy of human reason, and, perhaps, the incompleteness of the concept of justice: and we have it as a concomitant of dispensing justice, since, as we have already seen,[8] it is a rule of natural justice

[8] Ch. 3, pp. 43–4, and Ch. 4, p. 77; see also below, Ch. 7, pp. 161–2.

that one should decide like cases alike, so that in deciding a particular case justly, we are thereby legislating for similar cases too. The rule of precedents is a concomitant of rationality, and justice is rational. Whenever we reason, we are committed to reasoning similarly in similar cases. If I reason that the distant lake seen shimmering in the desert is not really a lake but only a mirage, then I am committed to explaining other phenomena similarly, unless some relevant circumstance is different. So, too, if I reluctantly decide against a man for compelling reason, I must, reluctantly again no doubt, decide against anyone else whose circumstances are exactly the same. And hence we have a formal requirement of justice that it treat like cases alike. If we abandon this principle, and treat differently cases that are apparently alike without being able to show some relevant difference, we abandon our claim to being rational, and therefore to being just. Hence, once we have given a judgement, we cannot decide similar cases differently, without forfeiting our right to be respected as a fount of justice. And, therefore, it seems, we are committed to the rule of precedents.

The argument, however, is not quite watertight. The first hole is that no two cases are exactly the same, and the second is that the dispenser of justice need not claim infallibility. No two cases are exactly the same. People are different; their attitudes, past histories and expectations differ. The very fact that something has been done once may make a difference to the way we look upon its repetition—there are many things which are unexceptionable if done only once, but actionable if done repeatedly. Although it might seem feasible to lay down just what features were to be accounted relevant, it has proved impossible. Since the time of the *Code Napoléon* there has been a determined attempt to specify by statute exactly what features shall be taken into account, so as to remove the need for, or possibility of, judicial discretion: but it has failed. Again and again particular cases have had features not catered for in the statute, for which no authoritative guidance has been laid down, and on which the judge must make up his mind; and however fully specified a statute was, there always might be some further feature still that altered the whole complexion of a particular case, so that the judge must be given some discretion. There will always be some cases where in the last resort he has to reason in accordance with the principle of equity, not that of legality.[9]

Judges can err. We all know that they do, and should not be shy about admitting it, even if we happen to be the judge in question. Although desirable, it is not necessary that the judgements of a judge be absolutely just, so long as they meet other, less exacting, conditions. An important part of a judge's function in society is to deliver authoritative decisions of disputes; and, within limits, it does not matter what the decisions are, provided they are available and adequately authoritative. Many regimes have proved tolerable in spite of manifold imperfections. A judge, therefore, can in retrospect admit that a decision of his ought to have gone the other way, without abrogating its validity or altogether destroying the respect in which his judgements ought to be held. His decision was still serving a useful social purpose at the time. It enabled a conflict to be settled without resort to fisticuffs. In many cases there was right on both sides, and if the balance of argument comes down other than was first supposed, there is still much to be said for the original decision, which is far from being very unjust. In such cases a decision subsequently seen to be wrong is not for that reason a bad decision. It was in its time useful, and still has much to be said for it. Provided the judge is trying to be just, we can trust ourselves to his arbitrament. We do not have to make out that it must be infallible, in order to be authoritative. We can, therefore, allow judges on occasion to correct their previous decisions—that is, to overrule their own precedents—provided other requirements of the judicial office are satisfied.

Nevertheless, the arguments in favour of the rule of precedents are strong. In the first place, the argument from equity is a qualification, not refutation, of the argument for legality. It shows that the rule of precedents sometimes requires some judicial discretion in its application, not that it always does. Although not every case is a clear case, some are: and although every fresh decision gives rise to new doubtful cases, it also settles many others that had been uncertain hitherto. Although we have to confer some discretion on judges, and although that discretion could be abused, justice requires that judges should not take into consideration irrelevant factors. From this it follows that we cannot always as a matter of logic find some relevant differences that will distinguish

[9] See above, Ch. 3, pp. 43–4, and Ch. 4, pp. 76–9.

each particular case from every other. Some cases really are, from the standpoint of justice, alike, and ought to be treated alike. This is not enough to establish that any two actual cases are alike, but, together with further consideration of the canons of relevance and irrelevance required by the principle of justice, it often makes it unlikely. In so far as the judges are trying to administer justice and not merely hand down authoritative decisions, they will indeed treat like cases alike, and will differentiate between cases only for good reason. In the second place, even if the judges were not trying to reach just decisions but thought their sole purpose was the social function of providing authoritative arbitration, there is still a social advantage in predictability, which will enable the parties to arrange their affairs so as not to come into conflict with each other, and, if they are in dispute, to settle out of court. Nor are most people concerned solely with predictability from an external standpoint, important though that is: they are concerned also with the internal aspect of law, as a guide to their own actions and not merely a predictor of other people's; and they want to identify with the judgements of a judge, understand them, and make them their own, whatever view he takes of them himself. This is why the judgement needs to be reasoned. And the reasoning once accepted as authoritative in one case becomes normative for all succeeding ones. It would be different if there were some other calculus or decision-procedure independently available. Then anyone could check up on the judge's reasoning, and reject it if it was wrong. But then also we should have little need of judges, save as enforcement officers. We turn to judges to decide cases, because we have no other recourse that will always be available whenever we need. Judges therefore are operating, at least on some occasions, in an area where the rest of us cannot tell which course is right, but need to know none the less. The judge's decision on these occasions has, therefore, the epistemological status of a convention. Once promulgated, it is accepted because there is no agreement on anything also. Even a bad precedent can give guidance, and may be, for most people, apart from the disappointed litigant, better than no precedent at all. People will know the law, as expressed in the precedent, and will be able to shape their actions in the light of that knowledge. The precedent will give them guidance for themselves and certainty with respect to the actions of others, and so will be valuable, even if leaving a lot to be desired as regards its substantive content.

Precedents are not only adjudications, but also legislations; and even though some may be bad considered as adjudications of particular cases, they are still valid, and to a large extent valuable, as legislation.

The rule of precedents greatly increases the knowability of the law: but most men's capacity for knowing the law is not very great, and soon the knowable body of law outruns most men's capacity, and law becomes a professional mystery known only to technical experts. Although law is still embedded in social life, in that you and I and most people know how to behave and know what each person's rights are in normal circumstances, there are a large number of special cases, to which you and I and most people have never addressed ourselves, on which the law has pronounced, and whose pronouncements we do not know. Worse, in view of the degree of conventionality introduced by precedents, the pronouncement of the law may not at all accord with what we find ourselves inclined to say when we have to address ourselves to some of the cases. Law ceases then to be the common possession of every member of the community, and becomes an external expertise we have to be told about by our attorneys and solicitors. And the more complicated it becomes, and the more given over to formalities and technicalities, the more moribund it seems to the layman, and the less concerned with membership of society and our common life together. Instead of the quickening judgement of Solomon, we have the musty tomes of the lawyers. Law is ossified justice.

We do not go to solicitors to seek moral advice. They give us legal advice on what we can and cannot do, rather than moral advice on what we should or should not do. Although law has its internal aspect, it differs from morals in having an external aspect too, which, in particular cases of extreme conflict, dominates the internal aspect. It is a defining characteristic of law that it will be enforced on me willy-nilly. And, conversely, I cannot but regard the law as something which may be enforced on me against my will, and therefore as being somewhat external. Although I may largely identify with the law, there is always a potential divergence. Justice being, as we have seen,[10] an "anular" concept, requires that we allow privacy of intention, and therefore cannot require a whole-hearted acceptance of its deliverances. And so I may see the law not as a guide but as a fetter. When I consult my solicitor, the

[10] Ch. 1, pp. 15–16.

divergence between my own real wishes and what the law allows will be prominent, and he will advise me how I can ease my fetters, and what I must do to manipulate the law to my own ends. Although it is not the only, or the original, or the essential, facet of law, it is an ineliminable one. Men will not simply put themselves under the guidance of the law, but will seek to use it and exploit it, and so will coarsen it and harden it. From this, ossification ensues. The law is not simply a collection of the judgements of a just judge arbitrating between good men, each of whom has much right on his side. Each decision will become a precedent which will be used by other men, not whole-heartedly good, nor altogether seeking to play fair in an impartial way, but rather seeking to use the law to bend other men to serve their own partial interests. This happens. It cannot but happen. The law recognises that it will happen, and must be allowed to happen, and, accommodating itself to the fact, constitutes itself as something different from, although still connected with, justice itself.

Laws, as well as individual decisions, can be criticized as unjust. Although we often need to supplement our imperfectly understood and acknowledged intimations of justice by the clearer and more indisputable pronouncements of law, and although not all laws can intelligibly be criticized as unjust, some can. Some laws are unjust, some very unjust. Yet they are laws, and lay some obligation on men to obey them. In particular, judges are under an obligation to administer the law as it is, and a judge who administers an unjust law impartially is, as we have seen,[11] both just, because he is impartial and does what a judge ought to do, and unjust, inasmuch as the law he is enforcing is unjust. It is one instance among many of the complexity of the concept of justice, and of the many different criteria for its application, and of its apparent ambiguity in consequence.

Laws, whether developed through cases in the common law or explicitly enacted as statutes, are not all of one type. Too often it is assumed that every law has substantially the same rationale, imposing similar costs and yielding similar benefits. Often in the Anglo-American tradition, it has been assumed that every law is *eo ipso* a restriction on liberty, and that the only justification of restricting liberty is to avoid harm to somebody else. But many laws do not fit this account, and even those that are concerned with the avoidance

[11] Ch. 1, p. 2.

of harm are of different types. In some cases the harm is immediate and obvious. Laws against murder and rape need no elaborate justification: simple concern for the potential victim is enough to persuade us that each and every deed of violence is a crime, a *malum per se*. Other laws create rather than recognise crimes. Often, as we saw in Chapter Three, we can express the rationale in terms of the Theory of Games. Some harm is avoided, or some good secured, by our all acting in a certain way, and although there is nothing intrinsically wrong in someone's acting otherwise, nevertheless breaches of the rule are wrong in view of there being a rule. They are *mala prohibita*, not *mala per se*. Among these we need to distinguish those whose rationale is the Prisoners' Dilemma from those whose rationale is the Rule of the Road. In the former case there is a restriction of liberty—each individual would like to park at his own convenience, and would do so if he were at liberty to do so: in the latter case the freedom forgone is an empty one. I have no desire to collide with other cars. My object is to know what they will expect me to do and will themselves do in consequence, so that I can drive without danger or embarrassment. This is far the more common case. Although sometimes I am tempted to go beyond, and do my neighbour down, far more often I simply need to know what to do so as to co-operate with him in avoiding awkwardness or achieving some common aim. The analysis of law offered by Protagoras, Plato, Hobbes and many modern thinkers gives the wrong emphasis. Our experience of life in society socialises us and leads us to internalise laws, rules and customs, much more whole-heartedly and less reluctantly than the Prisoners' Dilemma would. I do not grudgingly forgo my liberty of doing wrong on condition that everyone else shall do likewise, but eagerly assimilate the rules which will give me the know-how to act on my own. This explains the apparent paradox in the medieval view of law:

The higher one rose towards liberty, the more the area of action was covered by law, the less it was subject to will. The knight did not obey fewer laws than the ordinary freeman, but very many more; the freeman was not less restricted than the serf, but he was restricted in a different, more rational way. Law was not the enemy of freedom; on the contrary, the outline of liberty was traced by the bewildering variety of law which was slowly evolved during our period. The irksome rules and tedious grada-tions of society did not appear, as they did to a later age, as so many strangle-holds on liberty. High and low alike sought liberty by insisting on enlarging the number of rules under which they lived. The most highly privileged communities were those with most laws. At the bottom of society was the serf, who could least appeal to law against the arbitrariness of his superiors. At the top was the nobleman, governed by an immensely complicated system of rules in his public life, and taught in his private relationships to observe an equally complicated code of behaviour.[12]

The medieval view makes obvious sense if we take the motoring analogy. The better a motorist is, the more rules he observes on his own account, without having to be told. It is only the learner who has to be given instructions by someone else what to do. Skilled motorists—taxi-drivers—can keep the traffic moving even when it is congested, whereas bank-holiday drivers cause jams, and need policemen to tell which motorist to give way to which. Law, on this view, is internalised authority, with the function of authority being to extend knowledge, in the face of my otherwise imperfect information about what other men are going to do and their correspondingly imperfect information about what I am going to do. Law is seen not as abridging freedom, curbing our right to do what we naturally would want to do, but as an exercise of liberty: in freely adopting the law as my guide, I shall know what to do, and others will know what I shall do, so that I shall be able to achieve my objects with their co-operation. They will be able to understand me, and so will not get in my way, and my efforts will not be frustrated by our being at cross-purposes and having unintended collisions.

The Rule of the Road illuminates our understanding of the nature of law in other ways too. It shows that law is a matter of knowledge, and not only of will. In the Prisoners' Dilemma there is an obvious rationality in both keeping silent, and one could think that if only men were possessed of the good will, all would be well. The Rule of the Road shows us how far this is from the truth. There is no greater menace than the well-intentioned motorist who needlessly dithers at a roundabout in order not to push his way forward unfairly. Although moral virtues are sometimes in point, and then no doubt too little observed, the first requirement is not a readiness to give way, but an entirely predictable pattern of manœuvre. We need to know. And the need to know is as important as the need to

---

[12] R. W. Southern, *The Making of the Middle Ages*, London, 1953, p. 108; quoted by F. A. Hayek, *Law, Legislation and Liberty*, I, 1975, p. 157.

be nice, and gives rise to a different sort of law, to which different standards of justice apply.

Other uniformities are established not for any games-theoretical reason but in order to establish some conventions of significance or in order to manifest a common mind. There may be reasons leading towards one particular law rather than another, but there do not have to be. It may be simply an expression of corporate freedom. In much the same way as it is desirable that the individual should be able on occasion to make up his own mind for himself spontaneously and authentically, if he is to be really himself and not a rule-governed nonentity, so we have come to realise since the end of the eighteenth century, in reaction against the rationalism of the Enlightenment, that nations and peoples also had an individuality of their own, which found expression in, among other things, their laws, and that these national individualities were valuable, and ought to be cherished. Scots law is different from English law. Not only may it be none the worse for that—a point established by the previous argument—but it is a positive merit, contributing a further thread to the web of Scottish identity. Although there are advantages in a uniform *Code Napoléon* or Whitehall-drafted Statute Law, these are usually purchased at too high a price of impersonality and alienation. The diversity of peoples ought to be reflected in a diversity of laws, in order that we may all feel at home in our own laws; the anomalies of devolution are a small price to pay for our all being able collectively to do our own thing.

It is often, but not always, unfair to break the law. In the case of murder, rape or grievious bodily harm, the word 'unfair' is not so much incorrect as inadequate to express our condemnation. Such crimes are not merely wrong, but very wrong, and should be called 'wicked' rather than 'unfair'. But they are unfair too: witness the fact that we say it is unfair not to take precautions against committing these crimes. If I know that I am liable to run amok, then it is unfair of me not to put myself under supervision or to wander unsupervised where other men go. If drink makes me unable to restrain my sexual urges or to drive safely, then it is unfair of me to drink when women are going to be about or when I am going to drive. But these are peripheral uses. Crimes of this sort are too deliberate to be felicitously stigmatized by the word 'unfair' which suggests a casual unconcern with other chap's interest rather than a deliberate intention to do him down.

The word 'unfair' applies much more naturally to breaking a law whose *raison d'être* is to enable us all to enjoy the fruits of uniform forbearance on the part of everyone. In that case it is unfair if anyone secures advantage to himself by going back on an agreement everyone else is adhering to. We would all like to drive our cars into the main shopping streets and park them outside the shop we visit, but the result of unrestricted parking is intolerable, and it is better that none of us should drive or park, in order that we all shall not be driven or parked against. But then if you drive and park in the main shopping street, it is unfair to the rest of us who have forgone a similar facility, because you are enjoying the benefit of our forbearance without bearing the burden of similar forbearance on your part. You are benefiting at our expense, and are therefore acting unfairly as regards each one of us, who had only forgone the advantages of untrammelled action on the understanding that everyone else, yourself included, would too. You are benefiting at our expense, and are therefore acting unfairly as regards each one of us in general.

Laws whose rationale is explained in terms of the Rule of the Road, rather than the Prisoners' Dilemma, also create expectations and interests, and therefore also cannot be broken without unfairness. Although there is nothing intrinsically wrong with driving on the right-hand side of the road, and although I am not snatching any advantage by doing so—on the contrary I am running a foolish risk of smashing up my own car and losing my own life—it is none the less unfair, as well as foolish, to drive on the wrong side on the road, because other people are entitled to count on my not doing so, and I am therefore endangering their lives and property by my action if I fail to conform to the normal rules. Contrary to the opinion of the Greeks, the essence of injustice is not my having too much, $\pi\lambda\epsilon\text{ov}\epsilon\xi\text{í}\alpha$, but the other chap's having too little; and as you may suffer injustice at the hands of an official who, without gaining any advantage for himself, fails to pay due regard to your interests, so you may be unfairly treated by me, if I disregard your interests, even if I also am disregarding my own.

With other laws it may be wrong to break them, but can hardly be said to be unfair. In the United States there are laws protecting the American flag from disrespect. It is illegal to wear pants which look as though they have been made out of the Stars and Stripes. We do not have any laws in Great Britain protecting the Union

Jack, but we have other ones securing that due respect be shown to the Queen. It is perfectly reasonable to have such laws, and it cannot be complained that they are illiberal or unjust. Yet to break them, although illegal, is not unjust. If I were to parade down Madison Avenue with my legs draped in the Stars and Stripes, I should have behaved illegally, wrongly, offensively and discourteously, but not unfairly. The reason is that there is nobody who has been done down. Feelings may have been hurt, but no bones were broken. Injustice differs from rudeness or discourtesy in adding injury to insult, in not only manifesting disrespect but doing actual damage to definite interests.[13] Other people have no natural interest in what I wear, nor one created by a mutual forbearance pact—there is no natural temptation to treat the American flag with disrespect, and the laws securing it against disrespect are not a means whereby the American people can escape from a Prisoners' Dilemma, whereby each of them by forbearing from wearing a certain sort of garment on his nether regions secures an obvious advantage for everybody else. Rather, the laws are intended to manifest a common mind about the identity of the American nation and its importance. A deviant who is out on a limb on this matter may be taxed with disloyalty and made to conform; but his rule-breaking has not been in any ordinary sense to his own advantage, or to anybody else's disadvantage, and therefore, although illegal, is not unjust.

Equally in the case of laws enforcing morality, law-breaking is to be stigmatized as wrong, immoral, maybe wicked, but not unfair. It may be wicked to commit incest, break the Sabbath, or smoke pot, but it is not unfair. Cruelty to animals is not properly described as unfair, since unfairness presupposes that animals not only have interests but could enter into the reasoning behind our dealings with them.[14] We could, none the less, still have laws against cruelty to animals: indeed, even if we attributed no feelings and no interests to animals, it would still be possible to maintain that there should be a law against cruelty simply on the grounds that people should not be sadists—some of those who oppose fox-hunting would continue to do so even if a gallup poll among foxes showed that they really did enjoy it—and if that were the ground of the law, then to break it would not be unfair, though it would still be wrong.

Not only law-breaking, but law-making may be criticized on the

---

[13] See above, Ch. 1, p. 7.   [14] See below, Ch. 11, pp. 199–200.

score of justice. A law may be said to be unjust if it has been enacted without due regard for the interests of some or if it turns out to bear on them unduly hardly. Laws which do not impose burdens cannot be said to be unjust. Anglophobes could have opposed in Congress the bill to confer American citizenship on Sir Winston Churchill, but could not have complained that it was unfair, any more than the bill's supporters could have argued that justice required the bill to be passed. Most laws, however, do impose burdens, if only that of observing their provisions, and so can raise issues of justice. Complaints against them, however, are more difficult to sustain than complaints against individual decisions, because laws are general. From the general nature of law it follows in the first place that the reasons for deciding against an individual in any particular case are already individualised: that is to say he is not being picked on—he is being decided against because his case has features which are deemed to be good reasons for deciding not only against him but against all others similarly situated. It follows in the second place that the conventions determining people's expectations and their understanding of what is just will often be affected by the existence of a general rule enshrined as law. Whereas particular decisions can be unjust because they disappoint expectations or flout conventions, a law, once established as law, cannot. Hence, although it does not follow that a law, simply by virtue of its generality, must be just,[15] the onus of proof is on those who claim that it is unjust, not those who maintain that it is just.

In assessing a claim that a law is unjust, we need to consider, on the one hand, how heavy a burden is being imposed and how avoidable its incidence, and, on the other, the reasons for imposing the burden at all. Acts of Attainder and Forfeiture are unjust because they pin penalties on individuals without proper trial to determine whether they deserve it or not. They offend against the principle *Nulla poena sine judicio*. Other legislative measures which impinge on the interests of particular individuals—private Acts of Parliament—go through a special procedure—the private bill procedure—to enable those affected by them to make representations, so that they shall not be put to avoidable loss. The argument against retrospective legislation is similarly founded on the principle of avoidability. It puts a man in jeopardy of punishment without his having had a chance to avoid it. If Parliament makes it a crime to

[15] See further below, pp. 119–23.

drive at more than 70 m.p.h., then I can keep out of trouble by keeping to the speed limit. But if it enacts that it shall have been a crime, then I did not know in time to avoid incurring the penalty. So, quite apart from other legal defects, retrospective enactment of criminal legislation is unfair. But some care is needed in applying this argument. Even without a speed limit, it might be wrong, and criminal, for me to drive at more than 70 m.p.h., e.g. in a built-up area, because it was inherently dangerous. But then it would be necessary to establish that it was dangerous, and not rely on the simple fact of its being forbidden. We have to distinguish between different types of laws, and in particular between those creating *mala prohibita* and those recognising *mala per se*. If the reason why an action is wrong is simply that it has been forbidden by law, then its wrongfulness cannot be known until the law has been passed forbidding it. If, however, it was wrong independently of its being forbidden, then a man should have known better than to have done it even before it was prohibited. The war criminals of Nuremberg did not need a statute to tell them that genocide was wrong. Similarly in the civil law it would not contravene the canons of justice to enshrine by retrospective legislation an assignment of rights and responsibilities that was already justified by morality or recognised by social custom. Difficulty arises in intermediate cases, where some, but not all, citizens can see that an action is wrong, or where there are arguments either way, and it is not clear where the balance lies. Often it has been the function of Parliament to define the law, rather than lay down new law, and recently the Supreme Court has taken to ruling prospectively, and then it is harder to separate the prospective and the retrospective effects of the ruling. In a developed legal system we may argue that we should eschew retrospective definition as well as retrospective prohibition. We may argue for a rather low level of knowledge of what ought and ought not to be done, and that people should not be expected to know what not to do unless they had been definitely told. There is some force in such an argument, although it cannot be cast-iron, since no legal system is completely developed. But it is an argument of liberty, not justice. So far as justice is concerned, all that is required is that a person should not be punished, or made to suffer other adverse legal consequences, for doing what, at the time of doing, he could not reasonably have known to be wrong. If it was dubious, he could have abstained, and has only himself to thank if, not keeping clear of shady activities, he finds himself on the windy side of the law. Only if a man has good reason to suppose that what he was doing was lawful, is it unfair to decide subsequently that it was not and that he should be punished for it.

"Strict liability" is, generally speaking, unjust. It is unfair to hold a man responsible for mischances or the actions of others, because, once again, there is nothing he can do to avoid it. We are willing to make certain distinctions or exceptions, however, depending on the sort of responsibility and more general conditions of voluntariness. Civil liability is much less personal than criminal responsibility: and a distinction can be drawn between penalties, which carry no great stigma, and punishments, which do.[16] Up to a point it is fair to hold the manufacturer of explosives liable for any explosion, whether or not it was the result of some fault of his: after all, he did not have to engage in that business, and if he chooses to, it is fair that he should carry the risk, and not passing bystanders. Equally, it would be fair to make motorists liable for accidents, even genuine accidents which were not any fault of theirs. For in driving a car they expose others to risks, and though the particular accident did not arise through any failure on their part, the hazard arose from a free choice of theirs. They are not blameworthy, but have incurred a duty to indemnify others against loss.

By the time an accident occurs it is too late to avoid loss. The duty of care is therefore reinforced by criminal sanctions in addition to civil liability. It is an offence to drive a car with defective brakes or inadequate lights, or to omit numerous precautions in the handling of explosives. Often employers are made responsible, at the bar of the criminal law as well as in the civil courts, for the actions and omissions of their employees. By making them strictly liable, we give them added incentive to keep their employees up to the mark. But there are limits. We do not like holding a man responsible for the actions of others over whom he has no control, or for mischances which were clearly due to the fault of somebody else. If the penalty can be construed merely as an additional cost which the employer did not succeed in avoiding, then it may be tolerable, on the grounds that great administrative efficiency and effectiveness outweigh small injustices.[17] But if some stigma is attached, or if the penalty is great, then strict liability is uncon-

[16] See further below, Ch. 6, pp. 136 ff.
[17] See further below, Ch. 6, pp. 139–40.

scionably unfair, and cannot be sustained, even by explicit parliamentary enactment, for long.[18] In the one case it tells a lie—it
makes out that the man did something that he did not—in the other
it subjects him to great loss, without giving him the chance to
protest the truth or show why he should not be so treated. The most
that justice will allow is to reverse the onus of proof. If people
engage in certain activities, it is up to them to take reasonable steps
to ensure that certain untoward eventualities cannot occur. And if
none the less things go wrong, that is *prima facie* evidence that they
did not discharge their duty. But it cannot be conclusive. If we
convict them automatically, without listening to their defence or
allowing any consideration of the fact that they had done all that
they reasonably could, we are doing them down gratuitously. And
any law which requires us to do that is unjust.

Laws enacted retrospectively or imposing strict liability are
unjust because they impose burdens unreluctantly, making people
unavoidably responsible for actions, contrary to our understanding
of responsibility and agency. Other laws can be stigmatized as
unjust because they impose grave burdens for inadequate reason, or
confer benefits on some but not on others equally deserving,
meritorious, needy, entitled or enfranchised. The latter raise issues
of distributive justice, and consideration of them is deferred until
Chapter Eight. For a law to be unjust under the former heads, it
must impose grave burdens. Not every restriction of freedom or
every obligation is a grave burden. It does not make sense in
ordinary circumstances to criticize the Highway Code as unfair.
This is because of its conventional character. It establishes conventions, but does not abridge anybody's interests. Being forbidden
to drive on the right-hand side of the road is not a serious
imposition, since the left is just as good as the right. The whole
point of conventions is that they are arbitrary. We need them
because we cannot otherwise know what other men will choose. But

[18] See especially the judgement in *Sweet* v. *Parsley*, All England Law Reports,
1969, I, pp. 347–64. Inferior courts, however, are less ready than the House of Lords
to reconstrue Acts of Parliament so as to make them just. On December 29, 1976,
Harold Huxley was prosecuted at Uppermill Magistrates' Court, Greater
Manchester, for failing to send his sixteen-year-old daughter, Mrs Debra Anne
Groves, to school. In his defence, Mr Huxley told the court "For all practical
purposes the child is not under my control. The marriage vows she took were to her
husband and not to me", but Mr Fletcher, for the prosecution, said that the
obligation was on the parent to see that a pupil attended school even if she was
married, and the magistrates fined Mr Huxley £5, with £10 costs.

if it is so much a matter of indifference that other men cannot reasonably know what I should naturally do, I cannot be said to have an interest, and cannot complain that my interests have been adversely affected. If I have a great yen for driving on the right, I may bellyache at the leftward direction of the British Highway Code; but it is hardly an interest of mine, only an idiosyncrasy.

For the same reason, an American cannot complain that he is unfairly deprived of the right to wear pants emblazoned with the Stars and Stripes. It is not a natural want. A desire to wear pants emblazoned with the Stars and Stripes cannot be imputed to a man in the way a desire to wear pants, perhaps, can. If a man wants to wear red pants, he can; if he wants to wear white pants, he can; if he wants to wear blue pants, he can. It is only if he wants to wear red, white and blue pants of a special pattern that he runs foul of the law. There would be no point in his wearing pants of that pattern except for the significance of the American flag. And therefore he is not being deprived of any natural interest, but only of a right to flaunt disrespect of a common symbol which no member of a community could reasonably claim. Hence, any such legislation, whatever its merits or demerits, cannot be criticized as being unfair.

The controversy over "moral" legislation reveals the same point. Many communities enshrine moral principles or religious rules in their laws. Until recent times this was regarded as entirely un-exceptionable. Recently there have been criticisms, but mostly on the score of liberty or a restricted view of the functions of the State. Unfairness has not been alleged against such laws, except when there has been an alteration of our view on the natural wants or interests of man. In order to make out that the laws against homosexuality are unfair, it is necessary not only to deny the wrongfulness of the proscribed behaviour but to see homosexuality as a natural condition and sexual activity as a normal desideratum of human life. Granted those assumptions, laws against homosexual behaviour can be said to be unfair, inasmuch as they curtail for some men a human activity we can ascribe, as a desirable part of human existence, to men *qua* men. But if these assumptions cannot be taken for granted, the charge of unfairness falls, and the laws must be criticized, if they are to be criticized at all, as inexpedient or from the standpoint of freedom not that of fairness.

Many laws impose substantial burdens, and the question of unfairness then arises. In some cases—taxing statutes—the point of the law is to impose burdens. We defer until Chapter Fourteen a discussion of the issues of justice these raise. In most cases, however, the burdens are imposed in pursuit of the other purposes for which the law is laid down, and the first question then is whether the good the law is intended to achieve justifies the imposition of burdens it will entail, and secondly whether the burdens are falling on exactly the right individuals. As regards the first question, we are much readier to weigh considerations of utility and public expediency against those of individual interest and right when we are legislating than when we are deciding a particular case. It is partly due to an awareness of the logic of the rationale of one sort of legislation—to break out of the Prisoners' Dilemma. It is also because we have less need to fear for the many than the few. The isolated individual is in danger from the casual unconcern of the community, which may well trample on his interests, without realizing it, in the pursuit of some common objective. There is evident need of the coalition of all for each.[19] But there is no need of a coalition of all for all. Indeed, it seems almost absurd. If the burden laid on everyone by some law is greater than the common benefit secured, then we shall reckon the law is not worth having, and so shall not enact it. Provided laws are universal in application, generalised self-interest will prevent particular injustice. Hence all we need, or so it seems, is to insist that all laws apply to all citizens equally and generally.[20] Independent of this argument is a third, that burdens are more easily borne if they fall on many shoulders. And it is also pertinent that burdens imposed by legislation, being prospective, give people opportunity so to arrange their affairs as to avoid burdens thought to be particularly unwelcome.

These arguments are weighty, but not conclusive. They alter the burden of proof, but do not close the question completely. Whereas it is *prima facie* unfair to reach an adverse decision in an individual case for extraneous reasons, no matter how compelling, it is *prima facie* fair if those reasons have been individualised through the medium of general rules.[21] But the presumption in favour of the fairness of general rules can be rebutted. We are not always in a Prisoners' Dilemma, and some laws, even though general in form, can bear much more hardly on some particular individuals than

---

[19] See above, Ch. 3, pp. 69–70.

[20] F. A. Hayek, *The Constitution of Liberty*, London, 1960, Ch. 14, esp. §4, pp. 209–10.

[21] See above, Ch. 1, pp. 12–14.

people at large. There is, besides the danger of the coalition of all against each, the danger of a coalition of most against the rest. And not all burdens are avoidable, even though imposed by prospective legislation.

Legislation is often criticized because it makes irrelevant discriminations. It is not denied that the benefits obtained justify the imposition of burdens, but the burdens are being imposed on the wrong people. Age is only weakly correlated with driving ability, gender is not the same as the ability to give good military orders: it seems unfair therefore to have an age qualification for holding a driving licence or a sex bar on holding a military command. Justice would seem to require that we examine each youth's driving ability on its merits, assess each woman's effectiveness as a commander without regard to her sex. But age and sex are definite, driving competence and leadership-potential difficult to assess. Age limits, admittedly somewhat arbitrary, are none the less admissable simply because they are practicable, and not totally irrelevant to the issue. Equally the refusal to licence epileptics to drive, although a great deprivation, is justifiable because we cannot at present know which epileptics are liable to seizures, and which are quite safe to drive. The incarceration of Americans of Japanese descent after Pearl Harbor could be defended as fair, on the grounds that that class was the smallest which could be picked out and would include potential traitors. In these cases great deprivations are justified by their being the only feasible means of averting great evils. If the laws imposing them are to be criticized ás unfair it must be by showing that there is a feasible alternative which will achieve the same purposes equally effectively, without bearing unreasonably heavily on anyone else. Disqualifications based on sex have come under much fire recently, but the logic is the same—often sex is relevant, or is correlated with some feature that is relevant—and therefore although "sexism" and "ageism" can be unjust, they are not necessarily so.[22] To the initial question "Why am I getting worse treatment than him?", it is an adequate counter to cite a law differentiating between us. Only if the law is making manifestly irrelevant distinctions, or is evidently imposing unnecessary or unnecessarily heavy burdens, can it be impugned as unjust.

Often a burden imposed by law will not be unduly heavy. In the

[22] For fuller discussion see J. R. Lucas, "Because You Are a Woman", *Philosophy*, 48, 1973, pp. 161–71; reprinted in James Rachels (ed.), *Moral Problems*, 2nd edn., New York, 1971, pp. 132–43.

first place, as we have noted, a law is characteristically general. It applies not to one man only, but to all those who fall within its scope. The burden is placed on them all, and it is only a collective, rather than an individual, injustice that can be complained of, if the burden is wrongly placed. But justice is primarily concerned with the individual, and a collective injustice, although sometimes real enough, does not strike so hard as an individual one. If I am unfairly deprived of a licence on inadequate, but general, grounds, there are many others in the same boat, and I can take some comfort from our common predicament. Although it still could be that we were all being unjustly treated, in most cases there will be some justification in imposing disqualification on us generally, and our position is that of a sub-community having to shoulder a burden for the benefit of the community as a whole, rather than of an individual being done down. Instead of the question "Why pick on me, a fully competent and fairly mature driver of fifteen?", the question we have to ask is "Why pick on us fifteen-year-olds?", and there may be good reasons for disqualifying fifteen-year-olds generally, even though those reasons would not actually apply in my individual case.

In the second place, laws, as we have seen, are known in advance, and the individual can arrange his own affairs in the knowledge of what their legal consequences will be. I can avoid having to bear the burdens imposed by a law by taking care not to bring myself within its scope. Clearly, there are exceptions. I cannot, by taking care, avoid having Japanese ancestors or being an epileptic—hence our sensitivity to legislation which discriminates on the basis of race or age or sex or some other factor over which the individual has no control. "He cannot help the colour of his skin" is a good reason for reckoning that skin colour should in general not be a factor relevant in law.

From this it follows that although the burdens imposed by laws are likely not to be unduly great, they may be. There could be a law imposing penalties on blue-eyed Englishmen of the male sex whose name was Smith and whose age was greater than eighteen and less than forty-eight. Nor, as even Hayek admitted, would any rule of law requiring statutes to be cast in universalised form be a definite safeguard against it.[23] Quite apart from Acts of Attainder and Forfeiture, which pick out individuals by name for adverse treat-

[23] F. A. Hayek, *The Constitution of Liberty*, London, 1960, pp. 209, 489.

ment, laws often bear hardly and unnecessarily so on some people rather than others, and it is known that they will do but that fact is not seen as a reason against passing them. Tyrants have long oppressed their peoples, and in democracies majorities are too ready to gang up against minorities. In spite of the considerations adduced in favour of the presumption that the laws are just, it would be quite wrong to suppose that all laws are just. Unjust laws are a feature of life. Some are not very unjust, and can be borne by reason of a general justice that pervades the whole system. But both individual laws and whole systems can be not rather unjust but very unjust.

The extent to which injustice impugns the validity of a law or a legal system is a different question, which cannot be adequately discussed here. In the Middle Ages it was said *lex injusta non est lex*. That gives bad laws too short a shrift. Many injustices ought to be put up with—justice, as we have seen,[24] can never be altogether attained. Besides, it would mean that we would deprive ourselves of the most important term in our vocabulary of criticism. If an unjust law were a contradiction in terms, we could not intelligibly criticize a law as being unjust. We want to be able to do this, and we want to be able to draw a distinction between the formal criteria for the validity of a law and the substantive defects of it. Hart suggests that we should define 'law' in terms of formal criteria alone, and leave it as a separate moral question whether a formally valid law should be obeyed or not.[25] But this has the two defects of weakening the conceptual link between the statements 'This is the law' and 'This ought to be obeyed', and of making it out to be simply a matter of individual conscience whether a law should be obeyed or not. Rather than this, we should distinguish between individual conscientious objections that a particular person may have to a particular law, and the general non-recognition that any reasonable man should have to putative laws vitiated by gross substantive defects. We must therefore say that if it is a law, it should then be obeyed even though it is unjust, but that grave and gross injustice strikes at the *raison d'être* of law, and hence that *lex injustissima non est lex*.[26]

[24] See above, Ch. 1, p. 16; Ch. 3, pp. 36–7.

[25] H. L. A. Hart, *The Concept of Law*, Oxford, 1961, pp. 203–7. H. L. A. Hart and Lon Fuller, *Harvard Law Report*, 71, 1953, pp. 593–672; reprinted in Frederick F. Olafson, *Society Law and Morality*, Englewood Cliffs, N.J., 1961, pp. 439–505.

[26] J. R. Lucas, "The Nature of Law", *Philosophica*, 23, 1979, pp. 45–6.

6

PUNISHMENT

Punishment illuminates justice, as well as posing severe problems for it. Like justice it is backward-looking. Like justice it has complicated links with rationality. Like justice it is sometimes to be construed as a species of communication, and not merely a manipulative cause of desirable effects. But whereas justice is concerned with not doing individuals down, punishment seems a deliberate doing down, necessarily unwelcome to them and associated with moral obloquy and social stigma. The decision to punish is an adverse decision, whose justification is open to question. If justice is a reluctance to do a man down, we should expect a just man to be merciful, and peculiarly reluctant to impose punishment: yet it is often in the name of justice that retributivists insist that punishment should be meted out to wrongdoers whether or not any subsequent good will come of it. Some people see punishment as a negative reward, a requital for bad actions just as good actions deserve well of us: but this is too *simpliste* an account to accommodate all the strands of our understanding of punishment; and, in particular, justice, according to the rationale we have given for it,[1] is essentially asymmetrical, and cannot be simply inverted—a rational reluctance to do down cannot be simply transformed into a rational reluctance to do up. Contrary to what the retributivists maintain, it is not always unfair to show mercy. Joseph being a just man was minded to be merciful to Mary and not make a public example of her.[2] Yet often justice is opposed to mercy and argues for deliberately tough treatment of those who have deliberately done wrong.

Punishment is linked with many other concepts. Besides punishment we should consider the etymologically related pains and penalties and penance, and also the equally unwelcome fines, taxes and forfeits we sometimes have to pay; besides imprisonment we should consider conscription, hospitalisation and quarantine; and we should not only contrast punishments and penalties with rewards, recompenses, prizes and payments, but compare them with

[1] Ch. 1, pp. 8–10.   [2] Matthew, 1:19.

reprimands, rebukes, reproofs, reproaches and blame, themselves
the opposites of praise, credit, honour, thanks and esteem.

Punishments, along with pains, penalties, penances, fines and
forfeits, are unwelcome, to be avoided; what Aristotle termed
φευκτά. Although it seems a contradiction in terms, they need not
involve the infliction of pain nor of suffering in any but a highly
metaphorical sense. One would have to love money very much
indeed to regard a ten-shilling fine as an infliction of suffering:
one can barely describe it even as a piece of unpleasantness. All that
is essential is that given a free choice one would not have normally and naturally[3] chosen to pay ten shillings to the Clerk of the
Court. In the few cases where old lags commit crimes in order to be
sent back to prison, we feel uneasy: it is because people in general
do not want to go to prison that imprisonment is a punishment,
and if a man does want to go to prison, then imprisonment ceases
to be a punishment for him. More generally, it is absurd to punish
somebody by letting him do what he would have chosen anyhow to
do. I cannot punish you by giving you a ticket for the opera, or a
thousand pounds in cash, or the opportunity of becoming a
member of the MCC: for if you want to go to the opera or to be rich
or to join the MCC, you will regard these opportunities as desirable, and if you do not want them, then you need not avail yourself
of them, and are no worse off than you were before. Punishments
may or may not be good for you, but they must be what you would
not have chosen if left to yourself.

Not everything unwelcome, not everything that befalls us against
our will, is to be construed as a punishment. Punishments not only
must be against our will but must be brought about by the will of
somebody else. They must be meted out by men or God. Natural
disasters and accidental damages are not, save on one peculiar
theological view, punishments. Nor are the many hurts and frustra-
tions that men inflict on one another in the pursuit of their several
separate aims. The unwelcome attentions of another must be not
only inflicted but inflicted knowingly and with the deliberate
intention of their being unwelcome before they can be construed as
punishments. Punishments are adventitiously annexed to ill-doing,
not the natural consequences which flow from it in virtue of others
pursuing their normal purposes. I may cause a man great suffering
by reviewing his book unfavourably, or by giving him the sack, or

[3] See below, pp. 133 and 153.

by awarding a fellowship to his rival or a contract to his competitor: but I am not punishing him. Nor am I punishing him if I quarantine him, certify him as a lunatic, or take him into protective custody. For these things, although done against his will, are not done in order to hurt or frustrate him. My neighbour who builds a piggery on his land is unmindful of my interests, but he does it for the sake of his profits not my despite. When Belshazzar was weighed in the balance and found wanting, his kingdom was taken from him not in order to punish him but because the Medes and Persians were adjudged better instruments of God's purposes.[4] Adverse decisions, especially when they are justified by reference to previous performance, are often construed as punishments. But that is a mistake. Many actions are hurtful and known to be hurtful, and yet are done: but they are not done in order to be hurtful, and if there were an equally effective but less hurtful way of accomplishing the agent's purposes, he would be perfectly ready to adopt them. If we can, we inoculate people rather than confine them in quarantine, and give schizophrenics doses of chlorpromazine instead of incarcerating them in a lunatic asylum, and it is a test of protective custody's being what it claims to be that the police will take the man to a place of safety and then enable him to resume the exercise of his liberty. Punishments, by contrast, not only are unwelcome but are intended to be, and would lose their point if they were not. Moreover they must be recognised as such. I may, out of ill will, harm a person, but I cannot represent it as punishment unless he recognises that he has suffered. The drama is incomplete unless in the last act the truth is revealed, and the victim knows what misfortunes he has brought upon his own head. The distinction between perceived hurt and real harm is often obscured—the English word 'hurt' and the Greek word $\beta\lambda\acute{a}\pi\tau\epsilon\iota\nu$ carry both senses—and has led to some confusion. Plato[5] argues that it could never be the function of a just man to harm people, thereby making them less good, and although some retributivists would maintain that justice required those who did ill to be harmed even though they would never know it, our sympathies tend to lie with Plato. A punishment needs to be recognised as such, or it is not, properly speaking, a punishment at all. It is like language. It has to be meant, and has to be recognised as being meant. It makes

---

[4] See above, Ch. 4, pp. 92–3.   [5] *Republic* I, 335b–336a.

sense only between rational agents who can know that it is meant
and demand reasons why it is being imposed.

We have to be able to ask "Why?" of punishment, and the answer
has to be of a certain type. It has to be *for* something done. This is a
further ground of distinction between punishment on the one hand
and quarantine, certification and protective custody on the other.
With these latter, if I am asked why I am imposing them, my answer
is "in order to protect other people (or yourself) from possible
infection (or harm or assault)". With punishment, however, the
answer must run "Because you did . . .". The difference of answer
serves also to distinguish punishment from those other cases where
unwelcome attentions are deliberate. The sadist, unlike the quarantine official, wants to hurt, and would not choose any other course
of action less painful for the victim, but he is inflicting pain because
he wants to enjoy tormenting his victim, not because of something
the victim has done. In some spartan societies pain is intentionally
inflicted in the course of initiation ceremonies: but although in-
tentional, it is still not punishment, since the justification is not
what the boy has done but what it will do for the boy or what it
shows the boy to be. Quinton is right to argue that it is part of the
concept of punishment that people can—logically can—be punished only *for* something done.[6] Although of course we may be
mistaken, and although people other than the judge may think the
accused man innocent, and although in some foreign country there
may be a corrupt and cynical judge who knows the accused to have
been framed on a trumped-up charge, there is a logical impropriety
in a judge saying 'You did not do it, nor are you in any way
responsible for its being done, but I am punishing you none the
less.' No law of logic can prevent pains from being imposed on men
actually innocent; logic is concerned only with words, and forbids
only that the innocent should be punished *under that description.*
For what distinguishes punishment from other unwelcome attentions of agents is that when we ask 'Why?', the answer begins
'Because you have . . .'. Even collective punishments do not destroy
Quinton's thesis. There must be some wrong done, and some
connection between the wrong done and the person being punished

---

[6] A. M. Quinton, "On Punishment", *Analysis*, 15, 1954, pp. 133–42; reprinted in
Peter Laslett (ed.), *Philosophy, Politics and Society*, Oxford, 1956, pp. 83–91; and in
H. S. Acton (ed.), *The Philosophy of Punishment*, London, 1969, pp. 55–64. See
earlier, Hobbes, *Leviathan*, Ch. 28.

in virtue of which he can be held responsible for it. I may, intelligibly if often unjustly, be punished for what my children, my colleagues, my compatriots or my co-religionists have done, but not for what the flower children, the rotarians of Kansas City, the citizens of Peru or the ideologists of the Kremlin have done.[7]

Punishments, together with penalties, penances, fines and forfeits, are intended to be unwelcome and are for something done by the person punished, or at least, either erroneously or vicariously, imputed to him. Moreover, what was done must be a *mis*deed. It may be morally wrong, or socially wrong, or wrong merely because prohibited by some law or convention or rule. But unless the person who is punishing me is prepared to say that what he is punishing or penalising me for is—in some sense—wrong, he is as incoherent as he would be if he said he was punishing me for nothing. It is this that differentiates a fine from a tax. A tax may be levied on someone because he has done something. I may be taxed on having a window or a television set, or for bringing a foreign car into the country or using a cheque. And, although as we shall see, the prime reason for levying taxes is to raise revenue, some taxes are imposed to discourage some particular activity or consumption rather than to yield resources for the public fisc.[8] Nevertheless, even a tax primarily intended to deter is not a fine, a forfeit, a penalty or a punishment. For these latter are annexed to something that is forbidden independently of any penalties attached: whereas when a tax is imposed, there is, by contrast, no element of prohibition, and, provided I am prepared to pay the tax, I am free to go ahead and do what I want with a good conscience. The double yellow lines say "Do not park here: and, moreover, if you do park here, you will be fined." The parking meter says "If you want to park here, you must pay the scheduled charge." The message of the parking meter is in the indicative. It tells me the price I must pay for parking, and the result may, of course, be that I decide not to. But the decision is mine. And if I decide to pay the charge, I have disobeyed no injunction, broken no law. There is nothing wrong, so far as the law is concerned, with activities that are subject to tax. Society may, for one reason or another, look on them with disfavour, and seek to discourage them by making people pay for doing them: but if a tax fails to deter someone, there is no more to be said. If I like to pay the tax and buy a foreign car, good luck to me. A penalty, by

<hr>

[7] See further below, pp. 152–3.   [8] Ch. 14, pp. 231–2.

contrast, is not to be cheerfully disregarded; witness the facts that one cannot first pay the penalty and then be free to go on to break the law, that for a second offence a higher penalty is exacted, and that "professional fouls" are bad form. Penal consequences are intended to reinforce a prohibition, but the prohibition is there independently of the penal consequences annexed to it, and to disregard the prohibition is wrong as well as inexpedient. Hence the tag *Nulla poena sine crimine*, which should be seen as another of Quinton's conceptual truths distinguishing punishment from other concepts. Just as I cannot punish you for what you have not done, so I cannot punish you for what you have done, unless it was in some sense wrong to do it. It does not have to be wrong in a very strong sense, nor need I endorse its wrongfulness whole-heartedly. Mabbott cites the example of the Dean enforcing a College rule which he himself disagrees with,[9] and it is a common predicament. But although it may on occasion pose severe moral problems for the holders of office, it does not affect the logic of punishment, which is being imposed for an action which can, according to the relevant criteria, be described as wrong.

The fact that punishment must be for wrongdoing applies also in private transactions and helps us distinguish punishments, penalties, penances, fines and forfeits, not only from taxes but from other unwelcome actions undertaken in respect of what has been done. In any free society, some decisions are left to the individual to take, and he may bargain with other individuals, offering to take some decision they want in return for their taking some decision he desires. And conversely, I may decide adversely unless the person concerned acts in the way I want or refrains from acting in the way I dislike. "Either you come down to seventeen and a half thousand", I may say to the vendor, "or I shall break off negotiations." If such a threat proves ineffective and I therefore carry it out and break off negotiations, my action cannot be correctly described as a punishment, although it is intended to be unwelcome to the vendor, and has been undertaken in respect of what he has done or has failed to do. Threats and punishments, although closely allied, are distinguished at least by this: that I can, with at least logical propriety,

[9] J. D. Mabbott, "Punishment", *Mind*, XLVIII, 1939, p. 155; reprinted in F. A. Olafson (ed.) *Justice and Social Policy*, Englewood Cliffs, 1961, pp. 42–3; J. Feinberg (ed.), *Reason and Responsibility*, Belmont, California, 1965, pp. 336–7; H. B. Acton, *Punishment*, London, 1969, p. 42.

carry out a threat whenever the person concerned has failed to conform with my requirements, whereas it is logically impossible to punish except for wrongdoing. So, too, the blackmailer cannot be said to be punishing his victim when he exposes him, since the victim's failure to pay up could not be described even by the blackmailer himself as wrong.

Punishment is not revenge. Punishment is disinterested, revenge self-regarding. I punish you for the wrong you have done, full stop, whereas I revenge myself on you for the wrong you have done *me*. Only if your actions have in some way adversely affected me or mine can I say I am taking my revenge on you. Besides my own reputation and material interests, I may take to heart those of my family and friends, and perhaps those of my country and any other good cause I hold dear. Some identification with the wronged man is essential. Although the limits of identification are elastic and very wide, it is necessary that I construe the wrong done as a wrong done to me, at least vicariously, if I am to exact vengeance for it. If, asked why I am doing someone an ill turn, I explain that he had done me down, my action, whether or not it is estimable, is clearly intelligible. No further questions are called for. If it was not me, nor my wife, nor my child, nor my cousin, nor my friend, that was hurt but only his own dog, people may wonder why I took it upon myself to intervene. "What business is it of yours?", they may ask. If I cannot make out that my interests are involved, to the charge "it is none of your business", I can only reply that it is, indeed, my business, because I am acting out of a disinterested concern for the maintenance of virtue and the suppression of wickedness and vice. If I say this, my action becomes intelligible again, but at the price of exposing me to further awkward questions. I may be attacked, not on the score of my reasons for acting, but my right to act on them. "Who made you a judge over us?", I may be asked. One requires some *locus standi* to inflict punishment. Although in one sense, punishment is my business, as it should be of any other rational man, simply because of the disinterested and universal concern which leads us to impose it, I still have to explain why I, rather than anyone else, should take it upon myself to exercise that office on behalf of rational humanity. Punishment differs from revenge, in being imposed not only out of a disinterested concern but in a representative capacity.

It differs also in admitting of rational debate. We can argue with the man who claims to be punishing another not only whether it is right for him to be acting in this punitive fashion, but also whether the punishment he is meting out is proportional to the misdeed. It makes sense to argue that the retribution exacted is disproportionate to the offence originally commited. No such objection arises in the case of revenge. If a man insults me, and I kill him, nobody can say that my revenge is excessive. As far as vengeance is concerned, the more the better. As I see my lifelong enemy, who has often slighted me and spoiled my plans, carried off to an early burial, my cup is full, and all that is left for me to desire is that wild asses may dance upon his grave. Punishment, however, admits of argument. Even if it is established that the man did, indeed, do wrong, and that the man imposing the punishment is authorised to judge and to pass sentence, it is still possible to protest that the offence does not merit as great a punishment as has been imposed. There are great difficulties in working out any precise correlation between punishment and crime. We should not think of there being a tariff made up in heaven which will measure out the appropriate amount of misery for each misdeed. But it is a matter that admits of argument. We may not have the answers, but we can intelligibly raise the question. And this constitutes another criterion for distinguishing punishment from revenge.

Punishments, along with penalties, fines and forfeits, are thus actions undertaken deliberately by a disinterested person ácting in a representative capacity in order to bring about unwelcome consequences which shall be recognised as such by the person being punished, because of some wrong, supposed to have been done by, or imputed to, the person being punished. It is a form of communication, and makes sense only within a complicated dialogue. The person being punished does not welcome it, and, seeing that it is the consequence of an agent's actions, protests. "Look out", he says, "you are hurting me." "Yes, I know", comes the answer. "Why are you doing it?" "Because you have done wrong". "What is that to you?" "It is right that you should be punished." "Who made you a judge over me?"—this last question may be an exacting one, the answer depending on the nature of the community of which they are both members and the sort of sanctions imposed. If it can be answered, there may be further questions, on whether the punishment is commensurate with the crime, together with expressions of contrition and pleas for mercy. The whole dialogue is essentially a rational one, a sort of communication between judge and convict, between the authorities and bystanders, and between society and the victims. To the convict it is a form of reprobation, communicating condemnation and disapproval; to the bystander it is a denunciation and possibly a warning, indicating what the values of society are and the authorities' determination to uphold them; to the victim it is a disavowal and a vindication, conveying the message that the misdeed, although perpetrated by a member of society is not to be construed as being in any way an action of society, and that society identifies not with the criminal but with the victim and it is his right that it is determined to uphold. Penal sanctions are thus much more than deterrents. Punishments differ from deterrents in the same way as rewards differ from incentives. Much as rewards are tangible tokens of esteem,[10] so punishments are tangible tokens of disesteem. And therefore it is convenient to consider first what we might call the case of null tangibility, where the punishment consists of a simple reprimand with no further sanctions attached, which is to be compared to a simple commendation. Along with reprimands, we need to consider apologies, disavowals, forgiveness, pardons and condonation.

I often do wrong. Sometimes I admit it and apologize. Sometimes I seek forgiveness, and if it is granted I am again at one with those I wronged. I need to be reconciled, because my own wrongdoing stands between us. It manifests a different scale of values from those generally accepted, and while it stands, it shows that my ways are not your ways nor my thoughts your thoughts. If, however, I acknowledge that I have done wrong, and having owned up to my deed then disown it, the way is clear to a community of wills being re-established, if you will agree to it and not hold my misdoings against me, now that I have admitted my fault. It is not automatic. The fact that I have done wrong cannot be undone, nor can it be expunged from the historical record. But it no longer needs to stand between us, as it has to when I still stood by the action, and maintained it against your system of values. Once I have disavowed the action, it is open to you to make no more of it, without thereby compromising the values for which you stand; and if you do so, then we can again be of one mind about the things that matter, and regard each other as members of the same community. But of

---

[10] See below, Ch. 11, pp. 204–6.

course it often does not work out as beautifully as this. Even in ideal communities it is easy to say 'sorry', difficult to mean it. Often, therefore, in order to prove his sincerity, and to show his contrition in more than mere words, the penitent feels called upon to make some substantial sacrifice, over and above anything he has done in reparation for his misdeed. Penance is punishment voluntarily undergone, the willing acceptance of a situation naturally un-welcome. And some punishments are penances: people sometimes freely give themselves up to the authorities, because they think they have done wrong and want to clear their consciences; they plead guilty and accept their punishment, in order that they may thereafter feel at peace with society; sometimes they speak of having purged their crimes; we find the medical metaphor difficult, but if we see it as a disavowal of the values which the crime manifested, expressed in a way so costly that its sincerity cannot be impugned, then we can make sense of what they feel. Such cases, however, are rare. Few people give themselves up, or voluntarily seek punish-ment in order to show how sorry they are for what they have done. Many people, although sorry enough that they have got themselves into trouble, are not really penitent. They either will not admit their action to have been wrong, or will do so only insincerely. A reprimand represents the considered judgement of society, which can override the absence of apology and constitute, in the absence of the individual's disavowal of his action, a formal disavowal on the part of the public. I may not be willing myself to acknowledge that I have done wrong, but it is none the less made public knowledge that this is just what I have done. For many people the public disgrace is the worst part of punishment; and we now can see that it is an essential part. Ignominy is the expression of public disapproval of wrong. And for many people and in many circles it is sanction enough. But not for all. Some people are too hardened to care much, and are quite prepared to flout public opinion. On their scale of values they will have got away with it, unless the reprimand is given tangible forms in terms which are meaningful to them. Words mean little. They will be unmoved if the judge merely jaws at them. The point of punishment, then, is threefold: it is to make them understand that the reprimand is really meant; it is to express a determination on the part of the public authorities to vindicate its own values and not allow them to be flouted; and it is to make it clear to third parties, especially those who have suffered in consequence of the wrong done, that the public authority does not condone the action, but, on the contrary, emphatically disavows it.

The function of punishment on this theory is to give weight to reprimands. Although for some men words are weighty enough, they are not so for all men. A punishment, unlike a merely verbal reproof, cannot be tossed aside. The wrongdoer is stopped in his tracks. Whether or not he internalises the values of society, he is forced to take them into account from an external point of view. If he will not acknowledge that what he has done was wrong, at least he shall be forced to see that it was from his point of view a mistake. Even if he does not come to avow the values of the community after all, he is unable successfully to maintain his own values in opposition to them. The man who will not listen to reason, and is not sensitive to the values of the community, is addressed in terms he cannot ignore, and is made to realise that the disapproval is meant seriously. Because he is insensitive to the values of society, and is concerned only with his own interests, the language of reproof has to be expressed in terms whose value he cannot be insensitive to, just because they concern his own self-interest. Punishment is a language. It translates the disesteem of society into the value system of the recalcitrant individual.

Although the language of punishment is primarily directed to the wrongdoer, it is significant also for society and for third parties. It expresses society's determination to uphold its standards. The wrongdoer is presenting society with a challenge. If a society acquiesces in its values being flouted, it both betrays and generates a lack of confidence in them. Laws which are not enforced cease to be in force. It costs a lot of effort to maintain standards. Policemen have to exercise continual vigilance, and sometimes have to risk their limbs, and even on occasion their lives, to bring offenders to book. If at the end of this the State appears not to mind about the wrongdoing enough to make the wrongdoer mind about his misdeeds, the message will be that wrongdoing does not really matter in its eyes, and that therefore the effort in preventing crimes and apprehending criminals is not worth the candle. Those outside the machinery of law-enforcement will get the same message. In their case they will construe it less as an invitation not to co-operate with the authorities for the maintenance of law and order—although this may well be their response—than as a warning to them, as potential victims of wrongdoing, that the State does not really care for them, and will not identify with them, if they should be wronged, and vindicate their rights. The reason why many women in the Britain of the 1960s and 1970s have been keen on capital punishment is not so much that they feel in serious danger of their lives—the murder rate in Britain is still relatively low—as that they have a sense of solidarity with sub-postmistresses and other much-murdered classes. They feel a vicarious resentment on the part of the victim at the apparent uncaringness of the authorities, who, they say, have the welfare of the murderer so much at heart that they let him off lightly, but quickly forget about his victim. In imposing an appropriate punishment, the authorities not only express their own conviction of the rightness of their values and the wrongfulness of the misdeed, but make a public disavowal of the wrongful action. The point is well brought out by Feinberg's example from international relations.[11] If an aeroplane of one country violates the air space of another, and, say, opens fire on one of that other country's own aeroplanes, the injured country will make a diplomatic protest, demanding among other things that the offending pilot be punished. If he is appropriately punished, that shows that his actions are disavowed by his country. They were his actions only, not those of his country, and quite contrary to his commission, as one of his country's officers, to act on his country's behalf. If, on the other hand, the offending officer is not punished appropriately—if either he is not punished at all, or given only a nominal penalty—then the country is acquiescing in the actions, and making them its own. Every member of society is, so far as obedience to laws is concerned, an officer. His actions involve the good name of society. If they are not punished adequately, then they are not being disavowed. Society is acquiescing in those actions, and saying that they are all right by it. Or so it seems—the connection between what a society tolerates and what it approves of is not as tight as this kind of argument makes out; often there may be considerations, either of principle or of practice, for not prosecuting and punishing actions which are nevertheless disapproved of, and sometimes this disapproval is manifested in other ways. Nevertheless, in general and especially in flagrant cases, the argument is cogent. We do not want our society to acquiesce in wrongful actions, or it will appear to acknowledge them as its own. They must be emphatically disowned. And with human nature being what it is, we do not believe that

[11] Joel Feinberg, *Doing and Deserving*, Princeton, 1970, pp. 101–2.

mere words can carry the full weight of the disapprobation and disavowal that is required.

Punishments, penalties, fines and forfeits are intended to serve as tangible tokens of disesteem, to make sure the disapprobation really, registers. But there are many different forms of disapprobation, just as there are different forms of doing and hence of wrongdoing. Actions have a dual aspect. They both are manifestations of the mind of the agent, and bring about consequences in the world of cause and effect. And so, too, some wrongs are deliberate and manifest a mind at variance with the moral and legal standards of society: others are damaging, but betoken no ill will. The former are often also grievous, and to disavow them needs a radical re-orientation of mind on the part of the perpetrator and a spectacular show of determination on the part of the authorities: the latter are often also peripheral, even venial, and call for only a slight check to secure amendment in the future and to discourage others. It is useful to mark this distinction by saying that the former call for punishments and the latter for penalties: but it is important to remember that the distinction is not always observed in ordinary usage—we talk of the death penalty as well as of capital punishment—and, indeed, that it cannot be a hard and fast one, since the concept of action always has its dual aspect, and the likely consequences of an action affect the way the agent must look at it. Nevertheless, the distinction is useful, and we shall develop it. For the present we note that punishments carry a great stigma, penalties a slight one or none at all. It makes sense to speak of a punishment fitting the crime, but not of a penalty doing so. A punishment can—should—bring home to the criminal the nature of his crime and make him realise what he has done—in some primitive societies by making him exchange places with his victim and be at the receiving end of treatment similar to what he had himself meted out. More modernly and less retributively, we make dangerous and drunken drivers serve as orderlies in casualty departments. It would be quite absurd to think of penalties teaching any other lesson than that of the inexpediency of breaking regulations and the advisability of minding one's step.

The distinction between fines and forfeits on the one hand and punishments and penalties on the other is even less clear and less well observed in common usage than that between penalties and punishments. Fines are invariably expressed in pecuniary terms, and thus are less immediate than other penalties, and more like taxes; but they are not intended to be taxes, and if they come to be regarded as such, they are failing of their purpose. They impinge, however, on a man's way of life much less drastically than imprisonment or any of the other punishments that used to be imposed, and are suitable for offences which do not reveal gross wickedness or callousness of mind, and where we do not want to stop a man in his tracks altogether, but merely to show that he had overstepped the mark in one particular respect. They are a particular form, impersonal but convenient to offenders and the authorities alike, in which, in our money-based society, punishment and penalties are exacted. Forfeits differ from fines in not being exacted only after due process. I can forfeit property, reputation, or sympathy, on account of my ill-doing, without having any opportunity to argue my case or rebut allegations. Public enemies and political opponents in time past were often deprived of their property, and even their lives, by Acts of Forfeiture and Acts of Attainder, and legislation in force today sometimes has the effect of automatically depriving a man of his goods without a fair hearing. As we saw in Chapter Four,[12] it is difficult to specify the rules of natural justice for all cases, and it is possible to construct cases where it is evident beyond reasonable doubt that a man has done wrong, but it is impossible to carry through the procedures for trying the case and sentencing him: but such cases are rare, very rare; and it is reasonable to enshrine the principle *Nulla poena sine judicio* as a central tenet of jurisprudence, in part as a conceptual truth, defining' punishment as opposed to penalties and other penal consequences, and in part as a maxim to guide the authorities whenever any penal action is in issue.

To punish is to hold responsible and to blame. It is essential, therefore, that the person being punished was responsible, and that what he did was wrong. To go through the motions of punishing someone who is in fact innocent is doubly unjust: not only does he suffer some unwelcome consequences, such as loss of life, liberty, or property, but his character is besmirched; he is made out to be a person who acted disgracefully. A false conviction is a lie: it proclaims that the person convicted has done something he has not done. It is, moreover, a peculiarly damaging lie, in that in making imputations against a man's character, it impugns him as the individual he is, and assails his status as a responsible member of

[12] pp. 90–1.

society. To be an agent is to have a mind of one's own, and it is in what one has done and will do that one makes one's own mark on the course of events. To impute misdeeds is, therefore, to deny one's identity by making out that one is not the person one is. It is also to sully one's character and attack one's position as a member of society in good standing. To be branded as antisocial is half-way to being deemed an outlaw. The shame and obloquy of punishment thus impinge on the individual in a peculiarly intimate way, and hurt him *qua* autonomous agent and *qua* member of society far more than the tangible tokens of disesteem do in themselves. We often suffer pecuniary loss, sometimes—in military service—loss of liberty, and all of us sooner or later loss of our lives. These adverse consequences, although grievous, are part of the common lot of mankind, and those who suffer them can gain some consolation from the consideration that in so far as they are common they are relatively external. But punishment is meant. It picks one out as responsible and holds one up as a special object of reprobation and blame. And so this can be pinned on someone only after careful trial, in which any explanation or excuse is given proper consideration. Not only would it be grossly unjust to punish a man without making sure that he did the deed he is accused of and has no explanation or excuse, but it would be incoherent. Punishment is, as we saw,[13] a form of communication which makes sense only in the context of a possible dialogue, and if we rule out the possibility of dialogue we subvert the meaning of the concept. To hold a man responsible is, as the etymology of the word indicates, to require of him an answer, an answer to the question "Why did you do it?", and not to allow him to answer the question, either directly by justifying what he did, or indirectly by denying that he did it or by claiming that what he did was to be described in some other, less blameworthy, way, is to abandon the concept of responsibility, and hence that of punishment, altogether. And thus *Nulla poena sine judicio* is, granted a suitably wide interpretation of *judicio*, a conceptual truth.

Punishments, because they carry moral stigma, are difficult to pin on to people. There are many excuses and extenuations—"I did not mean to", "I could not help it", "I thought it would be all right", "I was labouring under a misapprehension", "It was a

---

[13] See above, pp. 131–2.

mistake"—which, if true, would exculpate the agent altogether. Crimes have to be deliberate if they are to be crimes. Without *mens rea* the criminal is not setting up his will in opposition to that of society. If there was no intention to flout the rules and standards of society, there is no need for a vigorous disavowal of the action on the part of the authorities or a radical change of heart by the lawbreaker. But much damage may be done by men who mean well, and often people will plead excuses which are not true but cannot be shown to be false. It is expedient, therefore, to have besides punishments for those who flout the law, penalties for those who for one reason or another fail to comply with its regulations. We penalise carelessness. We do not convict the careless man of setting himself up in opposition to society, but we remind him, with a greater or lesser degree of sharpness, to mend his ways and take better care next time. Although he did not intend to do anything wrong, he did contravene the regulations, and could have complied with them if he had set about it properly. He is responsible, not in the original sense that he can say why he did it, but in the derivative sense that he had a duty to see that the regulations were complied with. It is the same as with the civil law: if a tile falls off my roof and injures a passer-by, nobody would suppose that I had meant it to happen or caused it to happen: but still, I would be held responsible, and have to pay damages, because it was my roof, and it was my business to keep it in good repair and ensure that nobody was injured by it. Penalties are like damages: they rest on the wider sense of responsibility rather than the narrower. They are simply untoward consequences, adventitiously annexed to certain actions to tip the balance of advantage to taking care not to do them. And in such a case it is reasonable to make them like natural consequences, and not admit any arguments about whether I could help committing the offence or whether I meant to do it. If my brakes fail on a steep hill, I shall have an accident whether or not I could help it, and whether or not I meant it: if my factory catches fire, or effluent gets into my milk, I shall be out of pocket, no matter how much it was not my fault. Similarly, if my brakes are defective, if somehow or other a snail gets into a bottle of milk sold in my shop, if my factory emits fumes or my farm effluent there may be good reasons for making these states of affairs undesirable from my point of view, so that I shall have an incentive to try and prevent them happening. Even if in the particular case I could not help it, I shall be encouraged to make doubly sure it does not happen again, and so will others.

It follows that penalties do not require actual personal guilt to be proved to the same high standard as is required before punishment can be inflicted. Certain pleas—"I did not know", "I didn't mean to", "I could not help it"—are inadmissible. It would be absurd to put forward such a plea to prevent a penalty goal being given against one's side in football, or to demand that there should be due judicial process before the sentence is pronounced. From this it follows that *Nulla poena sine judicio* is not a conceptual truth if *poena* is translated penalty, and it is often inferred that it is not a maxim of justice either. In modern legislation there has been a strong tendency to impose "strict liability" for breaches of regulations, and effectively to turn penalties into forfeits. Under the Road Traffic Act, 1930, the owner of a car was liable to disqualification if he permitted anyone uninsured to drive it, and this rule applied even if he had been misled by the uninsured driver, so that if a man was taken in by a forged certificate of insurance he would still lose his licence. And that was manifestly unjust, and after many innocent men had been victimised, was finally changed by Parliament. It was fair to make the owner of the car responsible for seeing that only insured drivers drove it: but when that duty of care had been discharged, it was unfair to penalise an innocent man for deliberate deceit on the part of another. Penal consequences, although likened to natural consequences, are not natural consequences but stem from deliberate decisions of the authorities, who act unjustly if they decide against anyone automatically and without due reluctance. Moreover penalties, although not as condemnatory as punishments, still carry some stigma. Although they do not impute a guilty intention, they do proclaim blameworthy negligence. Not every plea exculpates, but some surely do. It may be my business to make sure my car is licensed and to display my excise disc, but suppose the authorities lose the application, or their computer goes slow, are they then to hold me responsible for their fault? Whereas in the civil law it may sometimes be fair to impose strict liability,[14] and hold a manufacturer of explosives, say, liable for any explosion, however caused, a penalty, because it carries some stigma, cannot be automatically affixed without injustice. If I proclaim him to be at fault without listening to what he has to say

[14] See above, Ch. 5, p. 177.

and without allowing myself to take any account of his defence, no matter how cogent it is, I am doing him down needlessly and manifesting my view that he is merely a manufacturer and not really a man at all. Justice requires that penalties should not be automatic, and that although we may focus on the consequences of actions rather than the motives, and therefore disallow some pleas and enlarge men's responsibilities in certain situations, we must not disallow every plea, or extend their responsibilities unreasonably or hold them responsible for events over which they had no control at all.

Punishments and penalties have not been distinguished in legal thinking, and some injustice has resulted from the confusion, sometimes, paradoxically, from insisting on over-elaborate, and therefore unworkably expensive, judicial procedures. People often pay the fine rather than go to the expense of contesting the case, even though they have a good defence. Although for serious crimes traditional judicial procedures are appropriate, it is possible to explain an undisplayed vehicle licence by letter, or to establish the truth about a defective bottle of milk without cross-examining witnesses under oath. In effect, the real decision whether or not to fine an offender is taken by officials of the executive, who decide whether or not to prosecute, not the judiciary, who are presented with open and shut cases that leave them no room for discretion. Justice is better served by a less ponderous process that can easily be invoked and will be actually used. What is important is that decisions whether or not to impose penalties are taken by men who stand outside the bureaucratic web of a department of the executive, and who can easily see things from the citizen's point of view. If they can receive representations from the individual, there is a better chance of unjust decisions not being reached than if those who have discretion are not likely to exercise it in a judicial frame of mind and those who are independent act as a rubber stamp in most cases and only very occasionally as a safety-valve.

We cannot, however, make a very sharp distinction between punishments and penalties. Although penalties are often the appropriate response for *mala prohibita* rather than *mala per se*, it is not the case that all laws whose rationale is given in terms of the Theory of Games should be enforced by penalties rather than punishments. Although there is nothing intrinsically wrong in travelling on a bus or train without paying, fare-dodging is wrong, and deserves to be punished. And conversely some *mala per se* are not very bad, and should be only slightly penalised: it is wrong to jostle or get in the way, and not because of any games-theoretical considerations, but only a misdemeanour, not a crime. Furthermore, the two shade into each other. To contravene regulations ordained by legitimate authority for the public good is in itself wrong, and the better known the regulations and the more obvious their rationale, the more blatantly unconcerned with the welfare of others is the man who ignores them. The traffic regulations may at one time have seemed pettifogging restrictions on a man's liberty of movement: but now that we know the toll that road accidents exact, to be negligent on matters of safety is to show oneself not merely foolish but criminal.

The principle *Nulla poena sine lege* is not a conceptual truth about either punishments or penalties as we have defined them, but is a conceptual truth for penal consequences attaching to *mala prohibita*. There is nothing wrong in itself about parking on double yellow lines or using a car in a city centre or travelling free on a bus or train: it is only because of certain regulations enjoining us not to do these things that they are wrong. Only if the regulations have been duly promulgated can the violation of them be any sort of misdeed, and so only on that condition can penal consequences be intelligibly inflicted. Legal positivists go further, and assimilate all law to regulations laid down by the sovereign. If that were so, then *Nulla poena sine lege* would be a conceptual truth so far as legal punishment was concerned: but, as we have seen,[15] law should be seen as a social phenomenon and not merely the ordinances of the sovereign, and people can know what they should and should not do without always having to be told by the sovereign. Exactly which misdeeds should be punished by law and which should be left to the reprobation of conscience or public opinion is sometimes unclear, and sometimes becomes clear through the decisions of the courts. In primitive legal systems, as well as in many domestic jurisdictions, there are relatively few explicit rules, and much is left to the good sense of individual members of society. The fact that there is no explicit rule forbidding an action does not render it incoherent to punish it, in the way that it would be incoherent to punish it if it were not in any way regarded as wrong. We may, however, commend the principle *Nulla poena sine lege* as a maxim

[15] Ch. 5, pp. 150–4.

of justice in so far as it is hard on a man to punish him for something he did not regard as wrong, and, especially in an age of moral confusion, many people do not recognise the same moral distinctions as do the authorities. By laying down an explicit law we give guidance to those that otherwise might remain in darkness, and enable them not to stumble into trouble through moral blindness. But this argument, although it carries some weight, is not as weighty as its proponents suppose. For the law of the land is not all that clearer or more accessible to the understanding than the moral law, and although lawyers are fond of saying that ignorance of the law is no excuse, ignorance of the positive law seems much more excusable than ignorance of the moral law. Hence, although it is sometimes fair to lay down definitely in advance exactly what the courts regard as wrong, it often makes it harder for the layman to mind his step. Thus, so far as justice is concerned, the principle *Nulla poena sine lege* is only a subordinate maxim even within a developed legal system, and barely applies at all elsewhere. On the score of liberty, however, a rather stronger case may be put forward. The principle gives content to a man's right to be wrong. It enables a man who wishes to be free of the shackles of morality and custom to know how far he can go without getting into trouble. It is a great enhancement of liberty to have all the laws written down explicitly and not locked up in the hearts of judges, no matter how just. But that is an argument of liberty, not justice.[16]

Justice bears not only on the conditions under which a man may be punished or penalised but the extent to which he should be made to suffer. It sets both an upper and, according to some at least, a lower limit. It is unjust to punish a man too much, more than the gravity of the crime warrants. Although it may be very effective to hang litterbugs and flay persistent parkers, it is unfair, because it is using them as examples without considering them or whether from their point of view it could be justified. Justice requires that an adverse decision be justified by an individualised reason; in the case of penal action by reference to what the individual has done wrong: and if what the individual has done is not very wrong, then it will not support taking severe action against him. Instead of

---

[16] For a contrary view see H. L. A. Hart, *Law, Liberty and Morality*, Oxford, 1963, pp. 6–12, criticizing the decision in *Shaw* v. *Director of Public Prosecutions* (1961) 2 A.E.R. 446; (1962) A.C. 223. See also J. R. Lucas, *The Principles of Politics*, Oxford, 1966, §§34, 35, 54.

asking the question "How can we best dispose of the individual to secure the enforcement of law and order?" as supporters of a deterrent theory of punishment do, we ask "In view of what you have done, can we let you off any more lightly without acquiescing in it and encouraging others to follow suit?". There is a minimalising slant to the question that, together with the emphasis on the individual, distinguishes a just theory of punishment from a deterrent theory; and it is on these two points that a purely deterrent theory must be accounted unsatisfactory.

The deterrent theory of punishment is based on its necessary unwelcomeness. Once we recognise that unwelcomeness is an essential feature of punishment we have to abandon the reformative and preventive theories. We may, of course, hope that punishment will reform someone or will prevent him from doing further wrong, but these are incidental desiderata; for means of achieving either of these aims could be successful but not count as punishment because they were not unwelcome—we may cure the inadequate housewife who shop-lifts by laying on a social worker to help her organize her finances, and prevent boys from hurling stones or insults at girls in break by rearranging the timetable—and a punishment would be intelligible even if there were no prospect of reform—an atheist can still inflict capital punishment. This is not to say that no regard should be given to considerations of reform or prevention in deciding what punishments to inflict: on the contrary, it is humane to choose punishments which will reform, and wise to choose those which at least secure some reduction of crime. But neither reform nor prevention constitute an essential aspect of punishment, whereas unwelcomeness does.

Unwelcomeness argues most naturally for a deterrent theory. Punishments are intended to deter; that is why they have to be unwelcome. We can go further, and explain why they have to be recognised as such, if we distinguish two senses of 'deter'. A man or an animal may be deterred by any difficulties which lead him to abandon some course of action. We can deter people, in this sense, by any means which make a course of action more difficult, or more dangerous or more unpleasant. By manipulating the adventitious circumstances, we can manipulate them. The other sense of 'deter' applies only to rational agents. These we can deter by giving reasons against a course of action. What reasons will deter a man depends on what he regards as cogent considerations. One man may be deterred by the thought that his action will cause somebody pain, another by the fear of doing wrong, another by the fear of public rebuke, and another only because of some adverse effect on his own interests. In the latter, rational, sense, it is analytic that punishment should deter; a "punishment" which does not afford any sort of reason against a man's undertaking the action penalised would not be a punishment at all. But there is a danger in sliding from this sense of deterrence, which applies only to rational agents, to a wider sense which applies equally to animals, because utilitarians generally take an external view of human beings, and treat them benevolently as pets, rather than reason with them as fellow human beings. In the debates on capital punishment in the 1960s utilitarians often argued that it was not much of a deterrent, because there were no figures proving that populations were less given to murder where capital punishment was imposed than where it was not. This may be an important consideration, but it needs to be distinguished from the rational sense of the word 'deter', where what is at issue is whether a rational man would be deterred from committing murder by the prospect of being punished by death for it. We need to be careful, in considering utilitarian arguments, not to slide into an excessively external point of view. Although external assessments have their part, and a sociologist may be able to give useful guidance in reducing the incidence of crime by altering social conditions, the concept of punishment is not itself intelligible from an exclusively external point of view. And it is important that deterrence, too, can be construed internally, as an argument addressed to a rational agent.

The deterrent theory has many attractions, and, at a somewhat high level of generality, expresses an important truth. But in its details it has difficulty in accommodating many retributivist feelings ordinary men have, and in particular the conceptual requirement that punishment can be only for wrong done. Although this objection can be circumvented by calling in arguments of natural or human rights, the theory of punishment that results is restricted to legal and quasi-legal contexts, and does not apply to domestic and personal situations, such as occur in family life. The deterrent theory also has difficulty in explaining why it is unjust, even when expedient, to visit very heavy penalties on the commission of minor crimes. It works better for penalties than for punishments properly so called, and even then tends to assimilate penalties to taxes.

Hart sees the general justifying aim of our having the institution of punishment as deterrence, but within that scheme we confine ourselves to punishing only those who have broken the law in order that a man may know that provided he keeps within the law he will not be liable to punishment.[17] More grandly, we may say the individual has a natural right to life, liberty and property, and the State is not entitled to use him as an example to others, however effective and expedient it may be, unless he has forfeited his rights by neglecting those of others. But the justification for making an example of the man who has forfeited his rights is simply that of deterring those who are tempted to break the law from actually making the attempt. Once he has overstepped the line and lost his immunity, there is no further reason based on utility or liberty for not treating him with the utmost severity. It is only if we have a continuing concern for the individual, even after he has broken his agreement and put himself in our power—only, that is, if we take the standpoint of justice, not that of deterrence on any utilitarian grounds—that we can account for our belief that excessive punishment is wrong. We may also point out that the general libertarian argument against punishing the innocent is, although strong, not as strong as it needs to be. It is good to know where one stands *vis à vis* the State, and to know that provided one minds one's step nothing very terrible will happen to one. But a reasonable security is all that is needed in order to be able to plan one's life, and is all that is afforded in other facets of the State's relations with the individual: we learn to live with the possibility of disaster, provided it is fairly remote, and some disasters—loss of one's house, one's job, one's career—are often due to the activities of the State. The argument from liberty tells against the State handing out punishments in a haphazard way, but does not account for our abhorrence at an innocent man's being made to suffer penal sanctions, or the conceptual link between punishment and previous wrongdoing. The argument from liberty, moreover, applies only to the formal legal processes of the State, whereas punishments are inflicted in many other communities—families, schools, colleges and clubs—and although the procedures are less formal, arguments of justice still

---

[17] H. L. A. Hart, "Prolegomenon to the Principles of Punishment", *Proceedings of the Aristotelian Society*, LX, 1959–60, pp. 1–26; reprinted as *Punishment and Responsibility, Essays in the Philosophy of Law*, Oxford, 1968, Ch. 1, pp. 1–27.

apply. The deterrent theory of punishment is therefore inadequate. It is based on the necessary unwelcomeness of punishment, but takes it as simply basic, instead of explaining it on the grounds that unwelcomeness, and unwelcomeness alone, expresses disesteem in a universal currency, capable of being appreciated by any and every man, no matter what his values are. Rather than being simply basic, unwelcomeness is a means of expressing disapprobation. Punishments are tangible tokens of disesteem, and what is essential is not that they should be tangible, but that the tokens should be understood.

Justice sets not only an upper limit to what may be visited on a man but a lower limit too. Justice demands, we say, that he pay the penalty for his transgressions, and it would be unfair to let him get off scot-free. If we ask "Unfair on whom?", there are four possible answers. In cases where the crimes consisted in wreaking some harm on a victim, it is unfair on him to make light of his hurt. He will be let down if the authorities let his assailant off. Although it is right and just that there should be continuing concern for the criminal and a reluctance to take unnecessary action against him, concern should not be focussed on the criminal to the exclusion of his law-abiding victim. When it comes to a choice, society must side with the victim rather than his assailant; else it fails to uphold the law and maintain the right of peaceful citizens, and ceases to be the common possession of all members of society and becomes simply the plaything of the sovereign. How heavy a sentence needs to be for society to be seen to be on the victim's side depends on circumstances, as we shall see. Justice does not require that there be a rigid tariff: but it does require that we do not forget the victim or indulge in easy third-party forgiveness at his expense.

Others, besides the victim, may feel let down if wrongdoers are let off too lightly. It is often burdensome to uphold the law; it costs much effort to enforce it and, in particular, to bring offenders to book. If at the end of the day the authorities pass over offences for no good reason, they appear to be conniving at them, and it seems pointless to put oneself out to police the law or apprehend offenders. If the judges, as official representatives of society, appear to overlook offences, they undo efforts of all those others who did not turn a blind eye. In addition to those who labour to enforce the law there are the very many other ordinary members of the public who keep it, sometimes against their own inclinations or at considerable cost. In much the same way as it is unfair to break the law, it is unfair to let law-breakers get away with it. Only if crime manifestly does not pay can we reasonably expect others to forbear from crime too: to let the fare-dodger off is unfair on all those who dig into their pockets regularly to buy their tickets and keep the transport system going. There are, finally, other offenders who have been, or will be, caught and made to suffer; and it would be unfair, in so far as their cases are similar, not to treat them the same. Hence to be lenient in any one case and not in all is unfair on the other offenders. For these reasons therefore justice can be affronted if an offender is treated too leniently as well as too severely: but the arguments are not symmetrical, and the objection to a punishment's being too heavy is quite different from—and much more pressing than—the objections to its being too light.

Justice is often thought to be retributive, demanding that evil deeds be requited and good ones rewarded: but, as we have seen, the case is more complicated than that, and straightforward retributivism is too *simpliste* to express the whole truth. Retributivism has the merit of being concerned with the individual, but the demerit of being often needlessly severe, taking no account of contrition and leaving no room for mercy. This is partly because it objectifies the matter. Instead of construing punishment as a form of communication it regards it as a sort of debt. It thinks in terms of a tariff or balance, entirely independent of contrition or apology, whereby every wrong done must be paid for by a wrong suffered, whether or not the subsequent wrong is recognised as being consequent upon the previous one. But it is hard to believe that a rational exercise of mercy is wrong. Where there is genuine contrition—where, for example, a man is driven by remorse to own up to a misdeed that would not otherwise be laid at his door—it would be unconscionable not to remit some of the penalty, and often in fact we reckon that where apologies have been proffered and amends made, the deed has been sufficiently disavowed and nothing further needs to be done. Moreover, if we objectify a tariff of punishments we are likely to hit on a very severe one because any less severe one would, under some conditions and with some people, fail to get the message across. In fact, with punishments as with linguistic communications, conventions vary. What at one time or to one person will seem absurdly lenient, will at another time or to another person seem grotesquely severe. The importance of conventions and the way they vary can be illustrated by our differing understandings of capital punishment. For some people—most people in time past—only by punishing a murderer with death could society repudiate the deed and make it clear how important in its own eyes was the sanctity of human life. But it now seems to many people that life-imprisonment is sufficiently awful to make murderer and bystander alike realise the abhorrence we feel at the crime and our total disavowal of it.[18] If this is indeed so, then justice requires only the lesser sentence. But if, as the retributivists would have it, there is to be only one standard for all time and for all persons, then we shall be impelled to adopt the one which will convey to the meanest intelligence and the toughest-minded operator the public reprimand and disavowal of the crime. It will not be enough that the criminal himself and the majority of bystanders shall get the message, but that the punishment shall be such that even the most insensitive and self-absorbed will be able to recognise its import. The most extreme penalty will be demanded, because only that is absolutely unmistakable in the significance it carries for everyone. Retributivist theories can lead to gratuitous suffering being imposed, and even where the suffering is not gratuitous, inasmuch as there is a rational justification for inflicting it, there may be too little concern about the future, and how good may be brought out of past and present ill. If the retributivist is right in saying that we ought not to ignore the past, it is right also not to allow ourselves to become prisoners of the past and ignore the future altogether. Moreover, retributivist theories are just as dangerous as utilitarian ones. Utilitarian theories are dangerous because they correspond too well with the instincts of rulers, retributivist ones because they correspond too well with the instincts of ordinary men. Utilitarian theories encourage bureaucrats in their natural propensity to push people around, manipulating them merely as means and not regarding them as ends in themselves: retributivist theories foster popular prejudice against the criminal, and can easily give rise to lynch law. Although retribution is, as we have shown, differrent from revenge, the two are easily confused, and our motives are often mixed; we burn, as we ourselves think, with righteous indignation, but to everyone else our actions seem to be fired by feelings of resentment and revenge.

---

[18] See Oliver O'Donovan, *Measure for Measure: Justice in Punishment and the Sentence of Death*, Grove Booklet on Ethics, No. 19, Nottingham, 1977, esp. pp. 20–2.

We should, therefore, be wary of adopting an entirely retributivist theory of punishment. Justice does demand that bad deeds be punished, as it does that good deeds be rewarded, but it does not rule out the relevance of contrition or the possibility of mercy. Justice is not concerned to balance the books in some heavenly ledger, but with the owning and disowning of deeds done in society. It is necessary that bad deeds be disowned, and that we make it adequately clear that we do not tolerate such actions and, where they have been done, we identify with those who suffer from them, not those who do them. If this calls for action against the perpetrators, so be it. There is reason enough for adverse action, and they have only themselves to blame. But we go no further than we have to in order to get the message across. Although in some circumstances we may have to go far indeed, or else fail to vindicate the victims of wrongdoing and uphold the standards of society, we do not always have to, and justice would have us go no further than necessary.

It remains to clear up three peripheral problems; the principle of double punishment, the concept of vicarious punishment, and the occasional cases where punishment is sought, not straightforwardly as a form of penance or purgation. The principle of double punishment is a logical one. The same man cannot be punished by the same authority for the same offence more than once. Of course, as we saw in Chapter Six, the powers that be subject me to any ill-treatment they see fit: but it will not be construed as punishment, if punishment has already been meted out by the powers that be, any more than it would if no offence were alleged. It is the same as with debts. "But I have paid it already" is, if true, a complete answer to a claim for payment of a debt; and similarly "But I have been punished by you already" is, if true, as complete an answer to an accusation as "I did not do it." This logical principle needs to be contrasted with the principle of double jeopardy, which is a principle not of logic, but of political morality. The latter is a development, in a particular direction, of the rule of definitiveness,[19] which imports for practical purposes to some decisions a degree of definiteness which they could not in logic otherwise claim. There is no reason to suppose that we always can reach a definite conclusion on a question of past fact, whether a particular man committed a particular crime or not; and, just as occasionally justice requires us

[19] See above, Ch. 4, pp. 96–7.

to reopen a case where a verdict of 'guilty' was wrongly given, so it might seem to require us, and certainly does not forbid us, to reopen a case where it emerges that a man really was guilty, in spite of a verdict to the contrary. The principle of double jeopardy is to be defended not so much on grounds of justice as on those of liberty. Men, even criminals, need to know where they stand. The jeopardy of a criminal accusation is great, and should not be endured twice. The rule against a man being put in jeopardy twice on the same offence contributes much to the security of the individual at only a small cost to justice. It therefore is a good principle to adopt, but should not be represented as an essential requirement of justice. Nor should either principle be construed as freeing the individual of every jurisdiction save one. I should not be tried, and cannot be punished, a second time by the same authority for the same offence, but I may be tried, and can be punished, by different authorities on charges arising out of the same actions. The same action may be a breach of the criminal law of the land, of the professional code of conduct for a doctor, of the etiquette of a barrister, of the rules of a university, or of the regulations of a factory. I may be punished, perhaps by a trivial fine, by the civil authorities, and much more severely—by being struck off, disbarred, expelled or sacked—by some other authority, which, with reason, regards the action more seriously. Moreover, these different jurisdictions may have different procedures, with different rules of evidence, and so may, without miscarriage of justice in either case, reach different verdicts. I may be found not guilty of an offence under the Dangerous Drugs Act, and yet guilty of unprofessional conduct with respect to dangerous drugs, because the jury accepted my explanation of what I had been up to, while my fellow doctors refused to believe that any doctor could in all innocence have acted as I did. It is not contrary to justice for a man to have to answer for his actions to different jurisdictions. He is, after all, a member of different communities, each avowing values in common. In cases where the common values are different, there is no question of his being accountable to one and not to others: in cases where the values are the same, there should not be any question either. The principle of double punishment can no more show that I cannot be punished by different authorities, than can a debt be argued not to be due to one man because a debt to another has been discharged. All we can argue for is not a principle of double punishment but a principle of sufficient punishment based on principles of humanity and justice: if a man has been, or is likely to be, punished severely by one jurisdiction, other jurisdictions taking cognisance of the same actions on his part should take into consideration also the condign consequences following upon them. For this reason, second punishments which are preventive—revocation of licence to practise, for example—or reformatory, are more acceptable than those which are purely deterrent or retributive. It may be necessary to strike off or disbar an offender: but if it is not, and if he is already being punished enough, then there is no call to add to his punishment simply for the sake of retribution or to signify the gravity of his offence and the severe view we take of it. That message has been rammed home already, and repetitions would be otiose.

We have great difficulties with the concept of vicarious punishment. It runs counter to the individualist tendency of justice that anyone should be punished for anything other than what he himself has done. Yet we are familiar with one man's carrying the can for another, and we distinguish vicarious punishment from harms inflicted for similar ends, but in the absence of any imputation of vicarious responsibility. A man can take the blame for another's actions. It is, as we have seen,[20] part of the concept of an action that it can be owned by more than one man, and that the actions of an agent may also be attributed to the principal. If I am in charge, and one of my subordinates makes a mess of things, it is still my fault, because I should have seen to it that he did not, either by giving him clearer instructions, or by monitoring his execution of the instructions I actually had given him, or by having chosen more reliable subordinates. Even when none of these conditions apply, a man may still be deemed responsible for actions taken in his name, although contrary to his wishes and effectively out of his control. The Queen is responsible for the actions of her Ministers, and her Ministers for those of their civil servants, though in each case the degree of control exercised is tenuous. It is rather different where there is no possibility of control. The fathers have eaten sour grapes, and the childrens' teeth are set on edge. Britons in East Africa today are blamed for the alleged wrongdoing of settlers before the war. The justification lies in some community of values and sentiment, often carrying with it a sharing of benefits, and therefore

[20] Ch. 3, p. 42, Ch. 1, p. 18.

arguably the burdens of collective responsibility. It is not that I did the action, or that I was in charge when it was done, or that I could have prevented it, but rather that having been done, it was never disavowed by me. I take on certain responsibilities by acknowledging my family name or by being a Briton, and in the absence of any specific disavowal, there is a presumption that I accept responsibility for the discreditable as well as the advantageous acts of those previously acting in the name which I now bear. In being a member of a community, I make myself one with my fellow members, and therefore acknowledge their actions as my own. It is not always so. Some communities are based on limited articles of association, outside which no imputation of similarity of outlook can be sustained. I am a member of this Aristotelian Society, but nobody should suppose that I in any way endorse the doctrines propounded by other members. But in more intimate and wide-ranging associations, such as the family, a college, or the State, there is some presumption of similarity of outlook, and hence of a shared responsibility for collective actions.[21]

Punishment, although necessarily unwelcome, is sometimes appreciated. It shows that the person inflicting the punishment cares what the person being punished does. Children quite often provoke their parents, because they want attention. For the same reason adolescents often misbehave, in order to reassure themselves that they are persons of consequence, and that it does matter what they do. It is far worse to be ignored than controlled. So, too, it is a phenomenon, common in novels and occasionally encountered in real life, where a woman craves for the company of a man who ill uses her, just because he at least takes some notice of her, and minds what she does. People want to matter. The mark of society's displeasure at one's wrongdoing, although unpleasant, at least shows that one signifies in the sight of society. Although the deed is disesteemed, the doer is recognised as someone who signifies. Punishment, although a disavowal of the action, acknowledges the agent as a member of the community, whose actions are the community's concern. Hence the double aspect of punishment, and the double thinking that sometimes goes with it.

[21] See, more fully, H. D. Lewis, "Collective Responsibility", *Philosophy*, 23, 1948; Joel Feinberg, "Collective Responsibility", *Journal of Philosophy*, 65, 1968; reprinted in Joel Feinberg, *Doing and Deserving*, Princeton, 1970; R. S. Downie, "Collective Responsibility", *Philosophy*, 44, 1969.

7

ADMINISTRATIVE JUSTICE

Many decisions of the authorities are not intended to penalise individual citizens but have adverse consequences all the same. If the Department of the Environment knocks down a man's house to build a road, or the Home Office refuses to allow a man to come into the country, or a fire officer says a school must spend a quarter of a million pounds on installing swing doors on each staircase, or the computer fails to produce a driving licence, or the Post Office cuts off someone's telephone, or the Department of Education and Science decides that only persons with degrees in eurythmics shall be allowed to teach in State schools, or the local planning authority refuses permission to build a bungalow in the orchard, or the health officer forbids a farmer from keeping a cow to supply his family with milk, the individual may suffer greatly in consequence: and although in none of these cases did the authority mean ill, or choose its course of action in order to inflict unwelcome consequences on the individual, the result from the individual's point of view is the same, and the message is likely to be much the same: even if the authority did not mean to do him down, it did not mind doing him down, and was careless of his interests in the pursuit of its purposes.

The authorities draw a sharp distinction between administrative and judicial action. Administrative action, in their view, should be completely unfettered by constraints of justice, and should be undertaken by the Executive—in effect the Departments of State—subject only to the accountability of the Minister to Parliament. Judicial action should be reserved to the judiciary, protected by elaborate procedures and traditions, and insulated from interference by civil servants or Parliament. In support of this distinction they stress the dissimilarity of the two types of action. In criminal trial the focus is entirely on the accused: the stigma, if he is convicted, is attached to him individually; and if he is acquitted, the case has little bearing on the authority's duty to maintain law and order, or on its ability to punish others who are shown to have broken the law. Administrative decisions are, for the most part, not focussed on the individual. The object of the exercise is not to stigmatize his wrongdoing: and the factors governing the decision are, many of them extraneous to his case. If the road cannot be built because somebody's house is in the way, the whole scheme may have to be scrapped. If people are allowed to enter this country it may put strain on housing or social services or cause unemployment. If the school does not install the fire equipment, children may get burnt. Computer technology is a good thing, and we must put up with the consequential delays. Telecommunications are a nationalised corporation with responsibilities towards the Treasury and the Unions, and cannot be expected to match the performance of the American Telephone and Telegraph Company. And so in all the cases, the reason for the decision is not an individualised reason, but none the less cogent for that. Not all reasons are individualised: not all cases are justiciable. We only darken counsel and clog administration if we confuse different types of decision-making, and introduce into the one considerations which properly belong to the other.

Some weight should be allowed to these arguments, but they do not yield the conclusion that administrative and judicial decision-making are entirely distinct. In the first place, as we have seen, administrative decisions can bear hardly on individuals, and in respect of important and central interests. It is quite absurd to provide elaborate protection against a man's being unjustly mulcted of two pounds for an alleged parking offence and allow him to be deprived of his house at the instance of a road planner. To make out that the interests of the individual should carry no weight against reasons of State and to give the individual no protection against the casual unconcern of officials is to manifest a scale of values which accords scant respect to the individual in comparison with the purposes of the community. The message which comes across is that the individual is nothing in comparison with the whole. He cannot rationally identify with society on that basis, or believe that his and its interests are really bound up together. The lamb is being invited to lie down not with a lion who will prey on him, but a leviathan which, without meaning him any ill, will not register his existence, and may well crush him as it lumbers on its way or obliterate him with a casual flick of its tail.

The second argument, from coherence, is also not decisive. Even if extraneous reasons bear on a decision, they are not the only ones, and should not be allowed automatically to override all considerations of justice. Moreover, we can often require that reasons be individualised, which has the effect of spreading the burden of the unwelcome consequences of adverse decisions required for reasons of State. We can forbid the press-gang, while allowing conscription. We can, more generally, think judicially even though allowing some weight—proper weight—to public policy and reasons of State. Considerations of public policy enter into even the criminal law. It is a mistake to suppose that the criminal process excludes all concern for the general good. It is also a mistake to argue that administrative decisions cannot be justiciable because they are not like criminal trials. The criminal trial, offered as a paradigm of the judicial process, is an extreme rather than a typical case. Rather than distinguish two sharply opposed paradigms, we should recognise a range of cases calling for greater or lesser concern towards individual interests; and rather than concentrate on the peculiar features of the criminal law, we should take as equally typical the less dramatic litigation of the civil law, in which one man's rights and interests conflict with another's, and a decision favourable to one is necessarily adverse to the other. True, a man in jeopardy of losing his job or his house is not accurately represented as being in the same case as a man facing a criminal charge; but it does not follow from this that no issues of justice arise. Rather, we should take as our exemplar of judicial decision-making not a criminal, but a civil, case, in which the public interest is opposed to some private interests, and can be achieved only at their expense. The case is more like *John Doe* v. *Richard Doe* than *Regina* v. *John Citizen*. There are, of course, differences. The public interest is not like the private interest of some one public person, say the Queen, and there is therefore and essential asymmetry between the parties, which is not present when two private individuals go to law with each other. But whether one of the interests involved is the public interest or not, it is not a foregone conclusion that the other interest must give way to it. Just as in a private case my interests may give way to your rights, so sometimes the public interest should give way to your rights. And the task of balancing public and private interests and public and private rights is a judicial one, which should be undertaken in such a way and vested in such persons as will best conduce to the right balance being struck.

We cannot lay down ground rules, either procedural or substantive, to govern all administrative decisions. Administrative activity is highly heterogeneous: some administrative tribunals such as those deciding the award of pensions, are very like courts of law, only less formal, and their activity is unquestionably a judicial one; most of what is done by the Ministry of Defence or the Foreign Office is executive in the traditional sense of the word, and is rightly kept free from the shackles of judicial thinking. Other decisions impinge on individual interests to a greater or lesser extent and in different ways. The extent to which decision-making should be undertaken according to judicial procedures and in a judicial frame of mind depends on the interest involved, the extent to which it is likely to suffer, the number of people involved, the background of convention and understanding about the matter, and whether or not the public interest involved is of overriding importance or great urgency. I shall not produce an exhaustive or exact account of all the different sorts of decisions that administrators take, but only some general arguments about the bearing of certain factors on the extent to which decisions should be arrived at judicially.

There is a *prima facie* presumption in favour of all decisions taken by the authorities of the State being taken judicially. This is because they constitute a natural monopoly and are backed up by the coercive power of the State. Transactions which are voluntary and where there is an effective choice available do not need much protection because the individual has a real alternative open to him if he is in danger of being done down. Where there is no alternative—either with a nationalised industry in Britain or with a privately owned monopoly like the American Telephone and Telegraph Company in the United States—the market provides no safeguard, and the individual needs some other protection against arbitrary action by the monopolist. The Electricity Board or Telephone Company cannot be allowed to disconnect or refuse to connect people at pleasure, nor should they be allowed to be guided solely by commercial considerations, because there is no parity of bargaining power between them and their customers. The railway companies in the last century were required to act as common carriers, which meant that they must offer the same terms to everyone. This is a minimal requirement, and in the United States, there is much more—perhaps too much—regulation of telephone charges. Equally important is provision for independent arbitration in cases of dispute. Usually at present the supplier is judge in its own cause. There is no justification for this. Independent arbitration is the first step to securing just treatment in the individual case.

What holds for a monopoly holds very much more for the State. Not only is there no alternative supplier, but membership is compulsory. I can survive without the telephone and—just—without electricity or gas. But if the State decides to take my house, it does not just refuse to supply me further, but uses bailiffs and bulldozers to force me out. There is no arguing with force. And therefore room must be made for arguing earlier along the line, and the individual must be allowed to urge reasons, and the authorities must be obliged to hear them, heed them, and give them full weight, while there is yet time, before decisions are taken, and Leviathan is set lumbering on its way.

Decisions of the authorities that endanger life or health are far more open to protest than those that impinge on more peripheral interests. Decisions that deprive a man of a particular piece of property need more safeguards than those that cause him merely pecuniary loss. Decisions that take away from a man what he already has need more safeguards than those that prevent him getting what he might otherwise have got. Decisions that disappoint chartered expectations are more to be avoided than those that disappoint expectations that are legitimate but unsecured, and decisions that disappoint reasonable expectations are more to be avoided than those that disappoint hopes. Again, obviously, the extent to which an interest is affected is relevant. The requirement that a man who fails the breathalyser test should give a specimen of blood does not require further safeguards, because it is seen as a trifling and entirely unhazardous invasion of a man's interest in his own body. If vaccinations and inoculations were similarly unhazardous we might be prepared to allow medical authorities to insist upon them, although we might also reckon that they could be seen by some as a breach of their bodily inviolability, and on grounds of insult rather than real injury, not to be imposed without due process.

Decisions that impinge on few people need more safeguards than those that affect a lot. It is partly a matter of expediency, partly of logic. If the authorities decide to call up all young men for military service, or to knock everybody's house down in order to build better roads, there is a possibility of redress through the normal procedures of politics. But the individual by himself has no such recourse. He is isolated and defenceless against the public juggernaut. True, he can vote against the government at the next election, but what is one vote among so many? Part of the rationale of justice, as we saw in Chapter Three,[1] is that it compensates for the weakness of the individual in the face of the hostility or uncaringness of the mob. But whereas a coalition of all for each makes sense, a coalition of all for all is not in the same way necessary: if we all suffer, we cannot all pass by on the other side.

It is possible for everyone to be done down by the State, not only in tyrannies, but even in democracies. By inadvertence or lack of foresight or lack of imagination, a democracy may adopt policies which gratuitously deprive people of life, liberty or property, or other important and central interests. Nevertheless, the argument over each particular decision takes a different form if everyone is in the same case from that if only one is or only a few. The question "Why pick on me?" does not arise, and needs no special answer. Although the fact that a general measure has been adopted is not conclusive evidence that it is good or wise, it is strong presumptive evidence of its being so. In order to show that it is unfair in its bearing on any one individual, it is necessary to show that it is a measure which is quite unjustifiable, and which society could not have any good reason for imposing on itself. And that is a different point from those normally at issue in questions of justice, and a difficult one to establish.

Much depends on the background of convention and understanding against which administrative decisions are taken. A decision not to promote me in the armed services affects me adversely and may disappoint a legitimate expectation of mine: but the *raison d'être* of the services is efficiency in war, and in entering them I accept that military needs should override personal ambitions. Equally posts in the Civil Service are not, *pace* the Civil Service Unions, good things to be distributed among their members as fairly as possible, but means to the achievement of public ends. It may be expedient for the Civil Service Commissioners to offer certain terms, and then of course it would be unjust not to keep to them: but there is no inherent right to appointment or promotion, and questions about these, even though they affect individuals

---

[1] pp. 69—70.

closely, are not justiciable. Equally, in the letting of government contracts, considerations of justice give way to those of efficiency and other public purposes. Of course, there would be objection if decisions about contracts were taken arbitrarily, corruptly or under the influence of fear or favour, but such objection would be on the score of maladministration not of unfairness. We object because public money is being wasted, and public servants are being idle, incompetent or dishonest, not because contractors have a right to receive contracts. The only rights they have are those that happen to arise from laws or guidelines themselves laid down to secure good administrative practice or to secure some desired public purpose.

The public interest is often invoked as a reason for dispensing with judicial safeguards. It is often improperly invoked. In the ordinary run of cases the conflict between the public and private interests should be brought out into the open and subjected to critical scrutiny on both sides. When the public interest is said to require a new airport or a new motorway, it is right to question the need, and see whether the arguments alleged in favour stand up to critical scrutiny. Equally it is right to probe objectors' contentions to see how well grounded they are. Often it will emerge that the need has not been made out, or that such need as there is could be met at much less cost to private interests or without trespassing on individual rights. The present British practice is defective on both counts. Public need does not have to be proved, but only stated: and great sacrifices are imposed on individuals when they could be obviated, or at least greatly reduced, by only minor concessions on the part of the public interest. For these reasons the present system of public inquiries is suspect. Fair consideration is not given to objectors. Where there is a conflict between public and private interest it is taken as a matter of course that the private interest should always give way. What is needed is partly a procedure but chiefly a background understanding by those in whom the decision is vested, whereby the claims of public interest and private right are brought into balance, with due regard being given to the individual, and a real reluctance to do him down manifested. This is not to say that private interests should always obstruct the public interest, or that no extra weight should be accorded to the public interest by reason of its being public; but only that undue weight should not be given it, and that some adjustments of public interest should be accepted in order to avoid great damage to the interests, especially the central interests, of the individual.

The fact that the public interest is often improperly invoked as a reason for dispensing with judicial safeguards should not blind us to its sometimes being a legitimate argument which may override other considerations. Cicero goes too far when he says *salus reipublicae suprema lex*: but the principle sometimes applies in the weighing of arguments. Sometimes, although not nearly so often as Ministers make out, there are arguments of national security for a particular action which override any interests the individual has, and make the normal judicial safeguards inappropriate. The Home Secretary may have his reasons for deporting a foreign spy which ought not to be subjected to cross-examination in public court, and which, if valid, could not be countered by any considerations of private interest. It would be quite wrong in such cases to insist rigidly on the rule *audi alteram partem*, or say the spy must be told of what the Home Secretary knows against him. But it is wrong also to leave it entirely to the Home Secretary to decide not only what ought to be done but whether to dispense with all safeguards. That makes him judge in his own cause in a bad way. Some protection is required, if only to make sure that the case is one where no fuller protection ought to be granted. An analogy with the modern practice of the courts over Crown privilege is apt. The judge does not leave it to the say-so of the Crown whether certain documents are not to be disclosed to the other side, but himself decides after seeing the documents whether they need to be kept secret. Similarly in administrative decisions where security issues arise we cannot confer on the parties concerned the same full rights which they have in normal court cases: but we can properly require that the decision whether the public interest is such that it cannot be subjected to public scrutiny and cannot be outweighed by any private interest or private right, should be taken by a judicial officer independent of the Department and the Civil Service generally, who can be relied upon not to take the Departmental view as a matter of course but to give full consideration to the rights of the individual, and only allow them to be overborne for good and compelling reason.

Historical accidents have combined to prevent our developing any clear idea of administrative justice in Britain. It is due partly to a mistaken doctrine of the separation of powers, partly to the fiction of parliamentary accountability, partly to the—in many ways admirable—reluctance of the judges to interfere with the ordinary business of government, and in part to the inadequacies of English legal practice and English legal thinking. We need to rethink. We need to recognise that administrators as well as judges are under an obligation to decide fairly and that the huge Departments of State cannot be effectively controlled by Parliament. Traditional forms of judicial review may not be the best way of bringing bureaucrats under the law. Often their reluctance to let the law in stems from a well-founded fear of the cumbersomeness of legal procedures and the ossification of legal principles—often it seems that a layman will reach a better and fairer decision on the merits of the case than a lawyer would let himself do. Again, although the rule of precedents is important, it is not all-important.[2] It is a great weakness of English law that judges, when faced by a new case, try and fit it into an existing pattern of old cases. Often it does not fit at all, and the whole logic of the decision is obscured or distorted by the attempt. In administrative law a large number of issues are coming up for the first time, and it would be better if they were decided by arguments based on underlying principles applied to new situations. In due course a new set of precedents will emerge which will gradually define boundaries between situations where one factor leads us to decide one way and those where some other factor leads us to decide the other way. But for the present we need to start with the principles of natural justice and a gradually forming consensus of what sort of extraneous considerations ought to be given greater or lesser weight when compared with individualised reasons, and work out ways in which we can arrive at decisions which will forward public policy and further public purposes without being insensitive to individual interests or doing any one down save for good reason whose cogency even the disappointed party is rationally obliged to acknowledge.

[2] See above, Ch. 3, pp. 43–4, Ch. 4, p. 77, and Ch. 5, pp. 104–8.

8

DISTRIBUTIVE JUSTICE

Distributive justice is traditionally characterized as being concerned with sharing good and bad things, benefits and burdens, among members of society. In the modern world we more commonly talk of social justice, but we should be chary of regarding the two terms as synonymous. For one thing, society, as we have seen,[1] takes many other decisions which raise questions of justice. For another, we need to distinguish, especially in view of Hayek's criticisms,[2] distributions carried out in the name of society as a whole from those undertaken within more limited organizations, such as firms, families or provident societies. The traditional term is on these counts preferable to the more idiomatic one, so long as we take care not to assume that burdens and benefits are *pari passu* when it comes to distributing them. It follows from the asymmetry of justice[3] that being offered benefits and being assigned burdens raise different issues of justice, which we shall mark by discussing the latter in a separate chapter under a new name.[4]

Not all benefits can be distributed. My feelings are necessarily my own. If I am happy, I can invite you to share my happiness, but my own happiness is not diminished thereby, but rather enhanced. No issues of distributive justice can arise over non-assignable goods, like truth, or non-privative ones, like happiness or knowledge. Distributable goods are typically assignable, privative and transferable, so that if I am to have more, you or someone else must have less, and it makes sense to maintain that you should give me some of yours, or vice versa. Money is the paradigm, but money raises special problems of its own, which we defer to Chapter Thirteen. In this chapter we consider the problem of benefits more generally, in which we may be dividing the spoils of conquest, sharing out conkers, cutting up cake, or allocating houses. There are other

---

[1] Ch. 2, p. 24.
[2] F. A. Hayek, *Law, Legislation and Liberty*, II, 1976, Ch. 9, pp. 62–100.
[3] See above, Ch. 1, pp. 8–10.
[4] Ch. 14.

goods, such as credit, prestige, power, education and health, which are not exactly or not completely transferable, but give rise to some issues of justice in their distribution or allocation. Fairness demands, I may say, that you should give credit where credit is due, and not take it all for yourself. Power is not exactly like money, inasmuch as my having it does not necessarily exclude your having it, but may, even, enhance it. Nevertheless, we can intelligibly call for power to be shared in a fairer way than at present. Egalitarian educationalists seem to be saying that it is unfair that some people should be able to write Greek, when others cannot even read English: we may find their utterances barely intelligible, and suspect that they are deeply confused about the nature and purpose of education;[5] but we should not dismiss out of hand all questions of educational policy as being entirely unconcerned with issues of justice.

There are many different grounds for the apportionment of benefits. Some are wholly irrational—if I bestow my favours by whim or caprice: others are rational, but not guided by the canons of justice—if I am guided by considerations of my own interest, or by utilitarian calculations, or again if I am guided by considerations of your interests alone (in which case, I am indeed being generous, but not just). To be just, I must be guided by reasons of a certain sort. For I must take each person seriously, and consider whether the solution is one that should be acceptable to him. I must ask whether his share is as large as it should be, and answer that question by reference to reasons which take into account, one way or another, his individuality by being based on the circumstances of his particular case. There are many sorts of individualised reason that satisfy this condition. Although, as I shall argue in Chapter Eleven, reasons based on the individual's deeds and agreements are in some way pre-eminent, reasons based on individual need, status, merit, entitlement or right are all, in appropriate circumstances, the proper basis of apportionment.[6] How much weight should be given

---

[5] See further, J. R. Lucas, "Equality in Education", in Bryan R. Wilson (ed.), *Education, Equality and Society*, London, 1975, pp. 39–40.

[6] Different writers put forward different potential bases of apportionment, Alf Ross, *On Law and Justice*, English tr., London, 1974, Ch. 12, §63, pp. 270–2, formulates the following principles:

Everyone according to merit

Everyone according to his performance

Everyone according to need

them will depend partly on the nature of the good, partly on the purposes of the association that has the disposal of the good in question. Williams argues that need is an obviously appropriate basis for distributing medical care,[7] and Vlastos similarly cites security against criminal assault as a good to be distributed according to need.[8] But need cannot be, as an example of Feinberg

---

Everyone according to ability
Everyone according to rank and station.
C. Perelman, *The Idea of Justice and the Problem of Argument*, tr. John Petrie, London, 1963, pp. 6–7, cites as some of the principles
  (1) To each the same thing
  (2) To each according to his merits
  (3) To each according to his works
  (4) To each according to his needs
  (5) To each according to his rank
  (6) To each according to his legal entitlement.
A. M. Honoré, "Social Justice", 8 *McGill Law Journal*, 1968, pp. 77–103; reprinted in R. S. Summers (ed.), *Essays in Legal Philosophy*, Oxford, 1968, pp. 66–81, itemises:
  The justice of special relations
  The justice of conformity to rule
  The justice of allocation according to desert
  The justice of allocation according to need
  The justice of allocation according to choice.
Gregory Vlastos, "Justice and Equality" in R. B. Brandt (ed.), *Social Justice*, p. 35:
  (1) To each according to his *need*
  (2) To each according to his *worth*
  (3) To each according to his *merit*
  (4) To each according to his *work*
  (5) To each according to the *agreements* he has made.
Nicholas Rescher, *Distributive Justice*, Indianapolis, 1966, Ch. 4, p. 73:
  (1) as equals (except possibly in the case of certain "negative" distributions such as punishments).
  (2) according to their needs.
  (3) according to their ability or merit or achievements.
  (4) according to their efforts and sacrifices.
  (5) according to their actual productive contribution.
  (6) according to the requirements of the common good, or the public interest, or the welfare of mankind, or the greater good of a greater number.
  (7) according to a valuation of their socially useful services in terms of their scarcity in the essentially economic terms of supply and demand.
which, except for No. 3, he cites from John A. Ryan, *Distributive Justice*, 3rd edn., London, 1942, Ch. 14.
  [7] B. A. O. Williams, "The Idea of Equality", in Peter Laslett and W. G. Runciman (eds.), *Philosophy, Politics and Society*, *II*, Oxford, 1962, pp. 121–2; reprinted in Hugo A. Hedau (ed.), *Justice and Equality*, Englewood Cliffs, N.J., 1971, pp. 127–8, and in Joel Feinberg (ed.), *Moral Concepts*, Oxford, 1969, pp. 153–71.
  [8] Gregory Vlastos, "Justice and Equality", in R. B. Brandt (ed.), *Social Justice*, Englewood Cliffs, N.J., 1962, pp. 41–3.

shows,[9] an appropriate basis for awarding a prize or a good grade in an examination; only merit or desert or performance in the competition or examination could be a logically appropriate basis for an award of that sort.

Status[10] is out of favour as a basis of distribution, but it is important none the less. 'Because he is your father', 'because he is your son', 'because he is your kinsman', 'because he is your compatriot' are perfectly intelligible reasons for determining a fair share, and sometimes the most important ones. I ought to consider my family first in allocating my time and attention and worldly goods. So, too, sometimes 'because he is a soldier', 'because he is a knight', 'because she is a woman', 'because he is a doctor', 'because he is a graduate', 'because he is a clergyman' are acceptable grounds for allocating good things. Men *need* places in lifeboats just as much as anybody else when the ship goes down, but women and children have prior claim on account of what they are, and not what they need or merit or deserve.

Merit is often understood in the same sense as desert, but it is useful to distinguish the two, using merit to refer to the personal qualities a man may possess, and desert to refer to the deeds he has done. We give scholarships on merit and military decorations on desert. It is reasonable to confer on a man educational opportunity, or membership of a prestigious club, or a desirable job, on the grounds that he simply *is* a good chap, although he may not have clocked up, perhaps through youth or lack of opportunity, many good deeds. Of course, we cannot know that he is good except through what he does and says, but having, perhaps after examination, reached the conclusion that he is good, we can on that basis prefer him, even though another has done more good deeds. By contrast, it would be absurd to award the Victoria Cross to a man, admittedly very courageous, who had never had occasion to perform some feat of gallantry, in preference to another, in general much more cowardly, character, who had, none the less, screwed himself up to an act of conspicuous heroism in the face of the

---

[9] Joel Feinberg, "Justice and Personal Desert", in Carl J. Friedrich and John W. Chapman (eds.), *Nomos VI: Justice*, New York, 1963, pp. 72–3. Reprinted in Joel Feinberg, *Doing and Deserving*, Princeton, 1970, p. 59.

[10] Under this heading I include Woozley's "Special Relationship"; see A. D. Woozley, "Injustice", *American Philosophical Quarterly*, Monograph No. 7, Oxford, 1973, p. 118.

enemy. Merit and, according to the retributivists, desert, can be the basis for assigning bad things as well as good. Young men are conscripted because they have the military merits that women, children and old men lack. Academics who have the misfortune to be competent administrators are pressured by their incompetent colleagues to assume the burdens of office on account of the very virtues that should earn them release.

Entitlement differs from need, merit and desert, in that it depends on antecedent conventions and awards. Often it depends on anterior agreement. If I buy a hundred shares in ICI, then I am entitled to a hundred dividends. I may not need them. I may be undeserving and lacking in merit. But it would be unjust none the less to deny me them, because I am entitled to them, and that is the relevant basis of distribution. In other cases the entitlement stems not from anterior agreement but authoritative arbitration. Feinberg points out that quite often the candidate who deserves to win does not, and that some other less deserving candidate nevertheless succeeds in satisfying the criteria and in being declared the winner.[11] In such a case he is entitled to the prize, and it would be unfair if he, like Antilochus, were to be deprived of his entitlement on the grounds of someone else's superior merit.[12] Merit is difficult to measure exactly. Often, to save dispute or subsequent recrimination, we replace unmeasurable merit by something more determinate or appoint judges whose decision is to be final. And then it is always possible that the substituted criterion may yield the wrong result or the decision of the judges be at manifest variance with the real merits of the candidates. But, however lacking in merit, the candidate thus adjudged the winner is entitled to the prize, and injustice would be done if he were not given it.

Merit shades not only into entitlement, but into rank, as the etymology of the word 'aristocrat' shows. Ideally, in assessing a man's merits, we should look into his heart, and see exactly what sort of man he was, and to what extent his characteristics were desirable or not: but the more definite criteria we are obliged to use in practice gradually oust any assessment of merit, and we come to regard as the important question not 'What sort of man is he?' but

[11] Joel Feinberg, "Justice and Personal Desert", in *Doing and Deserving*, Princeton, 1970, pp. 64–5, 72, 83–6.

[12] *Iliad* xxiii, ll. 536–5; see A. W. H. Adkins, *Merit and Responsibility*, Oxford, 1960, p. 56.

'What qualifications does he have?', and these, whether a matter of lineage and ancestry, as in times past, or of degrees and diplomas, as now, are more peripheral to the individual, and constitute his status rather than his real merit.

All these bases of apportionment are individualised. It would be unjust, a man can argue, not to give him such-and-such a share of some good, and the reason why it would be unjust is some fact about him—that *he* is a kinsman, a compatriot or a member of the society, that *he* is in need of that sort of good, that *he* possesses certain desirable qualities or looks like developing them, that *he* has done good deeds in the past or shows promise of performing well in the future, that it is assigned to *him* by virtue of some agreement explicitly entered into or some understanding we have implicitly accepted as part of the rules of the game. If we simply ignore such considerations, we are not merely being unreasonable, but are manifesting our disregard for him as a person, and are therefore being unfair as well. Unless we can argue against them, either impugning the facts or their relevance to the distribution in question, or showing them to be overridden by other, weightier considerations, we must, if we are to be just, acknowledge their force. And so, correlatively, we construe them all as being claims of right. A just distribution is one that gives each individual his right—*suum cuique tribuere*—but there are many rights, and they may conflict. Justice has often seemed in consequence to be an inherently confused and self-contradictory concept,[13] or at least an irreducibly pluriform one.[14] Michael Young puts it with characteristic vigour:

One could say it was wrong to pay one man more than another because there should be distribution according to needs. One could say it was wrong to pay the lazy scientist more than the diligent dustman because there should be distribution according to effort. One could say it was wrong to pay the intelligent more than the stupid because society should compensate for genetic injustice. One could say it was wrong to pay the stupid more than the intelligent because society should compensate for the unhappiness which is the usual lot of the intelligent. (No one can do much about the brilliant, they will be miserable anyway.) One could say it was wrong to pay the man who lived a long and serene life in Upper Slaughter as much as a scientist who wore himself out in the service of knowledge at

---

[13] Plato, *Laws*, IX, 861a.
[14] Renford Bambrough, *New Essays on Plato and Aristotle*, London, 1965, pp. 159 ff.

the Battersea Poly. One could say it was wrong to pay people who liked their work as much as those who didn't. One could—and did—say anything, and whatever one said it was always with the support of the particular kind of justice invoked by principles implicit in the statement.[15]

But this does not really prove that distributive justice is a confused concept or that no further elucidation is possible. What it shows is that, as in litigation, there are often arguments on all sides, which have to be considered and assessed before we can decide which of them are relevant to the particular distribution in question, and how much weight should be given them. It all depends. Sometimes the nature of the good or the purpose of the association may indicate one basis of apportionment unambiguously, but often there is room for dispute. A provident association will distribute its funds on the basis of need, a joint stock company on the number of shares held: but most associations exist for purposes that are not quite so explicit and exclusive, and there can be more doubt how the common purposes should determine the basis of distribution, and how much weight should be given to each. Even medical care, the paradigm example of a good to be distributed according to need, is not quite straightforward. As Nozick points out, there are many other goods and services—food and barbering—which are similarly defined in terms of human needs, but which are not apportioned simply on grounds of need.[16] Although need, in some fairly wide sense (else, what about cosmetic surgery?) is a necessary condition, and sometimes an adequate condition, for medical care, it is not always a sufficient condition—as when we have to decide who shall have the few available kidney machines. Moreover, besides conflicts between different bases for apportionment, there are often conflicts between individualised and other sorts of reason. Jobs are good things to have. People have rights in them, under the Protection of Employment Act, and rights to them under the Equal Opportunities Act. Nevertheless, it is part of the concept of a job that it is not primarily a good thing to be assigned to someone, but an activity undertaken for other, consumer-oriented, reasons. And these generate requirements which are at variance with indivi- dualised reasons. A person may need a job, deserve a job, be

---

[15] Michael Young, *The Rise of the Meritocracy*, Penguin, 1961, pp. 155–6, quoted, Hugh Stretton, *Capitalism, Socialism and the Environment*, Cambriddge, 1975, p. 165. Compare J. S. Mill, *Utilitarianism*, Ch. 5, Everyman edn., p. 43.

[16] *Anarchy, State and Utopia*, p. 198.

entitled to a job: but if he cannot do the work required, or if nobody wants the work to be done, or nobody is willing to pay for the work to be done, then, whatever the individualised reasons for his having one, they will be overridden by other reasons against. And so too in less extreme cases, appointments and reappointments are not simply questions of right, but questions into which other factors enter, and the only rights individuals have are to a certain degree of consideration, and certain procedures to secure it.

We find it difficult to be content with such untidiness. We yearn for a unified over-all system of justice, which shall determine what each of us is worth and give him then his due. If only there were a just king who would do by us as we ought to be done by, then we could rest assured that all would be well, and nobody would have to push his own interest or press his own suit. Such a demand is dangerous. It supposes too passive a view of man, denying our need for freedom to decide most things for ourselves, and it suggests a totalitarian view of society.[17] But although dangerous if unchecked, such a demand answers to part of our human nature and one facet of the concept of justice, and has greatly influenced men's thinking about justice. Some, Plato and Aristotle and more recently Sir David Ross,[18] have reflected back the unified justice they seek into a single basis—$\dot{a}\xi\dot{\iota}a$, which is usually translated 'worth' and corresponds approximately to our 'merit'—on which every just distribution should be grounded. Others fix on one of the bases listed, and exalt it over all the others. Popular morality continues obstinately in its belief that distribution ought always in justice to be according to desert. Strict egalitarians will have none of this, and insist on assigning equal shares to everyone within the relevant range of concern. Others, often also regarding themselves as egalitarians, would give to each according to his need. Liberals, extolling the value of liberty and the virtues of the market economy think that so long as contracts freely entered into are kept, justice is served. None of these contentions is absurd. Although they are only partial and inadequate explications of the concept of justice, each takes up and develops a strand of reasoning that is integral to the concept as a whole. We need, therefore, to appreciate the force of the arguments for particular versions of justice, as well as their limitations.

[17] See Ch. 9, p. 183, and pp. 173–4.
[18] W. D. Ross, *The Right and the Good*, Oxford, 1930, pp. 26 f.

9

JUSTICE AND EQUALITY

Justice is sometimes said to be the same as equality. This is a mistake. Justice is connected with equality, and sometimes arguments of justice lead to egalitarian conclusions, but justice is not identical·with equality, and can run counter to it.

At first sight, it is obvious that justice is not the same as equality. Justice is concerned with deciding between people, and therefore cannot deal with them all the same. It must mete out different treatment to the guilty from what it does to the innocent, and give judgement for the successful plaintiff and against the plaintiff who fails to make out his case. Aristotle attempts an etymological connection between the Greek words δικάζω to adjudicate, and διχάζω to divide,[1] and although the etymology is unsound, the conceptual point remains. To judge is to discriminate. It must involve differential treatment, and cannot be elucidated simply in terms of uniformity. This point is well brought out by a story Isaiah Berlin tells of Lord Halifax during the war, who found there was a leak from the Foreign Office, which could be tracked down to a certain typing pool, but no further to any particular individual. Lord Halifax went to the pool, and said "I am going to do something very unjust, but necessary in the interests of national security. There has been a leak from this pool. I do not know which of you it is. And therefore I am going to sack you all." Halifax had treated them all alike. If justice were simply equality, he need have had no scruples. The objection he himself felt to his action was not that he was discriminating between them but that he was failing to

[1] *Nicomachean Ethics*, V, 1132a 31–2. The sentence is awkwardly placed in its present position in the text, which requires it to be understood as an argument in favour of the identification of justice with equality. Aristotle compares δίκαιον with δίχα, suggesting that it is really δίχαιον, and that δικαστής is really διχαστής. δίχα means asunder, apart, differently and διχάζω means to divide without any special sense of dividing equally. The δικαστής differentiates between the two parties, rather than dividing things equally between them. The sentence may have been misplaced in the text, or it may be an attempt by Aristotle to nullify an earlier argument against the identification.

do so, and meting out to the innocent the same treatment as to the guilty; not that he was treating like cases differently but that he was failing to take into account the different merits of the different cases. So, too, if a ruler were to boil his subjects in oil, jumping in afterwards himself, it would be an injustice, although there would be no inequality of treatment.[2] Or, again, the suppression of, for example, *Doctor Zhivago*, in Russia is not only illiberal, but unjust, and would still be unjust if it applied to absolutely everyone, not only ordinary citizens, but members of the Politburo as well.[3]

The same point can be made with respect to distributive justice. The labourers in the vineyard murmured against the master in spite of their all having been given equal rewards, and he met their complaints not by maintaining that since their wages were equal they must be just, but by claiming that the relevant principle of justice in their case was contractual, not distributive, and that for the rest it was an exercise of generosity, not of justice, on his part.[4] If justice were simply identical with equality, the complaint of those who had laboured through the heat of the day would have been unintelligible. But, whether we agree with them or not, we can understand them.

So justice is not equality. But there is some connection, as even Plato and Aristotle allowed. We must at least treat like cases alike, else our decisions are not even rational, and so cannot *a fortiori* be just. It is, as we have seen,[5] none other than Kant's principle of universalisability. And this can be made to yield egalitarian results, if coupled with a robust scepticism about the relevance of any factors adduced to show cases not to be alike—and scepticism is not only easy in the present age but on strong ground where questions of justice are in issue, which require particularly cogent reasons to be adduced.[6] Thus Benn argues: "Egalitarians protest when ... they see no rational justification for differentiating a particular class for the purpose of allocating certain specific privileges or burdens."[7] Both the issue and the standard of justification

---

[2] William K. Frankena, "The Concept of Social Justice", in R. B. Brandt (ed.), *Social Justice*, Englewood Cliffs, N.J., 1962, p. 17.

[3] Gregory Vlastos, "Justice and Equality", in R. B. Brandt, op. cit., p. 62.

[4] Matt. 20:1-15.

[5] Ch. 3, pp. 43-4.

[6] See, for example, the argument in S. I. Benn and R. S. Peters, *Social Principles and the Democratic State*, London, 1959, Ch. 5, §III, pp. 114 ff.

[7] S. I. Benn, "Egalitarianism and the equal consideration of interests" in J. Rowland Pennock and John W. Chapman (eds.), *Nomos II: Equality*, New York,

required are left to the choice of the egalitarian. Thus discrimination between the sexes has been called in question in recent years "because, it is argued, no one has yet shown good enough reasons for thinking a person's sex relevant to the income he should earn—and the burden of proof rests on the discriminator".[7] But sometimes a practice is not called in question or is thought to be justified, as Benn goes on to point out: "On the other hand, discrimination according to sex for military service has been generally accepted without much question and is usually considered well grounded; so it is rarely called an inequality."[7] This principle, which Bedau calls the *presumption of equality*[8] is a clearly powerful principle, but open to considerable objection. It is easy to ask questions, and easy not to be satisfied with the answers given. But not all questions ought to be answered, and often merely by asking a question one is committed to waiting for an answer and not dismissing it out of hand. Moreover, without considerable qualification the presumption of equality is bound to prove internally inconsistent. It cannot be a presumption we are always entitled to make, and once we have to consider whether in any particular case it is justified, its bulldozing power is already gone.

It is easy to ask questions. Job asked God to justify his treatment of him, and modern man, especially modern young man, is fond of demanding that Society should justify itself to his satisfaction. But questions have to be addressed to someone, and it depends very much on the person to whom the question is addressed what sort of answer it is reasonable to expect. If you ask me, I may be able to explain why we have certain sorts of arrangements, but I cannot be called on to justify them unless I had some control over them and am therefore responsible for them. It is dangerously easy in seeking a rational justification to smuggle in an assumption of omnipotence. In our age of unbelief we tend to be "egotheists" and to assume that we, or the State at our bidding, can arrange everything as seems best. But not everything is possible to the State, nor should it be. If

---

1967, pp. 64–5; reprinted in Hugo A. Bedau, *Justice and Equality*, Prentice-Hall, 1971, p. 155. See also S. I. Benn and R. S. Peters, *Social Principles and the Democratic State*, London, 1959, p. 110; A. M. Honoré, "Social Justice", *McGill Law Journal*, 78, 1962, p. 96; reprinted in R. S. Summers (ed.), *Essays in Legal Philosophy*, Oxford, 1968, p. 83; or earlier, Leslie Stephen, "Social Equality", *International Journal of Ethics I*, 1891, p. 267.

[8] Hugo A. Bedau, "Radical Egalitarianism", in *Justice and Equality*, p. 173; or his "Egalitarianism and the idea of Equality" in *Nomos II: Equality*, p. 19.

we insist on the State's being answerable for all the arrangements of society, we implicitly concede to it absolute power. Unless we are totalitarians, we must be prepared on occasion to disclaim responsibility, and to refuse to offer a justification in the terms desired of some social arrangement which has attracted criticism. In an imperfect world inhabited by imperfect men, many things will go wrong, which are indubitably wrong, but which cannot be remedied except at the cost of much greater evils. Egalitarian sentiment leads easily to totalitarianism, and if we abhor totalitarianism we must be prepared on occasion to rebut the presumption of the egalitarians, and concede that not everything in our society can be justified.

Those disclaimers of responsibility are not to be always invoked. One of the reasons for the radicals' impatience with authority is authority's tendency to brush off awkward questions with unreasonable disclaimers. Nevertheless the tone of the discussion should change. Although we should think critically about our society, we should not be too strident in our questioning. There will be plenty of occasions when we shall have to probe and press our questions hard, and not be put off by easy evasions; but we should not assume that answers must always be forthcoming, or that nothing can be accepted unless it has been rationally justified to our complete satisfaction.

Benn is at pains to distinguish his egalitarianism from the radical egalitarianism, discussed by Bedau, which presses for the removal of all forms of differentiation, assigning, in Perelman's formulation, to each the same thing.[9] Having allowed that the conditions under attack may be contextually supplied and not explicitly stated, he protests in a footnote:

A favourite way of discrediting the egalitarian, however, is to make it appear that he seeks to remove forms of discrimination that neither he, nor anyone else, would for a moment question. Though the Levellers were concerned only for equal political rights, for removing monopolistic privileges in trade, and for legal reforms, they were frequently accused, despite vigorous disclaimers, of wanting to level property.[10]

But it is perfectly reasonable counter. If the egalitarian is entitled to call any form of discrimination in question, then the anti-egalitarian

---

[9] C. Perelman, *The Idea of Justice and the Problem of Argument*, tr. John Petrie, London, 1963, p. 7; quoted above, Ch. 8, p. 165 n.

[10] Benn, op. cit., p. 155.

can reduce the presumption of equality to absurdity by calling in question some form of discrimination the egalitarian is disposed to accept. American advocates of Women's Lib who believe that considerations of chivalry should secure them exemption from the Draft Laws *are* being inconsistent if they base their claim for equal treatment on a general refusal to allow that differences of sex can ever be relevant to the treatment meted out to a citizen by the State. Often in politics criteria of relevance are difficult to determine, and we have to take into account many different considerations based on different facts. The presumption of equality, however, focusses on just one factor, and ignores all the rest. But whether a distinction is relevant or not cannot depend on whether the egalitarian happens to question it or not. For one thing it makes for arbitrariness: for another it leads to inconsistency. If, at the choice of the egalitarian, one of the many fine differences of grey in political discourse is singled out and presented as a black and white distinction, rational debate is at the mercy of his whim. Moreover, if at his bidding, we set out to establish equality in one respect, we shall thereby establish some other inequality in another respect. Equality of opportunity in education leads to inequality of achievement. Policies intended to promote economic equality in Britain have led to great inequalities of power. These inequalities can be questioned too, but if they are, inconsistency results. The egalitarian is refusing to accept as justifiable the consequences of a previous application of the selfsame presumption of equality. It must, therefore, be, at best, a principle of only restricted applicability, and before the egalitarian can apply it, he needs to show that the case is a suitable one for its application. That is to say, it is not a presumption.

Not only does the argument lack presumptive force, but its conclusion is false. Equal treatment is often unfair, we have seen, because it fails to do justice to the individual's case. It is not enough that he should be treated the same as other people similarly situated: it is also required that proper account should be taken of the difference between cases, and that all, and not merely some, of the relevant factors should be taken into consideration in determining what treatment should be accorded to the individual in question. Else his individuality is being denied. He is being treated merely as one of a lump, not in the full particularity of his own case. Only if his treatment is differentiated in the light of the features of his case, can he feel that the decision is one he could himself identify with, since only then is there no relevant factor which has not been taken into consideration, and which, had it been taken into consideration might have had a bearing on the result. The current concern with differentials by Trades Unionists is not, as cynics suppose, simply due to greed. No doubt they are concerned, as most other men are, to improve their economic position. But the reason why it arouses fierce feelings is that an absence of differentials is construed as evidence of a lack of appreciation for a man's work, and this is not merely an injury but an insult. Justice demands not merely that we treat like cases alike, but equally important, that we treat different cases differently. Plato was the first to see this. In his attack on the permissive society in Book VIII of the *Republic*, he instances as one of its defects that it is undiscriminating, regarding everyone and everything as of equal merit, ἰσότητά τινα ὁμοίως ἴσοις τε καὶ ἀνίσοις διανέμουσα, assigning a sort of equality to equals and unequals alike.[11] A sort of equality: Plato had already realised that the concept of equality was itself equivocal, and that it could be construed in more than one way. In the *Gorgias*, he refers to a geometrical equality which applies to gods and men alike,[12] and from Aristotle's discussion in Book V of the *Nicomachean Ethics*, it is clear that what Plato had in mind—possibly having pondered it in the course of his researches into the foundations of Euclidean Geometry—was the fact that two figures can have equal angles but not equal, only proportional, sides. Aristotle tries to elucidate distributive justice—δικαιοσύνη διανεμητική—as requiring that each person's share should be proportional to his deserts, rather than that fair shares were, of necessity, equal shares. The important point that emerges both here and in his discussion of ἐπιείκεια—equity—at the end of Book V is the insistence that circumstances alter cases, and that we fail to do justice unless we recognise that fact, and take into account all the relevant factors in each individual case.

That justice is quite different from equality is also shown by our rules of natural justice, which are concerned primarily with procedures rather than outcomes. Equality does not insist on the principle *audi alteram partem: audi neutram partem* would be just as good so far as equality is concerned. Our rules of natural justice derive their force from our determination to regard each individual

---

[11] *Republic* VIII, 558c 5–6.   [12] *Gorgias* 508a 5–7.

as a separate entity who is entitled to be considered on his own account, and not merely lumped into some general category or class. We should be treating everyone equally if we gave none of them the opportunity of protesting their innocence or meeting their accuser's case. And our reason for thinking it unjust to treat them in this way all alike is not that we should be discriminating unfairly but that we were not giving full and fair consideration to each case, and thus not treating each person as an individual, an individual who may well turn out to be in the wrong, but who must not be assumed to be in the wrong, and therefore must be given an opportunity of stating his side of the argument. Again our reason for stigmatizing laws that impose strict liability is not that they discriminate unfairly, but unfairly fail to take into account certain crucial circumstances of some particular cases.[13] There may well have been a classification according to which Miss Sweet was in the same case as a man who knowingly and deliberately maintained a junkies' pad for pot parties: the objection was that it overlooked the difference that Miss Sweet neither intended nor knew the use to which her house was being put in her absence, and that this difference made all the difference to her being innocent or guilty.[14] Justice is concerned with the sort of things an individual has done, but for that very reason cannot confine its attention to the *sort* of things, but must also allow the possibility of the plea 'But I could not help it' which seeks to distinguish the particular case under consideration from others admitted to be blameworthy.

Justice in general then neither is, nor implies, equality. Although like cases are to be treated alike, different cases are to be treated differently, and justice requires that we be neither discriminatory nor undiscriminating in our response to individual cases. Distributive justice, however, is not the whole of justice. Distributive justice is concerned with the sharing of benefits among members of society, and it must be in his capacity as a member of the relevant society that each man should be allocated his share. And that, although an individualised basis of apportionment, is not individualised indefinitely far. Many—most—facts about an individual are not facts about him in his capacity as a member of society. In that capacity only fairly few facts feature. And therefore the principle of universalisability applies in its strong form

[13] Ch. 5, pp. 117–18, and Ch. 6, pp. 140–1.
[14] *Sweet* v. *Parsley*, All England Law Reports, 1969, I, pp. 347–64.

rather than its weak.[15] We cannot continue distinguishing cases indefinitely, but soon come to an *infima species* of cases, all of which are like one another in all relevant respects and ought, in consequence, to be treated alike.

The justice to be achieved in apportioning benefits and burdens is, therefore, only rather rough, subject to the crude requirements of the strong principle of universalisability rather than the more finely grained considerations admitted by the weak. Many considerations, although *prima facie* relevant, are rightly excluded, because, if allowed, every case would be a special case, to be given preferential treatment at the expense of the common cause, that is, at the expense of everybody else. We can be sure that some sort of justice is being done, only if the apportionment of benefits and burdens is according to rules, rules which are generally known and clear in their application. As in the law generally we often have reason to prefer legality to equity,[16] in order not to be at the mercy of the judge's discretion and in order to know where we stand, so in deciding how good and bad things are to be shared, we go by the book, this time to avoid jealousy and to enable each to see how he and everyone else stands, and to be satisfied that comparisons will not prove individious.

The word ἰσονομία in Greek carries the double sense of legality and equal distribution, and during the Fifth Century B.C. gave powerful support to egalitarian sentiment. There is a logical connection between the codification of law in rules and equality. Rules necessarily classify; and within each classification everybody is the same: the law brands all murderers alike as law-breakers, all takers of other people's property as thieves. As soon as the laws are codified and put in writing and published, and rulers no longer have discretion to decide each case on what seems to them to be its merits, the laws rather than the rulers reign supreme. All, rulers and ruled alike, are under the laws. The laws in this sense apply equally to all. Ἰσονομία "equallawness" expresses this aspect of the rule of law: there is Equality before the Law in the sense that nobody is above the Law, in contrast to autocracy, τῇ ἔξεστι ἀνευθύνῳ ποιέειν τὰ βούλεται, which is allowed to act as it pleases without being called to account.[17] If we value non-arbitrary and reasonable

---

[15] See above, Ch. 3, pp. 43–4.   [16] See above, Ch. 5, pp. 104–8.

[17] Herodotus III, 80:3. Pisistratus, who was anxious not to be accounted a tyrant, thought it incumbent on him to show willingness to stand his trial. See *Politics* V, 12, 2; 1315b 21, and *Athenaion Politeia*, 16.8.

government, as we should, we should value also ἰσονομία, equality
before the law; and from this a more general equality seems to
follow, assigning to all men "an equal share in all advantages which
are commonly regarded as desirable and which are in fact con-
ducive to human well being".[18] But it does not really. Although
laws make relatively few, relatively blunt distinctions, lumping, say,
all murderers together, or all thieves, they none the less make some
distinctions, and distinguish very firmly murderers from non-
murderers, thieves from those who do not take what is not their
own. As we have already seen with legality, formulating a legal rule
does not conclude the question of justice: although once the rule is
laid down as law, it is only fair to follow it in particular cases, it is
still possible to raise the question of whether the law itself is just.[19]
And similarly, although the rules for distributing benefits and
imposing burdens establish categories within which everyone
should, in all fairness, be treated the same, we can still raise the
question of whether the categories themselves are fairly
drawn—whether those cases are distinguished, as well as whether
those are accounted the same that ought to be so treated. To this
question there is, as we have seen in the previous chapter, no single
over-all answer. Different distinctions need to be drawn in different
associations, and with regard to the different benefits to be distributed or burdens to be imposed. All we can argue in general is that
while justice requires us to treat like cases alike, it requires us also
to frame our rules so as to take account of relevant differences, and
to respond to them accordingly.

An egalitarian may argue that there are in fact no relevant
differences not by merely doubting sceptically the relevance of any
differences that there are, but more by positively asserting that the
only relevant factor is bare membership of the society in question. It
is, in fact, the limiting case of distribution according to status, the
requisite status being simply membership of the society in question.
Perelman's 'To each the same thing'[20] is but a special case of his 'To
each according to his rank', where membership alone constitutes a

---

[18] A. M. Honoré, "Social Justice", *McGill Law Journal*, 78, 1962, p. 95; reprinted
in Robert S. Summers (ed.), *Essays in Legal Philosophy*, Oxford, 1968, p. 82.

[19] See above, Ch. 5, pp. 108–23.

[20] C. Perelman, *The Idea of Justice and the Problems of Argument*, tr. John Petrie,
London, 1963, pp. 6–7, quoted above, Ch. 8, p. 165 n.

relevant rank.[21] It may be membership of a particular association, citizenship of the State, possession of a common humanity, even bare consciousness of being discriminated against.[22] But, whatever the requisite status, parity of esteem is presumed for those with it: and its absence is a total disqualification for being eligible at all.

The argument for single-status egalitarianism is powerful. It is expressed in the slogan "No Second-Class Citizenship". If there were more than one rank, those not in the top rank would be done down: and equally, if there were any other criterion, some would fare worse than others, and could construe this as being done out of their citizens' rights. For any member of a society to be done by less well than he might have been can be regarded as an affront to his membership of that society, and therefore to be resisted on that ground alone. *Civis Romanus sum* expressed a claim to full respect by the authorities in the ancient world, and perhaps *civis humanus sum* does the same in the modern. The mere fact that a person is a member of our society, one of the "players" in an *n*-person game, someone with whom we can reason and enter into meaningful dialogue, is enough to establish his claim to our regard; and to give him anything less than anyone else is, in effect, to downgrade him and show that he is not considered to be as worthy of regard as other people. Justice, being by its nature concerned with the dignity of man, and not treating him with disrespect, cannot countenance anything derogating from anyone's claim. And therefore everyone is entitled to the same maximum as everybody else.

This argument has many variants. Most recently it has been formulated by Rawls in a highly sophisticated version, which merits a chapter of its own. Here we consider only the layout of the general argument which underlies not only Rawls's theory but that of most egalitarians today. Its strength lies in the ease with which the argument can be got off the ground. The preservation of human dignity is a concern we all share. As soon as we recognise anyone as a human being, we identify with him, and can understand what it would be like to be slighted, and we can see how any adverse decision could in some context be construed as a slight. But a *prima facie* case is not a conclusive case. The adverse decision may not be reached gratuitously, with cavalier unconcern for the in-

---

[21] See Gregory Vlastos, "Justice and Equality", in R. B. Brandt (ed.), *Social Justice*, Englewood Cliffs, N.J., 1962, pp. 45–52.

[22] A. M. Honoré, op. cit., pp. 83–4, 96–7.

dividual concerned. There may be cogent reasons, adequate and relevant to the individual case, for reaching the decision, which completely answer the initial complaint of apparent injustice. The egalitarian strategy is to make the protest, and then not to wait for any answer there might be, or even consider the possibility of there being one. But that is an ultimately incoherent approach. To ask questions is to presuppose the possibility of there being answers, and to commit oneself to listening to and assessing such answers as may be forthcoming. If the egalitarian will not listen to answers, others will not listen to his protests. Justice becomes circumscribed. Once it is acknowledged that if a decision raises any issues of justice, no justification will be accepted as being satisfactory, then there will be reluctance to admit the decision is justiciable at all: either it will be made out to be an exercise of liberty or of political or economic expediency from which considerations of justice are explicitly excluded, or ears will be stopped to every kind of protest. Both responses are evident today.

The egalitarian strategy not only abridges reason, and therefore justice itself, but also the range of concern. It is essentially unclear exactly who is and who is not a member of a society distributing good things. An n-person game can always be regarded as an $(n+m)$-person game, with an additional m persons playing a null part. If we deny, on egalitarian principle, that what a man did, or what he is, or what he needs, or what he is entitled to under antecedent agreement, could be relevant to how much he should have, we have no rational grounds for describing an n-person game as such rather as an $(n+m)$-person game, or, under the latter description, for discriminating between the genuine players and the null-playing passengers. Membership is everything, and there are no rational grounds for determining the relevant range of membership when it comes to distributing any particular good. As mere membership becomes more important, it becomes more contested. It may be no accident that ancient Athens began to restrict its citizenship about the time it started giving hand-outs and had good reason to limit its liabilities. Britain has become much more xenophobic as it has become more egalitarian. If everybody, merely by virtue of being here, is entitled to an equal share of the G.N.P., then it becomes important to make it clear that here does not include Ireland or Pakistan, and that West Indians must be sent back where they belong, for fear that otherwise they may qualify for income supplement at our expense.[23] The word 'peer' means 'equal': but the equality of the peerage gains its content by its contrast with all the rank outsiders who do not count at all. The intensity of egalitarian feeling is purchased at the cost of the extension of its scope. We start by saying that there shall be no second-class citizens: but since our sympathies, like our practical concern, is limited, we end by disfranchising many altogether, who, instead of being second-class citizens, will be placed utterly beyond the pale.

Need is a different basis of apportionment, but often is regarded as an egalitarian one.[24] If we give to each according to his need, then although we shall treat different people differently, the result will be to equalise their positions in some important respect. If each is given the food he needs, they will end up all equally full; if each is given the medical treatment he needs, they will end up, if not all equally well, at least more so than if some were not given needed medication. To this extent, then, need is an egalitarian basis of apportionment.

The doctrine that need alone is a proper basis for a fair distribution is a modern one: in times gone by it was often not regarded as constituting any claim in justice at all, but only one for pity or generosity. Like the strict principle of equality, it flourishes in a sceptical climate. Need is, by definition, capable of rational assessment, and therefore, although we may dispute whether this or that particular claim is one of need, or merely one of want or desire, we cannot dispute that needs, once established, constitute good reasons of some sort—whether of justice or of something else—for allocating benefits; and since they are individualised reasons, and since to harden the heart to a plea of need is to manifest apparent disregard, it seems natural to construe them as reasons of justice, reasons which, besides being by definition undeniable, are present and urgent. They therefore resist the erosion of the acids of scepticism longer than claims based on previous deeds or agreements, whose immediacy fades with the passage of time, or on assessments of merit whose adequacy and relevance can always be disputed. Distribution according to need, moreover, keys in with the passive

[23] See further, F. A. Hayek, *The Constitution of Liberty*, London, 1960, Ch. VI, §10, pp. 100–2.

[24] Gregory Vlastos, "Justice and Equality", in R. B. Brandt (ed.), *Social Justice*, Englewood Cliffs, N.J., 1962, pp. 40–3. A. M. Honoré, "Social Justice", p. 100; 88. See also A. D. Woozley, "Injustice", *American Philosophical Quarterly*, Monograph, No. 7, Oxford, 1973, pp. 114–15.

stance that justice easily engenders.[25] I do not create my own needs: they happen to me. If distribution is to be according to need alone, I do not have to exert myself, nor fear that I am being selfish or pushing my own interests. I cannot be accused of self-seeking or grabbing too much, because I am not *doing* anything, but merely letting justice take its course. My case rests on the facts, objectively known and impersonally assessed. And so I come before the judgement seat with a pure heart and clean hands.

The appeal of such an argument is powerful, but misdirected. It speaks to a moral consciousness, perhaps higher than, but certainly other than, and more restricted than, that to which arguments of justice are addressed. Justice does not deny self-interest or demand complete selflessness.[26] Plato was wrong in contrasting it with πλεονεξία, me-firstism: rather it is opposed to ἀλλότριον κακόν, otherchap-lastism; and thus, in spite of its passive aspect, is not altogether passive and not to be achieved by complete self-abnegation, but by a proper assertiveness acting on behalf of others as well as of oneself. There is, therefore, no special virtue in the impersonal character of need as a basis of assessment, as contrasted with the more personal bases of desert and agreement or possibly subjective assessments of merit. Moreover, although need once established constitutes a good, individualised reason for allocating benefits, it is not easy always to determine exactly what claims are, and what are not, to be allowed as claims of need. Standards vary. One generation's luxuries are another's necessities, and vice versa. We have differing criteria. So long as need is not the only basis of apportionment, ambiguity in its application does not matter too much, as decisions can often be reached on some other basis when need is uncertain: but once need is made the only, or the prime, ground, ambiguity in its application will give rise to much dissension and some injustice.

Need, therefore, although a logically proper basis of apportionment, is not the only, or the prime, one, nor is it suitable to be elevated into being the only one. Its appearance of being impersonally objective is in many cases specious, and is anyhow not a requirement of justice, which, being impartially partial to each party, is peculiarly concerned with personal factors, and is as much concerned with a man's personal merits, entitlements and deserts as with his particular, but in some sense impersonal, needs.

[25] See above, Ch. 8, p. 170.   [26] See below, Ch. 16, pp. 261–2.

The general argument from justice to equality is mistaken. We cannot discount in advance the relevance of differences between cases without implicitly denying the relevance of reason altogether, nor can we elevate bare membership of society or need into a sole basis for apportionment without imposing greater strains than either concept can bear. The strategy of egalitarian argument involves arbitrariness in the choice of discriminations found unjustifiable, and hence leads to inconsistency and a propensity to overlook other injustices not currently the topic of popular indignation. There is an implicit totalitarianism in the demand for absolute justice according to some single principle, and a tendency to make justice be more passive and less personal than it should be.

Justice, then, is not to be identified with equality, nor does it always imply it. Although, being rational, it must conform to the principle of universalisability, which, for distributive justice, may take a strong form, it cannot be identified with it, since there are many other exercises of rationality, which must also be universalisable, but are not, for that reason alone, just. Nor does justice imply equality. Although sometimes when we are distributing benefits, fair shares are equal shares, this is not always so. An equal distribution can be unfair. To give nobody anything is to give each an equal amount, but often would be unjust. If we give everyone the same, then someone who deserves more, or who merits more, or who is entitled to more, will have cause for complaint, and, as we shall argue in the next chapter, just cause for complaint, since he is being given less than he should, for no adequate reason. A decision not to give him what he deserves, or merits, or is entitled to, is an adverse decision, even as a decision not to give anybody else what he otherwise might have been given is a decision adverse to him. If he deserves much and is not given more than anyone else, then he is being given too little, even though it is not less than what others are being given. It is not enough to meet his complaint with the counter that he is being treated the same as everybody else, unless it can be maintained that he is in the same case as everyone else. For although the absence of irrelevant discrimination is a necessary condition of a decision's being just, it is not a sufficient condition: and the core of the concept lies not in comparing one case with another, but in simply putting to the question an adverse decision, and seeing whether there were sufficiently compelling reasons for taking it.

10

THE THEORY OF RAWLS

Much interest has been aroused by John Rawls's volume *A Theory of Justice*;[1] and it is appropriate to consider it from the standpoint adopted in our present work, the more so because Rawls denies any connection between justice and desert, and seeks to elucidate justice in a wholly different, egalitarian way.

Rawls's theory is a variant on utilitarianism. He shares the same conceptual scheme as the utilitarians, but seeks to mitigate the most obnoxious conclusions which they are forced to draw. Like the utilitarians, he believes that goods can be compared and aggregated, that states of affairs are to be evaluated in terms of goods, and that the prime concern of politics is to bring it about that desirable states of affairs obtain. Unlike the utilitarians, however, Rawls does not seek simply to maximise the total goods produced. He shrinks from the callous unconcern manifested by utilitarians towards particular individuals, whose interests they are prepared to trample on without scruple, so long as the sum of good is thereby increased. Instead, he focusses attention on those who are likely to come off worst, and to alleviate their lot. In the terminology of the Theory of Games, Rawls would have us pursue, subject to certain constraints about individual rights and liberties, a maximin policy.[2]

Rawls claims that his policy is the rational one for anybody to adopt if he were to make his choice without knowing how he was going to fare. If we were setting up a society from scratch, a prudent man, knowing that he could not know how he was going to fare, would opt for that constitution under which, if things went ill with him, he would be least badly off. Any other choice could work out to his greater disadvantage, and therefore, according to Rawls, would be a less sensible one to make. Hence, if we are wise, we shall all agree on the maximin strategy which Rawls commends. Not only is this the rational policy for us all to adopt, but it is the only basis of a social contract which could include everyone; and therefore an acceptance of it can be imputed to everyone, and

---

[1] Cambridge, Mass., 1971; Oxford, 1972. [2] Ch. 3, p. 66.

everyone can be held to it. The arguments of Locke are thus adduced to defend, not the rights of property, but the egalitarian measures of social democracy.

Rawls's recommendation of a maximin strategy carries some weight: but it seems to be a rational reconstruction not of justice but of prudence. If I found myself deliberating what constitution to set up, it would be wise to ensure that, if the next turn of the wheel of fortune went against me, I should none the less fare not too ill. But this counsel, thus presented, has little to do with justice. It is prospective, not retrospective: it is based on ignorance, not knowledge: and it is concerned with my own advantage, not others' rights. Prudence may suggest, but justice has not been shown to demand, a maximin strategy. Indeed, although a maximin strategy may be prudent, Rawls has not shown either that it is the pre-eminently rational one or that it is in fact widely adopted. It could be argued, with some show of reason, that it was better to run risks. Although a prudent man may seek to minimise possible losses, a man might equally wisely risk some losses for great gains. Rather than minimise losses, a rational man should, according to one course of reckoning, seek to maximise the expectation, in the technical sense elucidated in probability theory, of gain. Or he might chance his arm even further. He might be guided by Pascal instead of Rawls, and pursue a maximax strategy, reckoning that all the ordinary goods he could reasonably be sure of getting were of so little value that it was worth staking everything on some slim chance of achieving a break-through, and really making good. Certainly this is how many people reason, and although we can deem them imprudent, we cannot dub them irrational, and must admit that in the event they may prove wiser than we. Even if no pearl of great price comes their way, it is good to be able to hope. Hopes are as important as fears, and if it is good to know nothing very bad can happen, it is also good not to know that nothing very good can happen. We should not seek security at the cost of frustrating all our fondest dreams and highest hopes. And therefore men, who are rational rather than merely prudent, are ready to take risks, and sometimes trade in security for the possibility of great achievement. We cannot say that they are wrong, and even more surely we cannot say that they do not exist. Rawls cannot argue convincingly for social democracy on the basis that nobody ever spends money on the pools.

Non-Americans find contract theories unconvincing. There never was a constitutional convention in Britain: to suppose oneself a Founding Father is not only a counterfactual hypothetical, but an idle and totally unhistorical fancy. Nevertheless, contract theories are not to be dismissed simply on that score. Historically false, they still may be vehicles for conveying philosophical truth. And much of Rawls's argument can be separated from his account of what it would be prudent to choose in the original position behind the veil of ignorance. In particular, Rawls often seems to be engaged in a dialogue with the least favoured members of modern industrial society, seeking to reconcile them to their lot. The janitor in the university building, the driver in the streetcar, the attendant in the gasoline station, the unemployed in Harlem or Bronx, may feel deprived and believe that they are being ill done by, and ought, by rights, to have as much as a college professor. Rawls concedes their main, egalitarian point, and agrees that there is no *a priori* reason why they ought to have less than anyone else: but then goes on with an *ad hominem* argument that poorer though they are than many members of modern society, they would be worse off still if those other members of society were brought down to their level. The poor benefit from the crumbs that fall from the rich man's table. Business men, if they are allowed to get rich, will do so by meeting public wants as efficiently as possible, and we all benefit by their self-interested labours. And therefore we should not be jealous of the rich. They may be richer than we are, but we are richer than we otherwise would be, and if we tried to cut them down to size, we should only be cutting off our noses to spite our faces. As Abraham Lincoln said, you can't make the poor rich by making the rich poor.

It is a familiar argument in modern times, and, within its limits, a cogent one. It is a powerful dissuasive to extreme egalitarian measures, and should go some way to reconciling the victims of modern industrial society to their lot. Although they have come off worst, they have done better than they would have done in a pre-industrial society. They may have lost out, but the consolation prizes are quite large. But, once again, we protest that this is barely an argument of justice. Justice is more exact. It is concerned with particular individuals and their particular wrongs, and seeks to remedy these. Sometimes we may be willing to set off against admitted wrongs other uncovenanted benefits, and allow our complaints to be assuaged by a consideration of our credit account in blessings; but any such reckoning is only a rough justice, and it is noteworthy how unavailing such arguments have been in modern Britain. Time and again grievances have been pursued without any regard to countervailing advantages, and often entirely contrary to all counsels of expediency. Strikers, convinced of the justice of their cause, have continued their strikes, even to their long-term disadvantage: and public policy has often been governed by egalitarian considerations rather than those of economic efficiency or general prosperity. Rawls's argument with the worst off is only a partial answer to the politics of envy, more effective in America than in Britain, and is much more an argument of expediency than of justice.

Rawls's argument is, in fact, not so much *with* the worst off as *about* them. It gains force from its vicarious lack of actuality. Instead of pointing out to an actual Puerto Rican that he is, in spite of everything, better off in New York than Puerto Rico, we are agonizing in our own consciences about the poor, and whether we ought not to be doing better by them. Could not we make them unpoor by giving them our money? It is from this perspective that Rawls's theory comes nearest to being a theory of justice. It raises a question not of expediency but of right, and focusses it in the direction of those who look most like being badly done by, namely these who are worst off. But the worst off are not the only ones who may be badly done by, and arguments about what ought to be done cannot always be reconstructed in terms of what Rawls will allow as a cogent consideration. Anyone may be badly done by. Even the rich may be wronged. A theory of justice needs to concern itself with all members of society, not just the poor, and should seek to ensure that nobody is done down, and everyone can dwell at peace with society. And in deciding what are, and what are not, adequate reasons for reaching an adverse decision, we shall need to adopt different canons from those implicitly put forward by Rawls.

Rawls is concerned, commendably, with the underdog, but, less commendably, exclusively so. He wants the underdog to have as much as possible, even at the expense of the overdog. But it is not clear that this should be so. After all, overdogs have their rights too. There are many cases where men have conferred great benefits on their fellows, and would, according to common notions of justice, be entitled to a greater share of the good things going than other men. A grateful nation gave the Duke of Marlborough a palace at

Blenheim. Honours and prizes were showered on Sir Alexander Fleming and Lord Florey, the discoverers of penicillin. The inventor of the xerox copying machine made a fortune. Rawls would have to say that this was wrong, except in so far as it could be shown that they were only in it for the money, and would not deliver the goods unless they were going to be paid for it. Most people would reject this conclusion as perverse. If, fired by a love of humanity, I labour to devise a new treatment for the common cold, and on my efforts being crowned with success admit that I would not have been deterred from my efforts by the knowledge that I would not obtain any pecuniary advantage, then I ought not to be paid $\frac{1}{2}$p: but if I hold out at every stage for the highest financial return I can extract, often threatening, if my demands are not met, to go and do research into germ warfare for the Russians, or into the manufacture of beauty products for a cosmetics firm, then I deserve every thousand pounds I can screw from my fellow men.

Two arguments seem to lead Rawls to this result. The first is an extension of the dialogue with the worst off. At first sight, we might expect a dialogue with the best off, parallel to that with the worst off, designed to assure the best off that he was not being done down needlessly. Indeed, this is what justice would require, and Nozick is able to make much of the asymmetry of Rawls's concern.[3] If such a dialogue were carried out, it might transpire that some people deserved very well indeed of their fellow men, and ought, in justice, to be given a large share of the available goods. But Rawls alters the terms of the debate. Instead of discussing what society owes them, he discusses what they owe society.[4] And, of course, they owe society a lot. Not only do they depend on others for their breeding and nurture, as we all do, but they, more than most of us, depend on society for the ambience of their success. Marlborough could have won no victories, had not England provided him with armies. Every discoverer is able to see further than other men only because, like, Newton, he has stood on other men's shoulders. It would be difficult to invent xerox on a desert island, and pointless, as there would be no market for it. We can reasonably point out to any great man who is minded to make too much of his own greatness, and to regard himself as entirely his own creation and as such entitled to extort from society everything he can, that this is very

[3] Robert Nozick, *Anarchy, State and Utopia*, Oxford, 1974, pp. 192 ff.
[4] *A Theory of Justice*, p. 103.

far from the case, and that the great should be mindful of their obligations to those lesser breeds, without whom they would never have been able to be great. The great need society, and it would be unjust as well as inexpedient for them to drive a very hard bargain with society. But it does not follow from this that they should accept as fair any bargain society chooses to offer them. Yet, according to Rawls, this is what they are to do. Whereas the worst off are to be offered the best bargain that can possibly be given them, the great are to be offered only standard terms on a take-it-or-leave-it basis—without the option of leaving it. They need society, and society would not be society unless it included every-one, even the worst off: therefore, they must offer terms that will win acceptance even from the worst off, namely the best possible terms from the worst off's point of view. Instead of considering a succession of dialogues between society and each individual, Rawls has selectively identified with society when the dialogue is with the worst off, and with the great when society is engaged in dialogue with them, in both cases imposing a sort of *noblesse oblige*. We, who are unpoor, feel guilty when in our imaginations we are confronted with the poor, and we are conscious of what society ought to do for them: we, who sometimes like to number ourselves in the ranks of the great and the good, feel guilty when we remember how much we have entered into the labours of other men, and sense an obligation to labour for other men. Both obligations are real, but they are not *pari passu*. And if we are to give an adequate account of justice, we must set like in balance with like.

Rawls's second argument for dismissing the claims of those who deserve well is that they do not deserve to be the people they are. He says

The initial endowment of natural assets and the contingencies of their growth and nurture are arbitrary from a moral point of view ... the effort a person is willing to make is influenced by his natural abilities and skills and the alternatives open to him. The better endowed are more likely, other things being equal, to strive conscientiously ...[5]

And from this he concludes that talents and efforts are irrelevant to the distribution of the available goods. It is, again, a counter-intuitive conclusion, and the argument is far from clear. What does 'arbitrary from a moral point of view' mean? And what is its

[5] *A Theory of Justice*, §48, pp. 311–12; see also §§12, 17, pp. 74–5, 104.

relevance to questions of justice? Rawls seems to be wanting to eliminate all elements of contingency from the distribution of available goods. Marlborough was lucky. His great gifts might have come to nought if he had lived in another age, if he had not changed sides opportunely in 1688, if Louis XIV had not needed humbling, if a stray bullet or sudden fever had brought him to an untimely death. Therefore, Rawls seems to be saying, he should not have been given Blenheim palace, because he did not deserve to be lucky. But this is a *non sequitur*. Marlborough was being rewarded not for being lucky but for taking advantage of the opportunities fortune offered. In natural science as well as human affairs, causes are operative only against a background of conditions *sine qua non*. But this fact does not detract from the causal efficacy of causes.

Rawls yearns for a theodicy. To be morally acceptable, a distribution must be justified completely. It is not enough that a man has made, by his own efforts and abilities, a contribution to the success of a joint enterprise: we must be sure that no other extraneous factor enters into our calculation, which cannot be explained in a morally satisfactory way; and, if that hurdle be surmounted, we must also face the question why he has those abilities and made those efforts. Such a theodicy is neither possible within an ordinary conceptual scheme that accommodates the concepts of responsibility and desert, nor necessary. We are responsible for our actions: our actions are influenced by our circumstances, for which we are, usually, not responsible, and which are, in Rawls's terminology, arbitrary from a moral point of view; if their being arbitrary from a moral point of view precludes our being responsible for our actions, which they influence, then we are never responsible for our actions. Moreover, the question why a man has the abilities he has and makes the efforts he makes is not one that can be answered completely within the framework of moral responsibility. Moral responsibility is essentially a first- and second-personal concept. It means, etymologically, answerability; my answering you or your answering me, with respect to the question "Why did you do that?" Reasons—even good reasons—may be given, but they are essentially reasons from the agent's point of view, and when all such reasons have been given there is no room, from the agent's point of view, for any further explanation why the agent was able to assess the force of these reasons or chose to act on them. If the question is asked, it must be from the standpoint of the spectator, not that of the agent, and if it is pressed, it forces a corresponding shift of perspective. From the spectator's point of view there may be some explanation—though not, I believe, a complete explanation[6]—of a man's being able to, and actually choosing to, act the way he does. But this is a perspective which, if regarded as giving a complete account of the world, leaves no room for responsibility. It is essentially a third-personal view of man. It is a fair criticism of Rawls, that, like the utilitarians, he tends to regard people as pets, who have feelings and ought to be well cared for, rather than rational agents who act on their own responsibility. And in pressing the question why a man has the abilities he has and makes the efforts he makes, Rawls is insisting on seeing him from a third-personal point of view, in which agency and responsibility do not figure. It is not surprising, then, that a theodicy based on such an assumption is lacking. Fortunately, however, it is not needed. We do not have to have a complete explanation in order to have an adequate one. If you have green fingers, and spend a lot of time pruning and spraying your roses, and I have no way with plants, and spend my time in the pub, those facts constitute an adequate explanation of your roses being better than mine, and of your winning the prize in the village flower show instead of me. No doubt other factors had a bearing on the result. It was hard luck that the one time I did spray my roses there was a thunderstorm shortly afterwards which washed off the spray. You were lucky to have once been gardener's boy in Lord Wideacre's establishment, when I was wasting my time on O-levels. But these factors "so arbitrary from a moral point of view"[7] are irrelevant to the issue. In my prayers I may thank God that I am not as other men are, or, more modernly, bellyache that I was not born with the talents and advantages I suppose other men to have, but in the world of human affairs I am responsible for my actions and must accept the consequences of what I actually do or fail to do.

Rawls has an incoherent view of human nature. Although for the most part, as we have noted, he sees it from a third-personal point of view, in the same way as utilitarians do, he takes a strongly first-

---

[6] See J. R. Lucas, *The Freedom of the Will*, Oxford, 1970; and more specifically, J. R. Lucas, 'Pelagius and St. Augustine', *Journal of Theological Studies*, N.S., XXII, Pt. 1 (April, 1971), pp. 84–5, reprinted in J. R. Lucas, *Freedom and Grace*, London, 1976, pp. 13–15.

[7] *A Theory of Justice*, p. 72.

and second-personal point of view in the debates he supposes to occur in the original position when we are discussing what sort of constitution to have. In these debates we are all to be very rational, and any decisions we make are to be binding ones which we can be held to thereafter. But we are not to have a coherent view of ourselves, or know what we are going to do. The veil of ignorance is so thick that I, in my original rational capacity, cannot know what sort of person I am going to be; and hence should make a prudent choice to secure that I shall not fare too badly if I turn out to be a feckless and irresponsible type. But this concept of personal identity is so much eviscerated that it cannot bear any weight of subsequent argument. Knowledge of oneself and an ability now to form intentions about one's future conduct are essential constituents of personality. Take away all my peculiar traits and characteristics, and I am no longer me. Take away my power of deciding my future plans of action, and I am not a rational agent at all. Consider someone in the original position wondering what line to take on punishment. According to our normal way of thinking, he might rationally approve of some punishments—say life-imprisonment for murder—reckoning that it would diminish his chance of being murdered while leaving it open to him not to incur any risk of life-imprisonment by the simple expedient of not murdering anyone. But Rawls forbids that line of reasoning. I do not know who I shall be. I may be, for all I know, a compulsive murderer, in which case I should be far better off if there are no' punishments, or, at worst, only very light ones. Normally we need to distinguish the two choices:

(1) I choose that if I were to be a murderer I should be punished.
(2) If I were a murderer I should choose to be punished.

Rawls's veil of ignorance makes it impossible to separate them, because I have no continuing identity through the veil to distinguish myself with my actual choice from hypothetical persons with hypothetical choices. This confusion greatly strengthens his egalitarian argument. If I had been a Founding Father of the United States, I might well have voted for the Constitution on the grounds that, apart from its other merits, it provided a framework within which I could pursue my own happiness to the best of my ability. But if I had been persuaded by Rawls, I should have opted for some other system which gave me less freedom to rise or fall, on the grounds that for all I knew I might be congenitally unable to pursue my own happiness, and would fare less badly under a modern welfare state. If I were a born loser, I should want very different rules from those which would appeal to me if I were simply an ordinary man in the original position. Rational agents simply discussing what rules might be best for their society, might well reckon that the concepts of responsibility and desert should have their part to play, and that goods should on occasion be distributed on that basis. It is only if they cannot have any reason to suppose that they will continue to be able to act responsibly, and regard their future position as being not under control at all, that they will have reason to concentrate all their concern on ensuring that, whatever befalls them in the lottery of life, they cannot come off too badly. But that is an unreal supposition. In order to reach Rawls's conclusion realistically, we must construe his argument not as a debate in the original position employing a defective concept of personal identity, but as a dialogue with actual persons who are actually worst off. To them can reasonably be imputed a choice of constitution which will most alleviate their condition. If I am badly off I may well opt for that system which would do most for the badly off, whereas it is far from clear that otherwise I would opt for that system on the grounds that if I were to do badly, it would benefit me most.

Rawls is wrong, then, to concentrate exclusively on the underdog, and to discount altogether each man's responsibility for his own actions, and the corresponding possibility that one man may deserve more than another on account of what he has actually done, and the greater contribution he has made to the success of some joint enterprise. Everyone needs to be considered. As we saw in Chapter Nine, justice is not the same as equality, and it is possible that someone is given too little even though he is given the same as everybody else. We cannot rule out the possibility that some of those who are relatively well off are being given less than they should. In the present egalitarian climate of opinion it is worth paying particular attention to the plight of the overdog, and consider whether he has any legitimate complaint against society. True, he needs society. So does everybody. Like everybody else he has social obligations. But unless we accept the logic of Leviathan, and confer on the State absolute sovereignty, and deny to individuals any rights against the State, we cannot on that score justify placing disproportionately heavier burdens on the rich than on the poor. True also, and more pertinently, that the rich have often benefited from society more than the poor, and in particular that often society provides them with the matrix of their success. Latter-day advocates of *laissez-faire* overlook this point, and too readily assume that a man's achievements are all his own, and that he owes nothing to society for being enabled to put his talents to good use. These points may be granted, but they go no way to showing that the individual is simply the product of his society, or that his actions are not in any real sense his own. We feel a certain discomfort at Rawls's readiness to make out that, so far as the good and the great are concerned, their natural abilities are simply a "collective asset".[8] As Nozick points out, this does not take seriously the individuality of persons, and is tantamount to regarding these men merely as means, and not at all as ends-in-themselves.[9] Great natural abilities do not just come upon a man. They have to be cultivated and tended. There is much perspiration in genius. Those who achieve great things do so at great cost to themselves—if only of simple pleasures forgone and quiet low content not enjoyed. It is unrealistic to suppose that natural abilities could be exploited except on terms which were accepted as fair. Solzhenitsyn's *First Circle* is credible—just—as a work of fiction, because the scientists employed are both confined to very narrow tasks and are very anxious to continue being able to do science. Once we move to the wider range of general administration, it becomes altogether incredible: could Stalin and the supreme soviet have run Russia on *First Circle* terms? Rulers must be given power; and therefore cannot be simply exploited on terms they reject as unjust. Nor is this just a counsel of expediency. Rather, it reveals the nature of certain social transactions. They are essentially non-manipulative. I cannot merely manipulate rulers, administrators, thinkers, poets and playwrights: if I am to do business with them at all, it must be on a basis of co-operation, and therefore must be on terms acceptable to them as paying proper regard to their point of view as well as advantageous to me. Hence the need for justice, and a recognition of the validity of their claims to proper consideration as well as those of everybody else. If they have made a greater contribution than others, that fact needs to be taken into account. It is not necessarily the only fact, nor does it override all other

[8] *A Theory of Justice*, p. 179.   [9] *Anarchy, State and Utopia*, p. 228.

considerations. Other bases than desert are sometimes relevant to distribution: it is fair to take into the reckoning other goods that the great enjoy, and the fact that often they would have been unable to achieve great things themselves were it not for the opportunities society offered. But if we altogether discount desert, we are implicitly denying that it was due to them at all that they exerted themselves and exercised their talents on our behalf. And if we deny that, and make out that it was in no way up to them whether they gave themselves to our affairs or not, we are regarding them as not possessed of a mind of their own, and as not being really persons at all, but merely things. And that is to do them the most grievous injustice of all.

11

FREEDOM, RESPONSIBILITY AND DESERT

The relationship between justice and freedom is complex. At first sight they seem to be opposed. Justice lays down what treatment should be accorded to people, whereas freedom assigns the decision to an individual and allows him to make up his mind for himself. If I am just I must have regard for others, whereas if I am free I am allowed to decide regardless of them. But this opposition, although real, does not make justice and freedom exclusive. Although if I am free, I am free to be unjust, I do not have to be unjust, and can, and should, choose justly. Indeed, only if I am free and dealing with free men, does the question of my acting justly or unjustly arise. At a deeper level, too, there is an important link between justice and freedom. For only if people are free, are they responsible for their actions, and their actions are the chief constituent of their deserts: and, although there are other bases than desert for determining how people ought to be treated, desert is pre-eminent. People ought to be done by according to how they deserve, and how they deserve depends on how they have done, which in turn presupposes responsibility and freedom. Doing constitutes deserving, and deserving determines how justice should be done; and thus justice depends on freedom.

The opposition between justice and freedom is of profound importance. It means that we cannot guarantee them both. If we have freedom, men may use their freedom unjustly. In a free society, although men may exercise their freedom with due consideration of others, we cannot be sure that they will, and therefore if we want to ensure that our society is an entirely just society, we must abridge freedom so that no unjust decision can stand. It must be a society in which there are no liberties or rights, and no importance is attached to who should take a decision, but only to what decision should be taken. Such a society will be static, impersonal and stultifying. If, however, we admit liberty, giving some people some discretion to decide as thy think fit, then they may decide wrong. It may be in good faith—each man doing what is right in his own eyes, although to other men it seems wrong—or it may be done with blatant disregard for others—each man seeking to maximise his own profit, or doing what comes naturally or what seems fun: and although we might hope that a society of free men would be one in which they all freely reached right decisions, such an ideal never has been reached, nor, if we accept any Christian doctrine of original sin or any naturalist view of the innate tendencies of *homo sapiens*, ever will. Certainly, we must acknowledge that freedom may result in injustice, and, if we are realistic, we must recognise furthermore that it sometimes will. Absolute freedom and absolute justice are thus incompatible. In part, this should not surprise us. Absolute freedom is impossible anyhow, in any world in which there is more than one person: and justice, as we saw in Chapter One, is not the basic concept, but rather injustice, from which it follows that it is difficult in any case to make justice absolute. But the incompatibility cuts deep. It is not merely an absence of conceptual perfection, but will manifest itself in the presence of actual injustices and actual unfreedom. We are constantly having to make hard choices and compromise justice for the sake of freedom, or freedom for the sake of justice.

This opposition is of such great importance that it is sometimes misconstrued. It is supposed not simply that we cannot guarantee them both, which is true, but that we cannot have them both, which is false. Lovers of liberty, therefore, have been jealous of justice, and have sought to extrude it from political consideration for fear of its fettering freedom. They have engaged in a sustained critique of justice, which they regard as a left-wing collectivist concept inimical to individual liberty, and have sought to restrict it to simple rule-observance according to the principle of legality. Each man, on their view, is free, within the limits set by law, to do as he thinks fit, and therefore may reasonably be expected to do as he pleases in general, and in particular so as to maximise his pecuniary gain. This is a confusion, and a disastrous one. It confuses conferring on men the right to make decisions and inviting them to choose as they please, and also confuses what we expect men *to* do and what we expect *that* they sometimes will do.[1] In giving men the right to decide, we may expect them to decide rationally,

---

[1] A. D. Woozley, "Injustice", *American Philosophical Quarterly*, Monograph No. 7, Oxford, 1973, pp. 119–21.

responsibly or justly, or we may not: often there is a presumption in favour of the former, so much so that we specify explicitly "You are to do as you like", or "You are to spend it as you please" on these occasions where it is not to hold. In conferring freedom we are not excluding some understanding how it is to be exercised; we are only saying who shall take the decision, and that his decision, even though wrong, shall stand. It may be one of the conditions for the survival of a free society that most of the decisions taken freely shall be taken responsibly, and, where other men's interests are involved, justly, as well. Whether this is so or not, it is perfectly intelligible to expect men to exercise their freedom reasonably, although not having any remedy in those cases which, we expect, will sometimes occur, where men decide arbitrarily, irresponsibly or unfairly. It is a mistake to suppose that a free society is one in which decisions are expected to be, and are, taken with scant regard for justice; or to think of justice as necessarily opposed to freedom, or as a monopoly of the left. It is to read into men's motives an unconcern for the interests of others that need not and often does not obtain. Men are not made selfish by being made free: if anything, the opposite. We can hope—must hope, if society is to survive in tolerable form—that decisions freely taken will, by and large, be fair, and that although in some cases they will not be, and although we cannot reckon ever to have a society which is absolutely free and absolutely just, nevertheless a free society will not be grossly unjust and a reasonably just society can be achieved through free institutions.

It is evident that the question of just dealing on my part arises only if I am free: it is not so evident that justice presupposes freedom in those I am dealing with. Yet whereas I can, if I am free, be said to act kindly towards animals, I cannot be said to act justly. In order to act justly, I must not merely be nice towards them, acting with tender regard for their interests, but must be guided in my actions by a *rational* regard for them. My actions must be undertaken for reasons into which *they* can enter. And if they are creatures incapable of reasoning, then they could not possibly enter into the reasoning behind my actions, and validate it as just. So, similarly, I can be unkind to animals, but not unfair, except in so far as I have humanised them, and arouse legitimate expectations which I then disappoint. There is some difficulty over infants and imbeciles, who cannot reason but can be described as being treated fairly or unfairly. In the case of infants this is defended on the ground of their being potentially rational agents, although not actually capable of exercising reason yet. In the case of imbeciles the argument is extended further, and we view them as untypical instances of a type that is characteristically rational, and accord to them the same respect as is due generally to members of the human species. Imbeciles are, we are sure, human; it is only some abnormality which prevents them manifesting normal human capacities: and therefore, although granted this abnormality, they cannot understand reason, they are, essentially, of a kind to understand reason, and should be treated as such. It is not too far-fetched a counterfactual to think of an imbecile as being in possession of his senses; whereas to think of a ratiocinating dog is not really to think of a dog at all.

Rationality, then, is presupposed on the part of those being justly treated as well as of those who are treating them justly, because it is essential to the concept that both those who are doing it and those who are being done by should be able to agree with each other, since both can enter into the reasoning behind the action, and acknowledge its adequacy. For this reason also the previous actions of the man affected by the action are likely to be peculiarly relevant. In so far as he is rational, he is responsible for what he has done, and in the absence of special considerations to the contrary, deserves to be treated accordingly. Although there are other considerations, which may under some conditions override desert as a basis for determining what ought to be done, those other considerations are more extraneous, and less essentially part of the man concerned than his own actions. I can disown the legal system under which I live, or my parentage, or the colour of my skin, much more readily than I can disown my own actions. My actions are essentially mine, what I ought to own up to, and are therefore disowned only with extreme difficulty, on pain of great penitence and a complete change of heart. That apart, I must stand by my actions, more than by anything else, as peculiarly constitutive of my own identity. Being an agent, I am what I do, and therefore am, as of now unalterably, what I have done. The things I have done constitute the most uncontestable, although not the only, premisses for any argument about what should happen to me. Hence the fundamental significance of desert.

This argument does not establish the exclusive pre-eminence of desert. Merit could also lay claim to being equally constitutive of what a man is, and so equally incontestable as a basis for argument. A long line of liberal argument regards promises as the one safe ground for all moral reasoning, and would therefore reckon that agreements freely entered into were what we could fairly hold men to when distributing benefits. In our religious moments we know that what a man does is at best an uncertain reflection of his true moral worth, and that in any case the best things in life are beyond deserving, and must be given freely if given at all. We therefore are doubtful about desert. We are not quite sure what it is—whether, and if so how, it is to be distinguished from merit or moral worth—and we are uncertain about making it the pre-eminently fair basis of distribution. Under Rawls's concentrated gaze,[2] it seemed morally arbitrary that one man should do better than another, and outward doing appeared insufficiently intrinsic to a man's worth for us to be able to ground a final judgement on them.

We can concede the force of some of these doubts. The justice we are propounding is not a poetic justice, but only a very homespun one. Desert is not always the right basis of distribution: even when it is, it may not accord with the true moral worth of individuals. And, as we shall see in Chapter Sixteen, justice does not encompass all moral virtue, and there may be something objectionable in insisting too much on one's just deserts. But it is a weak argument to complain that desert does not correspond to some other, better basis of distribution, unless one is prepared to take that other basis seriously. Plato or Aristotle can reject mere deeds in favour of true ἀξία because they are prepared to distribute benefits according to this ἀξία. Modern sceptics, however, do not wish to replace desert by some other individualised reason which is, they claim, even more integral to the personality. They complain that it is not integral enough, and having rejected it on that ground, replace it by some other, much more extraneous basis, such as status. But this is an unapt argument to reach that objective.

That desert, although not the only, nor an unsurpassably ideal, basis for the distribution of benefits, is nevertheless a pre-eminent one, can be seen if we continue the argument of the previous chapter and consider further what goes wrong if it is systematically discountenanced. There emerges, in the first place, an incoherence between our treatment of men's individual and their joint enterprises. It would seem that if men do not deserve any share in the fruits of their co-operative labours, they do not deserve either to enjoy the results of the operations of their own unaided efforts. If desert is no sort of basis at all for allocating the yield of some n-person non-zero-sum game, then it is not so in the special case where $n=1$, in which we are dealing with the single man's game against nature. But this is deeply counter-intuitive, and would undercut the whole concept of action. Action differs from mere bodily behaviour in being "homeostatic". The feedback is monitored, and further movements made in the light of it, so as to bring about some state of affairs, fulfil some requirement, or maintain some condition. Actions, that is, are guided by some evaluation of them or their effects. If the agent could not evaluate them, he could not act at all. Action presupposes some evaluation on the part of the agent: that is to say, that the agent shall, in some way, enjoy the fruits of his labours. This is the conceptual foundation of Locke's insight that the paradigm example of ownership is a man's ownership of his actions, so that "mixing with one's labour" constitutes the original and most natural title to property. We may not follow Locke all the way, but unless we allow the link between doing and deserving, we subvert the concept of doing altogether, and with it that of responsibility. This illuminates at a deeper level our criticism of Rawls's theory, as of the utilitarianism from which it is derived, that it treats people as patients rather than agents.[3]

If we deny people their deserts, we are not really treating them as persons because we are taking them for granted. They are not in our eyes autonomous agents who had it in their power to act or not to act, but merely natural phenomena which we have been manipulating at our will. Thus we have our second counter-argument not only against Rawlsian scepticism but against any refusal to take desert seriously, namely that it implicitly denies personal agency and responsibility in the general n-person co-operative enterprise as well as in the special case where only one person is operating on his own. The success of the co-operative enterprise depends on a number of different people contributing their own efforts and expertise, and it was up to each individual taking part to decide whether or not to co-operate. Of course, there were good reasons why each person should. But there may have been also, for all we know, weighty reasons against making the necessary effort. In any case, we are not entitled to take it for granted that any man has no

[3] See above, Ch. 10, pp. 194–6, Ch. 3, pp. 65–6.

alternative but to act the way we want him to. Whatever the weight of argument, the final choice is his. He may well—we hope he will—act in a co-operative way, but he does not have to, and we owe it to him, in recognition of this fact, to acknowledge that the success of the joint enterprise, and the benefits brought thereby, are due, in part, to what he did. His doing was part cause of the common good, so that when it comes to distributing the good, we need to see it from his point of view, as something which he produced, in part, and could have chosen not to. The action must make sense from his point of view, as well as from ours, and must be one that it would have been reasonable for him, recognising both his point of view and ours, without their being in conflict, to undertake. The concept of desert stems from these two different views of a man's deeds. Each contribution is seen from our collective view as contributing to the success of the joint enterprise and from the contributor's point of view as his own action, which he was free to withold but did, in fact, contribute, and which was his very own contribution to the production of the common good. Because it served our purposes, it is a desert, and because it was his doing, it is his desert. And the rationale of taking desert as the basis of distribution is that on this basis we can most readily harmonize the two different views of a man's deeds. His deed was undertaken in order to forward the joint enterprise, true: that explained why it was undertaken and makes it a rational thing to have done. But equally, from his own point of view, if we impute to him a rational concern for his own interest, it should not prove utterly quixotic. Although he may not have undertaken it in order to forward his own interests, yet were the natural Adam in him to review his actions at the end of the day, his contributions to the joint enterprise will not be seen to have been from that interested point of view in vain.

The common thread throughout is a collective recognition of each contributor's individuality, and the legitimacy of his individual interest. We do not suppose that he is animated by interested motives, only that he reasonably might be. A man may merge his individual interest altogether in the collective interest, or may be fired by a disinterested zeal for altruistic aims: but it is for him to decide that, and not for us to suppose it on his behalf. In so far as we consider things from his point of view, we ought to consider the interests he might have if he were not altogether altruistic, in the same way as we and others, in enjoying the benefits of the co-operative enterprises, are serving our own, non-altruistic aims. If we are benefiting in respect of some assignable interest, so should he. Else we are acting as though our private interests are a proper object to be secured by collective action, but his are not. In so far as the collective action generates assignable goods, we should take care that since it is constituted by a number of actions on the part of individuals, each person should benefit individually from the collective action, on the basis of his contribution to it.

The correlative of desert is reward, and rewards are not simply incentives. Rewards stand to incentives as punishments to deterrents. A punishment is annexed to wrongdoing, but does not constitute its wrongfulness. We punish people because what they have done is wrong, and not vice versa. So, too, with rewards. Rewards are given for deeds which were good anyhow. The action does not become good because it is rewarded, but is rewarded for being good. By contrast, an incentive is offered in lieu of argument. I do not give reasons why you should act in a certain way, but only undertake to pay you if you do. There is a veil of ignorance between us, not about facts but about values. You are not privy to my aims and ambitions, nor able to engage in argument with me about what ought to be done, or how it should be accomplished, but only know what you have to do in order to secure payment from me. And therefore, although you are free to accept or reject my proposition, you are excluded from my counsels. This underlies much of the moral discontent with the free market economy. It seems to be a system of mutual exploitation rather than of shared endeavour. Where, however, the aims of a joint enterprise are shared, each person concerned has reasons for what he is doing other than the mere desire for payment, and therefore might be expected to do his bit without payment. Payment is not the prime incentive, any more than punishment is the prime deterrent to the commission of crime. Nevertheless, rewards, like punishments, cannot be totally dispensed with. Rewards are tangible tokens of gratitude, as punishments are of disapproval.[4] They express the communal attitude to the individual doer of deeds. And they do it, in both cases, by translating the communal assessment of the deed into the language of individual interest, so as to secure that if the individual should be

---

[4] See above, Ch. 6, p. 132.

minded to assess his actions from a limited individual point of view, he will see that just as crime does not pay, so well-doing does.

The analogy between reward and punishment goes further. Both are for what actually has been done, and not for attitudes, thoughts, dispositions or states of mind, nor for moral merits or demerits. If a man has actually done wrong, it is fair to punish him for it, even though another may be morally a much worse person. So, too, we reward the man who actually did what was needed for the success of the joint enterprise, even though another may be morally —or socially—a much better person. Again, some wrongdoing is not punishable, and some activities are estimable, but constitute no ground for a claim to a share of some distributable good. Just as we can punish a man without believing him to be altogether bad, and let off a man who is much worse, so we can reward a man without believing him to be thoroughly estimable, and without rewarding a much better one. Culpability and desert, being limited to actual actions, constitute only a limited judgement which may be at variance with either an all-in judgement or another limited judgement on a different basis. Although providing much ammunition to the sceptic, it should not alarm us, once we recognise the limited contexts in which the concepts of culpability and desert operate. We are not called to take upon ourselves the divine office or to anticipate the day of judgement. The only judgements we are called on to make are limited in scope. If it falls upon us to distribute benefits, we need to consider how those benefits came to be. They seldom arise purely fortuitously, but are usually produced by careful contrivance and hard labour. They do not, as Nozick puts it, fall from heaven like manna.[5] Windfalls are few, and most good things have to be worked for, and because they are the result of many labours, perhaps by many hands, arrive on the scene fully structured, with strong indications of appropriate bases of apportionment. It is, in the absence of other considerations or agreement to the contrary, right to have regard to what people did towards the production of the benefit, and not the other things that they did, or their personal merits or ultimate moral worth, because that is what was relevant to the production of the benefit and so should be relevant to its distribution. Although other judgements are possible about the other things that they did—just as the criminal may have done many acts of kindness, and the man who keeps on the right

[5] *Anarchy, State and Utopia*, p. 198.

side of the law may have none the less committed many odious sins—and the final assessment of his character may be quite different from the limited assessment of his desert in the particular case in question, the limited assessment is in this particular case none the less the right one. What he actually did is integral to his individual identity although not exhaustive of it. We can allow that there are other, more intrinsic facets of his individuality still, but should not disown his deeds for him. They are undubitably his. They were incontestably done. And it was on account of them, and not anything else about him, that the benefit came to be. And therefore, when that benefit is being distributed, what he did towards its production is the relevant individualised reason by which his share should be determined.

Desert is difficult to determine. For many large co-operative enterprises it is hard to know what everyone is doing, let alone assess its contribution to the activity as a whole. Often the principle is more important than the practice, and then some conventional measure is, for reasons which will emerge in Chapter Thirteen, acceptable. Sometimes there is a scale of fees, sometimes the market provides a standard. But the market really measures indispensability rather than desert. In conditions of perfect competition, a man will be paid as much as it would cost to find a substitute, and the more indispensable he is, the higher he is paid. This half represents our thinking about desert. In a complicated activity there are many jobs which are essential—the patient will die if the anaesthetist dozes off or the maintenance man fuses the operating-theatre lights, as well as if the surgeon cuts an artery; but we regard them as less constitutive of the joint activity because more standard. Gross negligence on the part of maintenance men—or a signalman or a sentry—could cause disaster: slight negligence on the part of an anaesthetist could be fatal: with the surgeon there are no guidelines, and he is always having to use his own judgement, and the slightest error of judgement will kill the patient. More, therefore, depends on the surgeon than on the anaesthetist, and much more than on the maintenance staff. Again, it is part of the logic of action that one man is responsible for what another man does, if he had told him to, advised him, or put him up to it. We therefore see those who organize or supervise as being more responsible than those who are organized or supervised, and the actions of the former as being more closely identified with the joint activity as a whole. Generals deserve a larger share of the booty than do privates.

The principles can be refined. Besides responsibility and supervision, much attention is paid to skill, qualifications (especially, in the modern world, paper ones) and seniority; these are criteria for determining, admittedly still only imprecisely, what different people's deserts are. The concept of desert is not, *pace* Rawls, a wholly indeterminate one, and can therefore be a basis for distributing the benefits and burdens of a joint enterprise fairly. It is not the only one, and it can be waived altogether. But in the absence of agreement to the contrary it is, in a wide range of cases, an appropriate one, and to ignore it altogether is implicitly to deny the individuality of the contributors and their status as autonomous agents, who make full rational choices and are responsible for their deeds.

12

PACTA SUNT SERVANDA

The concept of desert is vulnerable from the right as well as from the left. It is criticized by Hayek and Nozick as being indeterminate and incoherent, and therefore to be replaced, not by some species of equality, but by agreement.[1] Justice consists in keeping one's agreements. Men are free to enter into any agreements they choose, and good things are to be distributed in accordance with their entitlement under those agreements. All other bases of distribution either can be subsumed under some antecedent agreement, implicit or explicit, or are to be rejected as unwarranted interferences with existing contracts or men's freedom to make future ones: they are hangovers from an earlier, tribal stage of human development, and are to be discountenanced as irrational and economically counter-productive. The ideal of distributive justice should be entirely eliminated in favour of that of commutative justice, and we shall fare better under a *laissez-faire* market economy than under any other system.

Many of Hayek's and Nozick's criticisms of contemporary thinking about justice are cogent. They are right to fear their totalitarian and illiberal presuppositions. It is a mistake for the State to attempt to give to each man a fair share of wealth or income according to some over-all scheme of distributive justice; and once we allow people freedom to make their own effective choices, the result will not fit any special pattern of supposedly just distribution. As we shall see in the next chapter, these points are of great importance for the understanding of economic justice. But they do not show that all notions of distributive justice are mistaken, but only that entitlement arising from antecedent agreement is one valid basis, and that, therefore, no other basis can be absolute. It can, however, be further argued that the admitted indeterminacy of desert can best

[1] F. A. Hayek, *The Constitution of Liberty*, London, 1960, esp. Ch. VI; *Law, Legislation and Liberty*, II, London, 1976, esp. Ch. IX; *New Studies in Philosophy, Politics, Economics and the History of Ideas*, London, 1978, Ch. 5, "The Atavism of Social Justice", pp. 57–68; Robert Nozick, *Anarchy, State and Utopia*, Oxford, 1974, Ch. VII, §1.

be remedied by a rational reconstruction which replaces it by agreement, and that this reconstruction, being *ex hypothesi* agreed to, is necessarily just. Moreover the classical analysis of the business bargain is simple and clear, and therefore much to be preferred to the vague and uncertain determination of desert.

Desert can easily be represented as being based on agreement, because it often contains a large conventional element, and can in any case be waived. The analogy with the law is instructive. Trades Union officials argue about differentials in much the same detailed, and sometimes pettifogging, way as do lawyers about rights. In each case the conventional element is large, but for different reasons. Law is, in large measure, conventional because of our need to know where we stand, and supplement our imperfect information about the intentions of others by common agreement on how we should act in specified circumstances.[2] Desert is, in large measure, conventional because it is expressive. It says 'Thank you'. It shows that we are not merely taking someone else for granted, nor simply exploiting him, but are recognising him as a fellow contributor to the generation of some distributable good. But there are many languages of gratitude, and 'thanks' can be expressed in different tokens. So long as they carry the meaning required, we are not manifesting disregard of the individual concerned or slighting his efforts. And that is largely a matter of convention.

Although, as we shall see later, claims of justice cannot always be waived, claims of desert are peculiarly open to being waived. This is because desert is based upon doing, and doing is largely constituted by intention. In order to describe an action, we need, not to characterize merely the bodily behaviour, but to specify the reasons for which it was undertaken. And my reasons can be unimpugnably altruistic. Although motives usually are mixed, they do not have to be. It may be the case that, even with assignable goods, my scale of values is, idiosyncratically, such, that if the outcome is that goods are assigned to others, my pay-off is as great as if they were assigned to me. Indeed, not always idiosyncratically: a man values his wife's good as much as his own, a mother her child's health, a father his son's success. In assessing desert we impute a self-interest, which is right in general to do, because self-interest is legitimate and to have regard to it manifests our respect for the individual, but which may be wrong in the particular case, simply because, as a matter of fact,

[2] See above, Ch. 3, pp. 58–9, Ch. 5, 104, 110–11.

the man is moved by entirely disinterested motives. To insist, against his every protestation, that he must be animated by self-interest, is, in yet another way, to disregard his individuality. If the outcome of the joint enterprise is already just what he wanted, we insult him if we assume that he could not have been so high-minded. If he has rendered some signal service to the common cause, but indicates that that fact alone is sufficient reward, nobody need feel thereafter that in not rewarding him according to his deserts he is taking him for granted: for it is he who has granted his services, and therefore to that extent, himself. There is no sense of exploiting the enthusiastic volunteer for a good cause. Although he is being used, he wanted to be used, and is achieving his own ends thereby.

It does not follow from all this, however, that desert can, or should, be always subsumed under, or replaced by, agreement. Although desert, like legal justice, often needs to be specified by conventions, it is not the case that any convention whatsoever is just. Laws, although duly enacted, can be unjust: bargains, although freely entered into, can be unfair. Laws seek to articulate principles of justice, applying them definitively to difficult cases: schemes of distribution should allocate fair shares to all concerned, determining what their desert is, so as to avoid jealousy, repining or subsequent dispute. More definitive than our crude intimations of desert, they should be in broad accord with our ideas about it. To deny desert altogether and to replace it entirely by agreement is to misconstrue the complexity of co-operative endeavours. It fails to accommodate the fact that the individual is acting, but within a co-operative framework. If we oust desert altogether in favour of agreement, we lose either the sense of individuality or that of co-operation. In the example just considered, where good men give their services free, waiving any claim to reward, because they so much identify with the common purpose that the success of the joint enterprise is all that they desire, their individual desires are being merged in the common aim, and for that reason there is no room for the application of desert. The replacement of desert by agreement can, however, lead to the opposite extreme where the parties see the bargain entirely from their own separate individual standpoints, and not from a joint point of view at all. Each then sees his actions as motivated exclusively by his desire to achieve his own, individual ends, and not in any sense as a contribution to a joint enterprise, and in so far as he serves others he does so merely as a means to secure their compliance with his own plans.

With this we reach the classical analysis of economic transactions. It is, fairly clearly, a different one from that in terms of desert, since it does not seek to accommodate the interplay between the individual and the collective point of view. But it has the great merits of simplicity and clarity, and many thinkers would have us use it in place of any based on desert, rejecting all other notions of the just wage or the just price as mere nostalgia for the obsolescent past. Many of their arguments are arguments of freedom or of economic efficiency, and do not concern us here—we have already seen in the previous chapter that we must sometimes compromise justice for freedom, and vice versa: equally we may sometimes see need to compromise justice for economic efficiency—and sometimes economic efficiency for justice. What concerns us here is the contention that a bargain freely entered into is *eo ipso* a fair one and that therefore commutative justice both is easily determined and should always replace claims based on desert. The contention is based on Aristotle's dictum, ἀδικεῖται δ'οὐδεὶς ἑκών,[3] nobody willing is wronged, which gave rise to the jurisconsults tag, *volenti non fit iniuria*. Since injustice is a matter of protest, I can choose not to protest, or debar myself from subsequently protesting. But not always. For there is a certain vicariousness in the concept of justice. Others may wax indignant on my behalf, even though I choose not to, and my placidity need not assuage their indignation; nor am I always totally debarred from complaining. It depends on how far the transaction was entered into purely as an exercise of my individual, perhaps idiosyncratic, will, and how far it was a standard situation to which a reasonable response might be expected. For the one-off transaction—the stranger exchanging beads for copra, or the rich business man commissioning his portrait from a fashionable painter[4]—it may well be true that a free bargain is necessarily a fair one. But it does not seem obviously true when we consider the garage charging an extortionate rate for petrol to a man hastening to visit his dying mother, or the grocer trebling his prices to a harassed housewife just before closing time.[5] If I take advantage of a man's temporary need, he may have no

---

[3] *Nicomachean Ethics*, V, 9, 6, 1136b 6; and V, 11, 3, 1138a 12.
[4] F. A. Hayek, *The Constitution of Liberty*, p. 136.
[5] See further below, Ch. 13, pp. 216–19.

reasonable alternative except to agree to my terms, but I am exploiting him none the less. He is, in effect, agreeing under duress, not the same duress as that suffered by a man whose life or children are threatened, but duress none the less in view of his situation and his normal pattern of life and expectations. We cannot, therefore, maintain that simply by agreeing to my terms he has waived all right of protest. And since we commonly do distinguish fair bargains from hard ones, it follows that the question whether it was just or not is not foreclosed by the fact of its having been entered into freely.

Underlying the distinction between the fair bargain and the free bargain are two different apprehensions of the nature of business and the nature of man. Classical economics offers an atomistic analysis of business transactions, and is usually, although not necessarily, based on an atomistic view of human nature. Most business transactions, however, are not isolated bargains but part of a general pattern of activity, typically involving standardised units of pecuniary value. Hence economic justice, as I shall argue in the next chapter, is not to be analysed in terms of a number of bilateral bargains each negotiated entirely separately on a take-it-or-leave-it basis, but is subject to certain third-party considerations and certain requirements of universalisability. Human beings also are not so separate as liberal theorists have commonly supposed. They share, to some limited extent, a common rationality and some common values. A man's decision to hasten to the bedside of his dying mother is one I can understand, enter into and identify with. Although each individual has a mind of his own which he can make up differently from everyone else, and though each of us must on many occasions make his own decisions without any assurance that others will endorse them too, many of our choices are shareable in the sense that others would regard them as natural and reasonable. To that extent there is an independent standard of choice other than the actual choice actually made on a particular occasion, and therefore others can feel vicariously for the agent and wax indignant on his behalf even though he makes no protest himself, and he can intelligibly disown his actual agreement as being unreasonably forced on him by the intransigence of the other party, and so not constituting a conclusive bar to his protesting himself at the unfairness of the terms he was offered and had no real alternative but to accept.

The market economy cannot be defended as being necessarily just. It does not follow that it is necessarily unjust. Indeed, sometimes we should be acting unjustly if we denied men the right to enter into contracts, even disadvantageous ones, freely. Justice, being concerned not only with men's interests but their rights, must accord to them some liberty which they may use to their own, as well as to others', disadvantage. It is not fair on men always to treat them paternalistically, forcing them to act in their own interests, because that is not to regard them as rational autonomous agents, capable of making up their own minds on what to do. Hence there is an argument from justice for countenancing even unjust contracts. But the fact that we—at least sometimes—allow even unfair contracts to be made and enforced does not mean that they are not unfair. They have something of the same ambiguous status as unjust laws. In extreme cases they cease to bind. It is somewhat easier for the courts to set aside very unjust contracts than to acknowledge the invalidity of very unjust laws, but in general they do men despite if they will not recognise their word as being their bond. To this extent, then, justice upholds the sanctity of business obligations. We may go further, on grounds of liberty or economic efficiency, and agree to govern our affairs by means of a market economy, and then, again, justice will require that we abide by our agreements. But it does not follow that there are no arguments of justice on the other side, or that no criticisms can be made of the market economy on the score of justice.

The market economy is fundamentally unsuitable as a way of resolving problems such as the Prisoners' Dilemma and the Battle of the Sexes.[6] In practice we find it unapt for producing public goods, for dealing with neighbourhood effects, or on account of the exclusion of third parties. We have evolved a number of political and social institutions to deal with these problems and need to develop further ones: and they will be typically resistant to the classical analysis, and will give rise to considerations of justice that cannot be altogether subsumed under the heading of agreement. Hayek concedes that "In a spontaneous order undeserved disappointments cannot be avoided. They are bound to cause grievances and a sense of having been treated unjustly, although nobody has acted unjustly."[7] Nozick allows that a succession of separate

---

[6] See above, Ch. 3, pp. 46–58, 60–1.
[7] *Law, Legislation and Liberty*, II, p. 127.

bilateral business transactions may disadvantage an individual, just as one person may be left out in the cold if everybody else pairs off together, but seeks to non-suit the complainants. "Against whom", he asks, "would the rejected suitor have a legitimate complaint? Against what?",[8] but this is to give too short a shrift to complainants. Although not all disappointments give good ground for grievance, and many misfortunes are not injustices, we cannot brush aside all complaints against the market economy or make out that to say the system is unfair is unintelligible. It is perfectly intelligible to say a game—e.g. roulette or *vingt et un*—is unfair,[9] and likewise it is intelligible (though not necessarily correct) to say that the *laissez-faire* system is unfair, because if all entitlements depend on previous bargains, there will be a great premium on bargaining power, so that to those who already have will be given more, while from those who have not will be taken away even the little they had. Nozick draws an analogy between his "justice in transfer" and rules of inference, inasmuch as the one preserves justice as the other does truth, but this analogy is uncomfortable on the score of how holdings may justly be acquired in the first place.[10] William the Conqueror and his barons may have won the Battle of Hastings, but that hardly constitutes just title for them and their heirs, and if we adopt an entirely historical view of justice, it would be open to those who regarded themselves as the successors to the Saxons to reopen the question of who really had the right to England's wealth, much as we can allow that certain conclusions follow logically from given premises but deny that either the premises or the conclusions are actually true. On these or on other grounds we may maintain that the market economy is unfair either in general or in certain particular respects, and the complaint cannot be always non-suited on the grounds that no one person is responsible, nor estopped on the grounds that we had earlier agreed to be bound by its operations.

The general contention that the keeping of covenants constitutes the whole of justice, and that the market economy is not only the freest and most efficient form of organization but of necessity the fairest too, is mistaken. It neither exhausts, nor excludes, justice. The rational reconstruction of desert in terms of agreement is

---

[8] *Anarchy, State and Utopia*, p. 237.
[9] See above, Ch. 1, p. 6.
[10] *Anarchy, State and Utopia*, p. 151.

neither called for nor capable of being carried through adequately. Agreement is a different concept from desert, and a cruder one, since it fails to represent the interplay between the individual and the collective point of view. Although sometimes a man may settle by agreement with another how their deserts shall be defined, or may by agreement waive his own claims based on desert, identifying his individual with the common interest, he may also, if he is not careful, be doing just the opposite, ignoring every other interest than his own personal one. To do this is to deny justice quite as much as is done by the collectivists who accord no weight to individual interests, but consider only some common interest or some impersonal principle of distribution. As, when the egalitarians deny its validity, they are implicitly denying the individuality of autonomous agents; so, when libertarians deny its validity and seek to replace it entirely by agreements freely negotiated between two parties each seeking to obtain the best possible terms for himself, they are manifesting an unconcern for each individual's own point of view and own interest. And that, too, is unjust.

13

ECONOMIC JUSTICE

Economic justice is usually taken to be the same as distributive justice, but is really a distinct species, in which the communal activity that generates a distributable good is of a very special kind, and in which purely distributive considerations are tempered by those of liberty and what Aristotle calls commutative justice. This is largely due to the nature of money, which is a peculiar sort of good, whose very logic imposes its own conditions on how it is to be distributed.

It is difficult to give an adequate account of money. Most economists trace its development from prehistoric barter to contemporary credit transfers, but leave it unclear why modern money works. Unlike other goods, it is entirely conventional. It was not always so, when sovereigns were golden, and *argent* really shone with a silver gleam, and then one could understand why people wanted to possess it and would accept it in exchange for earthenware pots or finely wrought ivories. But for a long time the currency has not needed adventitious attractions to enable it to fulfil its economic functions. Nearly all currencies now are merely nominal tokens with no other attraction than that they carry a conventional value, and are to be coveted by any one man just because they are coveted by others. From this it follows that the classic paradigm of the isolated bargain is inadequate. If I exchange a pot of olive oil for a chunk of yellow metal, the transaction could be viewed in isolation, and construed as a simple exchange. But when I fill up my car, and tender a piece of paper or a credit card, it is clear that this particular transaction can only be understood by reference to certain conventions and within the context of many similar transactions. Money is not a function of just the two contracting parties, but of the whole society. From this there flow important, collectivist, consequences. But they, though important, do not constitute the chief moral to be drawn from the nature of money. For money is not just conventional, to be valued merely because others value it, or the confidence trick would soon be exposed, and money pass out of fashion. Although its value depends on social confidence, it is maintained not only by its social utility but by its serving individual purposes. Money is valuable for me not simply in that other people value it, but in that, because it is valued by other people, it confers on me a certain freedom of choice. That is, I value money not primarily because, since other people do, I shall acquire prestige in their eyes by possessing it, or make them envious, or bolster my own ego—though these motives play their part—but because I can spend it. And the reason why spending is good is that it enables me to exercise choices I otherwise could not exercise. Although I may have mortgaged some of my freedom of action, I can in general spend my money as I choose. And hence it is necessarily a good. Ability to achieve one's ends is the paradigm good, just as imprisonment is the paradigm punishment. There may be other things we all regard as good—gold or silver or strawberries or music—just as we all dislike being burnt or beaten or subjected to electric shocks. But we do not have to regard the former as good or the latter as evil, even though in fact we all do. Whereas, if we are rational agents at all, we must all want to be able to do whatsoever we want to do. Our other values may vary—each man may seek highly idiosyncratic ends. But whatever ends he seeks, he must want to achieve them. Hence ability to make effective decisions is necessarily regarded as a good, whatever his other ends are. And therefore money, if it is to serve its purpose of being impersonally valuable, and if it is to be valued independently of something we all happen to value, such as gold, must be conceptually tied in with ability to choose.

Money provides a conventional measure of value which is, by convention, impersonal, and can be assigned, transferred and accumulated. Although it does not fit our actual personal values—one person values ten loaves of bread more than a pair of shoes, another less—it provides a common standard. A poor man may set greater store on £1 than a rich man, but the monetary value of their pounds is by definition the same. We can always ask of money whose it is, and its ownership is necessarily and intentionally privative. Other goods—health, happiness or prestige—are assignable, but not essentially exclusive. They are not always shared or shareable, but do not have to be privative. My being healthy does not exclude your being healthy, and if the glory is mine, it can be yours too, and you can bask in my reflected glory. But money differs from them all in that if some money belongs to me, it necessarily does not belong to you (this does not exclude joint ownership—but if some money belongs to us jointly, then it does not belong just to me). Money has been fashioned to be peculiarly privative. It is part of its *raison d'être* that it should be uniquely and exclusively assignable, and therefore every allocation of money is a non-allocation to somebody else. Although at any one time it has a unique owner, it can be transferred but does not have to be. It can be transferred in order to induce people to do things we want, to render some return for the services they have rendered us, or to discharge some legal, social or moral obligation: or it can be kept, so as to defer until later, when many present uncertainties will have resolved themselves, the decision how it is to be used. While we have it, it constitutes a perpetual possibility of choice. This is why it is inherently valuable. It is encapsulated choice.

Because money is a conventional token of value established and sustained by society, it follows that its use and distribution is a legitimate topic of social concern, contrary to the teaching of Hayek and Nozick. They argue that each business transaction is the business only of the contracting parties, and of no concern to anybody else. I may be put out if Jill chooses Jack instead of me, but that is just my tough luck, and so, too, if Standard Oil undercuts me, and puts me out of business.[1] But the cases are not comparable. Marriage is highly personal and necessarily exclusive: business transactions are impersonal, and normally part of a repetitive pattern. As we noted in the previous chapter, it is a weakness of the classical analysis of economic transactions that it takes as its paradigm the visiting trader exchanging beads for copra, or the rich business man wondering whether to have his portrait painted by a fashionable artist at an exorbitant price.[2] These are casual, once-only transactions, in which the mutual commitment of each party to the other is minimal, and where either can afford not to go ahead with the bargain if it does not suit him. Most transactions are quite different. They are regular and relied on, in which each party has a number of commitments to the other, and

---

[1] Robert Nozick, *Anarchy, State and Utopia*, p. 237.
[2] F. A. Hayek, *The Constitution of Liberty*, pp. 136–7, allows that in some cases—in times of high unemployment or in a mining town where the company has a monopoly of employment—the weaker party is, in effect, "coerced" by the stronger; but argues that such cases are rare.

where one or both depend very much on the transaction going through. If the milkman fails to leave his morning pinta, I shall not be able to have coffee at breakfast, and shall be out of sorts all morning. If the firm sacks its old employee, he will have nothing to pay the rent with, and may be quite unable to find another job. The milkman is part of the neighbourhood's way of life: the employee has given years of faithful service to the firm, and both are bound to each other by ties of mutual obligation. This is not to say that the obligations are absolute or the way of life sacrosant; the obligations may be overriden by other factors, the way of life may need to be amended: but in either case the relationship is not a casual one, and the obligations should not be lightly disregarded nor the way of life wantonly altered. If I go to a shop and try on a hat and do not like it, I do not buy the hat and there is no more to be said. But if on my rounds I decide not to leave milk for Mr Ovambo Ishago, or if it no longer pleases me to employ the services of John Doe, there is more that needs to be said by way of justification or excuse. This is not to deny all liberty of choice, only the absolute liberty claimed by some classical economists. Although liberty is essential if money is to have any meaning, it needs to be exercised in accordance with certain canons of fair and equal treatment. A tradesman is carrying on his trade in the public domain, and ought to be available to all comers, else those discriminated against may be altogether deprived of what is generally available to others in their place. If society makes available to him conveniently standardised tokens of value, it is fair that he should have to meet society's requirement that he provide goods and services on somewhat standardised terms. What these terms should be, and what exceptions may reasonably be made, will depend on conditions obtaining in a particular society, and may be open to dispute. Often the prescriptions of *laissez-faire* may work best in practice, competition being more effective than regulation in securing fair dealing. But that is a question of practical politics not of principle. Regulation of trade cannot be ruled out on principle, although often inexpedient in practice.

Although the public have a legitimate concern in business transactions, it does not follow that it should or could be a total concern. For though money is a function of society, it only has value inasmuch as it enables individual choices to be effectively made. It has built into it the possibility of being disposed of in other ways than those that are in accordance with justice or approved of by society. If I have money, I may choose to spend it on Jill rather than on Jane, even though Jane deserves or needs it more and society does not approve of Jill receiving so much attention. As we have seen in Chapter Eleven, freedom, although presupposed by justice, can also conflict with it. And since money encapsulates freedom, and would cease to be of value were it otherwise, no system of economic justice can conform to a totally collectivist ideal. A totally collectivist society may ration all the distributable goods available, or make some other authoritative allocation of them, but it cannot use money or delegate to individuals any right of altering, by mutual agreement, their respective allocations; else, people will start making their own arrangements, and some may fare better than others. I may give all my sweet ration to Jill and none to Jane, or you may swap your butter for points with one family, and at a more favourable rate of exchange points for butter with another, ending up better off than others. Money introduces freedom and therefore non-conformity and anomaly into the collectivist scheme of things, and thus disrupts collectivist ideals of distributive justice. A society in which money is allowed to circulate freely will take a form which depends on innumerable individual choices, and is unlikely therefore to conform closely to anyone's assessment of what people ought to be paid. It will be at best only an imperfectly just society according to any canons of distributive justice, although it may none the less be so arranged as to avoid great injustices in the distribution of benefits and burdens.

The imperfections of justice engendered by money may be reckoned too high a price to pay for the undoubted advantages afforded by money: many thinkers have thought so, and have sought to banish money and money-mindedness in order to establish the just society. Money and money-mindedness are, indeed, the root of many evils, but as a defence against the charge of subverting the possibility of social justice it can be argued that considerations of distributive justice cannot in any case be extended to the whole of society. The concept of distributive justice is applicable within the context of limited associations, with limited and definite aims held in common. Such aims give guidance how the fruits of common activities should be distributed. In the case of society as a whole—at least in the form of the modern nation-state—the aims are unlimited and indefinite, and therefore invariably vague and sometimes conflicting, and altogether an inappropriate foundation on which to base any just apportionment. Society as a whole cannot say whether nurses should be paid more than pop-singers or less, since society as a whole does not have, and ought not to have, a well-worked-out system of values which would enable us to say which group deserved to be paid more.

This argument traces its ancestry back to Aristotle, and is weighty. But we need to distinguish two forms, a milder one, which only denies the possibility of a complete scheme of social justice, and a stronger one which denies the coherence of the concept altogether. The milder version is correct, and constitutes a powerful defence against criticisms based on a yearning for absolute social justice: but the stronger version, which would, if correct, rule out every argument of social justice, is misconceived. Although society as a whole differs from more limited associations, in having aims which are vaguer and more varied, and although these sometimes conflict, they do not do so always, nor are they altogether vacuous. A nation-state can espouse definite values. Some—a concern for justice and a love of liberty—are grounded in the nature of civil society itself. Others can vary from society to society, but are none the less definitely avowed within some one society. Englishmen once valued country life, while Frenchmen aspired to urbanity and elegance. Some basis of shared values is available on which to base judgements of social justice, if need be. Only, they will not be always available, nor can they be anything other than rough. We have to decide how much policemen, Members of Parliament, and the Queen should be paid—there is no market in Queens—and we can make a rational decision in the light of the nature of society and its common aspirations. And, as we shall see in the next chapter, in deciding how burdens, most notably taxes, are to be imposed, the State is making decisions which raise important issues of justice—as Hayek himself allows.[3] What we cannot do is to extend our range of judgement to every walk of society, or pretend that we can make precise and correct calculations of what each man—banker, teacher, miner and farm-worker—ought to be paid. So long as we exercise our judgement relatively rarely, and acknowledge the extremely approximate nature of our conclusions, we may hope to escape gross error—there are plenty of alternative employments open to those who find our conclusions quite unacceptable, and many will be able to accept them by reason of their admittedly not being an

[3] *Constitution of Liberty*, p. 322.

exact assessment of what the job is worth. But once we aim at a complete scheme of social justice which shall give everyone exactly what he ought to have, then we presuppose some over-all purpose in society, on which such judgements could be grounded; and no such over-all purpose exists.

Economic justice is difficult to do, not only on the large scale, but on the small scale too. This is because the shared purposes, instead of being unlimited, are too limited. A business transaction—a catalaxy, as Hayek calls it[4]—should not be seen as a simple bargain, but rather as a joint enterprise, though of a special sort. No shared benefit is engendered. It may be advantageous to both parties, but the advantage to each is assignable only to him, and therefore there is no basis of co-operative activity on which to base an apportionment of distributable goods. In an army or a factory there is a natural rhythm of activity which gives some guidance as to how the spoils or the pay-roll should be divided: but when it comes to negotiating a contract, it appears to be a much more competitive affair, with each side trying to get the best of the bargain at the other's expense. Sometimes, indeed, this is exactly what is happening, and it is important to recognise that possibility and to see why it is valuable to provide for it. Most economists, however, see this not simply as a possibility but as the standard case, and base their whole economic analysis on the assumption that each party is always aiming to get the best of the bargain. Yet it does not appear like that to many, and they reject the whole view of business that makes them out always to be trying to do the other side down. Fair dealing is for them not an idle phrase, and it is important that we should elucidate what it means.

In any business transaction, both parties benefit—otherwise they would not go through with it. But the benefit may go much more to one party than to the other. There is a wide range of terms on which it would still be more advantageous to clinch the deal than not to, and although this range is narrowed by competition, it is seldom in practice, and only dubiously in principle, narrowed to the point of setting a definite price on the goods or services exchanged. One may get the best, or the worst, of the bargain, and, as we saw in the

---

[4] F. A. Hayek, *Essays on Philosophy, Politics and Economics*, London, 1967, p. 164, and *Law, Legislation and Liberty*, II, London, 1973, p. 108, who refers back to Richard Whately, *Introductory Lectures on Political Economy*, London, 1855, and L. von Mises, *Human Action*, New Haven, 1949.

previous chapter, the fact that the bargain was freely entered into does not mean that it was therefore fair. The difference between a fair bargain and a hard one is that while both serve the actual purpose of the contracting parties, a fair bargain is one both can approve of, taking into account the interests of each, whereas a hard bargain is to be seen by each individual only from his own point of view. Before I can decide whether a bargain is fair or not, I have to consider not only the simple question whether, when it comes to the crunch, I am prepared to go ahead with it, but the more complicated question of whether, in view of what each is contributing, the advantages gained by each are distributed in a way both can reasonably endorse. We see the transaction not as a simple exchange, but as a limiting case of co-operation. Each contributes: as a result, both are better off. The benefits engendered are assignable goods, and may accrue much more to one party than the other, and so money may need to pass, in order to restore the balance. The question is how the co-operators' surplus is to be divided. Neither the entirely individualistic account of classical economics nor the collectivist account of the egalitarians is adequate. Justice requires that the division be one which should be acceptable to each according to standards common to both. Like the analysis of classical economics, it considers co-operation from both points of view separately, and takes each seriously, but its assignments, like collectivist ones, should have a validity no matter from whose point of view it is considered. In taking each person's view seriously, it asks if his pay-off is as much as it should be, rather than concerning itself solely with the collective total, as classical utilitarianism does, or with some simple formula of distribution, as egalitarians do. But in answering that question, it seeks not the maximum which might be extorted, seen only from that individual's point of view, but what is reasonable, and should be accepted as reasonable by others as well as himself, having regard to the contributions made by him and by the other party. To put it very crudely, the questions are individual, the answers collective.

Theories of the just wage and the just price are connected, but the just wage is the more fundamental concept. This is because the individual question that springs most readily to each party is 'How much do I get?' not 'How much should I pay?' The latter question invites consideration of alternative ways of seeking satisfaction, and how much I would have to pay if I looked elsewhere:

and hence the just price is more easily eroded by competition, and is only with difficulty distinguished from the market price. The question of how much I should get is both more interesting and more individual. It invites answers referring to my own contribution, and the concept of desert has the complexity required to enable us to give individual answers to collective questions. We need, however, to distinguish arguments based on desert properly so called from other arguments which may be adduced in answer to the question of how much I ought to be paid. In the first place there are arguments of need. A wage may be less than it ought to be not because it is unfair in view of the work done but because it is inadequate to provide the means of life. If an incompetent and unreliable worker with a large family to feed cannot make ends meet, we feel that he ought to be paid more on account of his need. But that is a claim of humanity, not justice. Needs and family circumstances may constitute good reasons for paying him more, but they are extraneous to his work and cannot be construed as part of his contribution. The concept of the just wage is different from that of the living wage.

There are, secondly, arguments of compensation. These, although not based on desert, do enter into our reckoning of what would be a just return. Better pay should sometimes be accorded to a job because it is unpleasant, risky or monotonous, or carries some other disadvantage. The business man works long hours, is always having to think of business affairs, and is liable to get a coronary thrombosis, and therefore ought to be paid more than the clerk, who can watch the clock by day and switch off at night, and generally lead a peaceful, unstressful life. This may mean that the business man is contributing more, but it need not. In voluntary societies, where claims based on desert are waived, we still reckon to meet people's expenses, and in recent years this has been extended sometimes to cover loss of earnings. We should distinguish the two arguments, that of desert proper—"He contributed greatly to the success of the joint enterprise, and so should have a corresponding share of the distributable goods engendered by it"—and that of compensation—"His contribution cost him a lot, and so we should, as a first charge on our funds, make it up to him, so that he is not out of pocket or in any other way at a disadvantage in consequence of having helped us." Together with compensations, we may need also to consider satisfactions. It is often said that those who take the responsibility of directing an enterprise are thereby rewarded. We like bossing people about. Instead of being compensated for the burdens of responsibility, top people ought to have their pay docked to take account of their enjoyment of power, which should be regarded as a sort of payment in kind. There is something in this argument, but not nearly as much as is made out. There are satisfactions, sometimes, in the exercise of power—or of some special skill—as well as, often, burdens. Both should be considered, and set off one against the other, leaving a balance, perhaps of satisfaction, perhaps of worry, to be seen as payment already, or as needing compensation. But these are different from strict considerations of desert.

If an economic transaction is seen as a limiting case of a co-operative enterprise, the bearing of desert on economic justice will be illuminated by mixed cases of co-operation where both distributable and undistributable goods are generated. A doctor may treat a man because that is his vocation. In the terminology of the Theory of Games, the outcome of men being healed has a pay-off for a doctor independent of any pecuniary advantage or personal advancement for himself. Nevertheless, there is also an assignable good generated, namely the patient's health, which is the patient's alone. In war we all share the aim of winning victory or at least staving off defeat; but sometimes there is booty to be divided—as always there are costs to be carried—and there are assignable benefits and burdens. In the everyday transactions of private life, we often give a hand and receive neighbourly help, motivated by general benevolence: but in many cases where the benefits are all on one side and the benevolence mostly on the other, we think that benevolence deserves its true reward.

The doctor is not primarily concerned to make money. If a society or some segment of it is deeply impoverished, he still will have reason to render what services he can, and will not expect to be paid what he could have counted on in happier circumstances. Before the advent of the National Health Service doctors often used to give their services free or for a purely nominal sum to poor patients, and to recoup themselves by charging Robin Hood fees to the wealthy. Medical missionaries are content with very meagre pay, and do not take themselves off to lucrative practices in more prosperous countries. In this professional men differ from merchants. Nobody would sell a television set cheaper to a slum-dweller in a poor country, if he had the chance of selling it at a higher price to a more prosperous man who was better able to pay. But although a doctor should be prepared to give his service free if need be, it does not follow that he ought not to expect any reward when a reward can perfectly well be paid. It is one thing if I have been mugged on my way down from Jerusalem to Jericho for you to take pity on me and come to my aid: it is quite another thing if I am a prosperous business man, and roll up in my Jaguar and want a doctor to attend to my indigestion or nurses to clean up after my bilious attack. If in the latter case I expect them to do it for free, I am exploiting them. I am using them, trading on their good will, imposing my needs on their freedom of action, but not allowing their needs, rights or interests to impinge on my freedom of action. I am demanding that I should have value in their eyes, with the consequence that they should put themselves out for my sake, but I am showing that they do not have value in my eyes, because I am not making any sacrifice of my interests on their behalf. A reward is a tangible token of gratitude. It is a mark of appreciation. If resources are straitened, a simple 'thank you' is enough. But if, thanks to the efforts of others, I am enjoying substantial benefits, I am showing unreasonable unconcern for the burdens they have borne and the contributions they have made, if I do not give them any share of the benefits that have accrued as a result of their endeavours. I am manipulating them, regarding them as part of the furniture, treating them merely as means to my ends. If I am to recognise them as independent autonomous beings in their own right, with their own interests, and free to act as they think fit, then I must see that not only I but they could have acted otherwise, and that the benefits of our having acted in concert did not depend solely on my decisions and should not be appropriated by me alone, but belong to us all, and should be distributed among us, so that nobody is left out and nobody's contribution is ignored or taken for granted.

It is the same with the spoils of war. It was not for their sake that I engaged in battle. I am satisfied if my home and family come through safe from the enemy. But if there are spoils of war, and if they are appropriated by others without my having a share, the message is clear: my contribution is not appreciated; I do not count; my point of view is not regarded. Again, if a man spends a lot of time getting my car going, it is a great benefit to me. It would be unreasonable and wrong of me to assume that it was of great benefit to him also. If he were my brother, my friend, or my neighbour, then I may be right in assuming that my good is *eo ipso* his good too. But in general this is not so, and it would be taking him for granted to assume that it was so. If I pay him for his pains, I am not taking him for granted: but if I merely "make it worth his while", I am still manipulating him. I am exploiting his need of money to get my car mended and he is exploiting my need of having a car mended to screw some money out of me. We are essentially alien and external to each other, and if I get the best of the bargain he gets the worst, and vice versa. If, however, I have considered the transaction from his point of view, and have asked myself whether he is getting as much as he should, and he has considered the transaction from my point of view, and asked himself whether I am coming out worse than I need, and if the answer is a commonly accepted one, then there is no conflict between us, and we can each regard the other as an ally not an enemy. Unlike the utilitarian, I am treating him as a partner. He is not merely a unit, quite possibly an insignificant unit, in my calculations of the sum total, but an individual, with his own interests and own point of view, and I identify with him to the extent of looking at the transaction from his point of view, asking the question which he might naturally ask, viz. "Why not more for me?", and, if the answer is unsatisfactory, remedying matters by seeing that he gets the more that he ought to have. And since he is similarly looking at the transaction from my point of view, and would similarly remedy matters if I were being done down, I can relax my guard against him, just as he can against me, and we can each trust the other to do as well for him as he would himself.

Economic transactions differ from other co-operative enterprises in not generating any undistributable goods, apart from each party's being glad to have been of service to the other. The *raison d'être* of the transaction was the generation of an assignable good, and in the typical case the whole benefit would, in the absence of money passing, accrue to only one party, and the whole contribution was provided by the other. In order to determine how much money should pass, both the contribution and the benefit need to be evaluated. Very often we take the market price as indicative of the value of the benefit, and quite often we regard the market as also setting a monetary value on the contribution, particularly when the transaction is a simple sale of goods, and the contribution and the benefit are regarded as identical and priced identically by the market; and if, as in some one-off transactions, there is no market, we employ an expert valuer to fix a price "as between willing buyer and seller". But the market price, although often a valuable guide, cannot be taken as giving a definitive value—for then there would be no transactions, since the parties would be no better off after than before. Rather than regarding the market price as somehow reflecting "the real value", we use it as showing what is the going rate for goods and services in situations relevantly similar to the actual one. If a man is buying petrol from a garage in normal hours, the fact that he needs it desperately is not relevant, and he should be charged the same as any other customer who could, if need be, do without it. If he is after hours, and knocks up a garage attendant to serve him, it would be fair to charge him more, depending on the trouble incurred (a lot if dragged from bed in the small hours many miles away, only a little if taken from watching the television in the adjoining house). We abstract from the actuality of the given situation, with its personal needs and pressures which ought to be irrelevant to the transaction, and consider instead what would be reasonable terms for other people similarly situated. And if both parties can agree that the terms are reasonable when seen from this universalised standpoint, then neither need feel done down by them or complain that they are unjust.

There is a large element of conventionality in economic justice, as there is in distributive justice. The reason is the same. It is all too easy to construe a bargain as a zero-sum game in which one person's gain is the other's loss. But, we feel obscurely, this is false to the more fundamental fact that bargains are to both parties' benefit, and therefore are co-operative, rather than competitive, enterprises. In order to avoid the appearance of trying to get the best of the bargain, we are often willing to agree to any established formula, which we both know of and can understand, and which will yield a definite result that is unlikely to be grossly disadvantageous to either party. There is a faint analogy with the development of the law. We do not want to go to law with our neighbour, and are willing to accept any—not absolutely any, but almost any—agreement which will obviate the need for litigation: and if, in something of the same spirit, we do not want to haggle, then any—not absolutely any, but almost any—price which is fixed independently of us will be fair enough.

Although a fair bargain is characterized by each party's considering it from the other's point of view, it is important not to push this
point too hard, or we shall be giving an altogether too cosy account
of business relationships. They are "non-tuistic" as Wicksteed[5]
terms it. When I negotiate a business deal, there is a clear demarcation of responsibilities. It is not my business to look after the
interests of the other side: that is his business. My business is to
look after the interests of my side, and make sure they are not
disregarded. If we were all minding one another's business, we
should for ever be getting in one another's way, and might well
neglect our own responsibilities. Better let each concentrate on his
own job.

There is force in this argument. The prime responsibility of each
party is to his own side. There is no general obligation to buy bad
goods because it would benefit the other side to do so, nor to buy
what is not wanted. Only the buyer can know precisely what he
wants. In that sense *caveat emptor* is a necessary truth. There are
many facts outside the immediate transaction which cannot be
known to the other side but are relevant to the question of whether
to go ahead with the transaction or not. Only a lifelong partnership
could be totally tuistic. A respect for privacy requires that each
should mind his own business, and not try to manage the other's
affairs for him. But we need to distinguish the unconcern which
privacy requires from the unconcern which justice condemns. It is
none of my business as milkman or garage mechanic or accountant
to know everything about my customers or clients. I need only
know some of their wants, and leave it to them to decide whether
they want to spend their money on milk or petrol; but inasmuch as
they do business with me, I cannot but see them as having certain
interests. If they buy milk, they have an interest in its not being
watered. It is these interests, which arise out of the nature of the
transaction, and often can be imputed on the strength of the
transaction alone, which justice requires us to consider. It is a
somewhat impersonal concern with the other person. We could say
that in normal business relations we should reckon them to be
"non-tuistic" but not "non-vousistic".[6]

Economic justice thus resembles other forms of justice in its
somewhat impersonal concern for the interests of others. There is

[5] Philip H. Wicksteed, *The Common Sense of Political Economy*, London, 1910,
Bk. I, Ch. V, p. 174.

[6] Compare Ch. 1, pp. 15–16.

less than complete identification of interests, but not complete unconcern either. The principles which move the just man in economic affairs occupy, as we shall see more fully in Chapter Sixteen, a middle range of morality, more sensitive to the interests of others than the merely honest man, but not as concerned with them as the altruistic man. The honest man abides by the rules. He keeps faith, and does not lie or cheat. But he drives as hard a bargain as he can, and does not scruple to exploit the folly or weakness of his associates. The altruistic man is dedicated to serving the interests of others and does not seek for any reward save that of knowing that he is doing good. In modern life we often oscillate between these two standpoints, often castigating the former as entirely immoral and pretending that only the latter is truly moral. But this is a mistake. Even the merely honest man is observing some principles, and it is not always right to intrude one's altruism on other men's affairs or take their concerns too much to heart. Often we are wise to settle for the minimal standard of rule observance of the merely honest man. Although the market economy is often felt to be morally unsatisfying, it offers security against great evils, and is often efficient. The great virtue of the market economy is that it preserves some liberty of choice, so that it is always possible to say No. The possibility will sometimes be abused, and a man will say No to a fair bargain, and will only say Yes if we allow him to drive a very hard bargain with us. Yet this is a small price to pay for freedom. Moreover, inasmuch as economic justice is, on its own, indeterminate, we need there to be a market to give guidance in general on what would be just in any particular case. We cannot have a complete scheme of the just wage or the just price for the same reasons as show the impossibility of a complete scheme of social justice. It does not follow from this, as often is maintained by classical economists, that all talk of the just wage or the just price is vacuous. But it does follow that we can apply concepts of economic justice only within limited contexts, and that market prices often provide the boundary conditions. We often determine the just price and the just wage by reference to the market: as, indeed, in the opposite direction, market prices and salaries are often determined by reference to what is generally felt to be fair.

14

FISCAL JUSTICE

Fiscal justice is concerned with how the burdens of a communal enterprise should be imposed. In the modern world we impose taxes, almost all of them to be paid in money: but we can also exact a tax on men's time, thought, energy or responsibility; and along with monetary taxes, we should consider various forms of conscription—the *corvée*, the draft and jury service—the "liturgies" of ancient Athens, the duty of voting in modern Australia, and unwelcome promotion in the professions, as when a priest is made to become a bishop, or an academic is pressured into being Vice-Chancellor, Chairman, Proctor or Dean. Taxes are sometimes imposed on people direct, sometimes imposed on the purchase of certain commodities or the pursuit of certain activities, such as driving a car or possessing a television set.

The main reason for levying taxes is to raise revenue, but some are levied for entirely other reasons, and often extraneous considerations influence the incidence of revenue-raising imposts. Tariffs are intended to make imported goods more expensive. Dog-licences are a negligible source of revenue, but may do something to keep down the dog population and to foster a sense of responsibility among dog-owners. The taxes on alcohol, tobacco and petrol yield a lot, but are justified not on that ground alone but because the consumption of these substances is socially undesirable, either as endangering the well-being of those who consume them or as having undesirable neighbourhood effects on others. Such taxes not only raise revenue, but act as deterrents. There are grave objections, of principle as well as of practicality, to complete prohibition of alcohol, tobacco or petrol. We need to countenance them, but at the same time to discourage them, and therefore tax them, in order to leave each man free to make his own decisions, while shifting the balance of cost against large-scale consumption. A tax, unlike a punishment or a penalty, carries with it no stigma of wrong having been done, but affords good reason none the less for not doing it; and therefore can be used to discourage when we are not prepared to forbid outright. In a somewhat similar fashion the Muslim conquerors refrained from persecuting their Christian and Jewish subjects, but made them pay an extra tax, to encourage conversion to Islam, and to show the lower status of those who failed to follow the teaching of the Prophet.

It is often said that there is no equity in taxation. Although, as we shall see,[1] there is a sense in which this is true, it is not true in the commonly accepted sense, where it is taken to mean that justice has no bearing on matters of taxation, which is held to be simply the exercise of arbitrary sovereign power, and not at all an adjudication of right. According to the historic principles of the British Constitution, tax bills are different from other legislative bills, receiving the Royal Assent with the words *La Reine remercie ses bon sujets, accepte leur benevolence, et ainsi le veult* instead of simply *La Reine le veult*, and it is argued that considerations of justice do not apply to taxation, because taxes are voluntary contributions by the people, agreed through their representatives in Parliament, to the Crown. But that is a fiction. There is nothing voluntary about my payment of income tax, and taxes generally involve not only the voluntary contributions of cheerful givers but the involuntary surrender of valued assets, done grudgingly and under threat of sanctions. And hence, although there are important differences between taxes and other laws, both raise issues of justice, because both may lead to people being done down.

Even though it is conceptually appropriate to raise questions of justice about fiscal policy, most arguments are couched in terms of expediency alone. That is a mistake. Although some questions are purely questions of expediency, issues of expediency and of justice often interpenetrate. As with law in general, so with tax law in particular; they are to be seen not as an order backed by sanctions imposed by the sovereign on his subjects, but as being primarily the way citizens arrange their affairs, with the sanctions coming into play only as a last resort to bring recalcitrants into line. However large we make Leviathan, and however many eyes he is able to acquire, he cannot see everything, and will not be able to secure observance of his ordinances without the free co-operation of ordinary members of the public: and however many Inspectors of Taxes are appointed by the Inland Revenue, and however many Vatmen by HM Customs and Excise, they cannot keep under

---

[1] Below, p. 240.

surveillance all the multifarious transactions between one man and another unless they are disposed to declare them. Tax law, like other forms of law, depends on being generally accepted for its being generally observed. Although some taxes can be exacted in the teeth of public opposition, just as some criminal statutes can be enforced on an unwilling public—and it is a counsel of fiscal expediency to choose levies that can be adequately exacted with a minimum of co-operation—public support for a tax is invaluable, and its absence in the long run fatal. Nobody likes paying taxes, but if the tax, and the tax system generally, is just, few people will go so far as to evade them, and those who do will keep quiet about it. If, however, either a particular impost or the whole system is unjust, those who are being done down by it will not see any reason why they should not escape, by any effective stratagem, being mulcted. First avoidance, then evasion, will become respectable and widespread. And, as we shall see later, once people begin to think that others are not paying their share, they will resent being dunned themselves. There is then a widespread collapse of confidence in the tax system, with taxes being regarded as the arbitrary impositions of rapacious tax-gatherers, which everyone should do his utmost to fend off, ending with a general collusion on the part of the public to defeat the requisitions of the public fisc. The only reliable protection against avoidance and evasion is public opinion and private conscience, and therefore, even if our ultimate concern were only that of expediency, justice would still be, fiscally speaking, the best policy.

Although in some respects like retributive and distributive justice, fiscal justice differs from them both. It differs from retributive justice in that taxes, although often unwelcome to the individual, are not intentionally unwelcome and not directed specifically at him. A tax is not a punishment. A punishment may or may not fit the crime, but it would be nonsense to ask whether a tax was fitting or not. Nor is it a penalty. If a penalty is regularly incurred, it is a sign that it is too low and ought to be raised to a level that will be an effective deterrent, whereas it is an argument against increasing a tax that the total yield will be less. Even in cases where taxes are imposed to discourage rather than to raise revenue, there is still, as we have seen,[2] an important distinction between a penalty and a tax, and in the standard case, where the prime purpose is to raise revenue, there is nothing the taxpayer has done *for* which he is being penalised.

[2] Ch. 6, pp. 128–9.

Although he can properly ask the authorities "Why am I being charged?", he cannot ask "What am I being charged for?", and their answer will not be in terms of what he has done, but only will show that according to some appropriate criterion, he falls within a chargeable category. A criminal trial is focussed on the accused, what *he* has done, and whether in consequence *he* ought to be deprived of life, liberty or property: a taxing measure, by contrast, is concerned primarily with general classes of persons, commodities or activities on which is laid a duty to contribute to the Revenue, and only secondarily, in borderline cases, with the question whether a certain individual, commodity or activity falls within the schedule laid down. He cannot plead "I could not help it" to rebut a tax charge, as he can to rebut a criminal charge; and whereas a plea in mitigation of a penalty is always appropriate, a plea in mitigation of a tax is inappropriate, and would, if successful, be unfair on all other payers of the tax. Again, the criminal law is avowedly avoidable. It is highly praiseworthy to act so as to avoid falling foul of the law. But tax-avoidance is not similarly praiseworthy. Although allowed by the law, it is held in public esteem to be on par with tax-evasion, and was until recently regarded as discreditable, because it seemed that the individual was shirking his share of the common burden. In short, the prime concern in taxation is that the tax levied shall secure goods for the use of the community, not that it shall be unwelcome to the individual: and to that extent the canons of retributive justice, with their intense focussing on the individual, are inappropriate.

Nevertheless, a tax, especially a direct tax, may well be un-welcome to the individual, and therefore it should be levied with due regard for the principles of natural justice. A man should not be mulcted gratuitously. The fact that the money is being taken from him ostensibly for the public good does not alter the fact that it is being taken from him. The question whether or not it should be taken from him is one which he is entitled to raise, and which ought to be answered adequately. If he has reason to believe that tax is being wrongly demanded of him, his reasons should be heard by an impartial man, who should take into account all the relevant circumstances and not be influenced by extraneous or improper considerations, by undue zeal for the Inland Revenue or by cor-porate *amour propre*.[3] If the decision is adverse, reasons should be

---

[3] See above, Ch. 4, pp. 83–4.

given, and it should be possible to discover in advance with some degree of reliability and accuracy what the consequences of different courses of action will be. The procedure should be open, and subject to review. And it should be timely and definitive, so that taxpayers can settle their affairs in reasonable time and have some security against new tax bills being sprung on them in respect of matters already settled.

Fiscal justice differs also from distributive justice in that it is burdens rather than benefits that are being apportioned. When benefits are being distributed, each person may be presumed to want his full share: but when burdens are being assigned, each person would like to be let off with as little as possible. It can be misleading to talk as if the canons for distributing burdens were symmetrical with those for distributing benefits. Since justice is concerned with people not being done down rather than with their not being done up, there is no symmetry between the allocation of burdens and the allocation of benefits. Nobody is done down if someone waives a benefit due to him, but we are all disadvantaged if someone disowns his burden. Rather than talk of burdens being *dist*ributed *to* people, we should think of a tax as being *con*tributed *by* them. The taxpayer gives of his money, or his time, or his thought, in order that together we may achieve certain purposes. And therefore, although the consideration of how burdens should be allocated has been thought to be an aspect of distributive justice, I think the difference of logic should be marked by a difference of nomenclature, and propose, with apologies for the neologism, the name contributive justice.

Contributive justice is based on the logic of the Prisoners' Dilemma,[4] tempered by a lively sense of the individual's point of view, and a tender-mindedness towards it. The Prisoners' Dilemma shows how, under certain conditions, we can achieve a common good only by forming a coalition and subordinating the choice of individuals to a common strategy. There is a conflict between a more limited and a wider rationality. If each individual considered only his immediate interests the result would be less good than if they all pursued the common strategy, but each is tempted to opt out, benefiting from the co-operativeness of the others, while not co-operating himself. If we all park in the town centre, traffic will be congested and the streets unpleasant: but if everyone else refrains

[4] Ch. 3, pp. 46–58.

from parking, it will not make much difference if I alone bring in my car. If nobody paid the fare, public transport would cease to run: but if everybody else does, and I alone travel without paying, public transport will still run, and I shall save the cost of the fare. So long as other people subscribe to the National Trust, I shall be able to enjoy unspoilt landscape and beautiful scenery. But everyone is in the same position as I am, and has the same incentive not to pay. I am, therefore acting unfairly if I make an exception for myself, not because of the damage done to other people by one's parking, or travelling without paying, or not subscribing—this may be minimal—but that the parker, fare-dodger and the non-subscriber are letting other people down by conning them. Other people also would like to park—and if they did, there would be nowhere available for the parker to put his car—would also like to travel free, also have other calls on their funds than subscriptions to common amenities. The parker's and the fare-dodger's game is to get the other people to make sacrifices for his benefit on the false pretence that he is making sacrifices too. They are being done. And for this reason, rather than on account of any damage actually caused, they can complain that they are being done down, and that therefore he is acting unfairly.

Justice requires that each should pull his weight, but that is not what justice is. The logic of the Prisoners' Dilemma requires a coalition of all against each: but justice is, rather, a coalition of all for each. It requires us all to see things from the individual's point of view, and do as well by him as we reasonably can. Although we recognise the rationality of the solution to the Prisoners' Dilemma, we recognise too how precarious its rationality is from the individual's point of view, and how attractive it would be to take a more limited view. If we are to address ourselves to the individual we must secure that the conditions under which it is rational for him to contribute hold, and that he can know that they hold. Although short-term expediency suggests that the rational strategy is to dodge paying one's fare and be a "frée-rider", a deeper analysis shows that the rational meta-strategy is to pay on condition that others do too. Contributive justice therefore requires that each contributor is assured that others are contributing their share, and that he is not simply being called upon to make a sacrifice for the good of others, but that there are individualised reasons, which are rationally cogent for him in as much as they form part of a meta-strategy it would be rational for him to adopt, why he should make this sacrifice. There are reasons and reasons. The common good, although a reason for requiring a sacrifice on the part of the individual, and one that to a utilitarian would be conclusive, is not an individualised reason, and so will not make it just, for it does not show why it should be he, rather than anyone else, who is to be asked to shoulder the burden. To be just, the common good should not bear immediately on any individual, but only through the medium of a common policy which bears on all. The common good, that is, does not itself constitute a reason why I should be called upon in all fairness to make sacrifices, but, rather, constitutes a reason for there being individualised reasons which make it fair for me, and for everyone else, to do our bit. If we do not have a common policy, we cannot count on the burden being shouldered at all, because each individual can opt out, since there are not sufficiently cogent reasons, applying to him specifically, why he must put himself out: and so, *per contra*, if the burden is to be reliably discharged, it must be by means of a common policy; and the logic of this, as we saw,[5] is that every individual should subordinate some of his own interests to the common policy, and must be able to count on everyone else's doing the same. Only if we all act together, forgoing in this matter, individual liberty of action, can we achieve anything. But in acting together, we need to remember that each man may be sacrificing some cherished interest, and should not be called upon to do so needlessly, but only if it is an essential part of a common strategy in which he can be sure that others as well as he are playing their part.

The Prisoners' Dilemma reveals different facets of rationality, and a conflict between them. Contributive justice recognises that there is this conflict, and seeks to minimise it. It recognises the validity of the individual's point of view, in which the contribution called from him is a real cost to him, but seeks to establish conditions under which the perceived cost will be as little as possible and the arguments of enlightened self-interest and communal altruism will be as strong as possible. Even though costly, burdens may be undertaken voluntarily, as sometimes were the "liturgies" in ancient Athens, and some forms of promotion to public duty in modern Britain. The ancient Athenian had an opportunity of displaying his wealth and exercising his taste. The

[5] Ch. 3, pp. 50–58.

modern Briton may earn kudos or obtain power by accepting office,
or he may value the common good achieved so greatly that it offsets
the sacrifices involved. Many men volunteered to fight in the war.
National Health contributions can be regarded as a "good buy" in
the way of health insurance. Some taxpayers are glad to pay their
bit towards making Britain the sort of country it ought to be. The
more public purposes command general assent, the more readily
members of the public will contribute towards realising them. The
claim "No Taxation without Representation" never was, and never
could be, valid: but it expresses an important insight none the less,
that taxation depends in part on a general willingness to identify
with public purposes, which can often be best achieved by involving
the public in their articulation and adoption. Simple identification
with the common good, however, is not always forthcoming and
cannot be enough to make every fiscal demand welcome. A man
may grudge his contribution. However altruistic he may be, he
cannot but be aware of some interests of his that are being forgone.
So long as they are not very central or very great interests, he will
not repine too much, but if they are important to him, he will
question the imposition, and it is inherent in the concept of justice
to take the individual and his own individual standpoint seriously,
and address its answer to the question he is likely in that capacity to
raise.

Two maxims of fiscal justice follow. Contributions, wherever
possible, should be light and should be avoidable. A small charge is
not worth making a great issue of. Few men see themselves as
individuals so single-mindedly that they will not put themselves out
at all for the common good. If the matrix of the Prisoners' Dilemma
were—

Prisoner B Prisoner A	keeps silent	confesses
keeps silent	both jailed for tax $\frac{1}{4}$ $\frac{1}{4}$	B let off: maximum jail for A 10 0
confesses	A let off: maximum jail for B 0 10	both jailed with reduced sentences 9 9

instead of as tabulated in Chapter Three (p. 46)—many would find the temptation to confess easily resistible. If import duties were 1 per cent, few travellers would bother to smuggle. Burdens are also less burdensome if they are adjustable. If a summons for jury service will brook no excuses, and prevents me taking my final examinations or taking my family on their annual holiday, I shall find it a far greater hardship than if I can arrange to discharge my duty at some other time. Taxes paid in money are more adjustable than taxes on one's time, and to that extent preferable. Indirect taxes are more adjustable still; barring very few taxes on absolute necessities, like the salt tax of old, they can be avoided altogether by the simple expedient of not consuming the dutiable commodity or not engaging in the chargeable activity. I have much more choice whether to pay duty on spirits than whether to pay a poll-tax: if I do not want to pay for a television licence, I need not have a television set. There are, as we shall see, other respects in which indirect taxes are more open to objection than direct taxes: but there is an element of voluntariness about them which goes far to non-suit potential protests, and avoid awkward questions being raised.

Not all taxes can be negligible. Few societies are so fortunately placed that they can function without exacting larger contributions than many would willingly give, and often, in time of war, men have been called upon to sacrifice liberty and life for the sake of their fellows. To the individual's question "Why is such a sacrifice demanded of me?" we return the collectivist answer "Only if you, along with everybody else, make that sacrifice can common good be obtained, or common disaster averted." Contributive justice tempers this answer by still giving the individual's question as much consideration as possible. We recognise that the sacrifice is real, and do not want it to be greater than necessary. And we recognise that each man is entitled to be assured that his sacrifice is necessary, and that he is not being called upon to bear a disproportionate burden by reason of others not bearing their share. It is not enough that the logic of the Prisoners' Dilemma calls for everyone to forgo some individual good: it is requisite also that the system be so structured that each man can perceive the logic of the situation and the rationale of the contribution required of him. We need to commend not simply the general strategy of our all forming a coalition, but the individual meta-strategies[6] of each one of us joining the

[6] See Ch. 3, pp. 51 ff.

coalition provided everyone else does. Once that point is made, the emphasis on togetherness becomes much sharper. It is not merely an appeal to merge the standpoint of the first person singular in that of the first person plural—though it is that—but also an indication to each of what he had best do, provided all the others do. The condition focusses attention on the others, considered from the outside; the concern of each is simply that they shall do their part, and he can see that from their point of view his doing his part is a condition of their joining in. Although we are together in contributing, we are apart in the view we take of one another. This accounts for that unconcern for the individual which characterizes contributive, like distributive, justice.[7] It is not I in my individuality that am involved, but I as a member of a community; and therefore factors peculiar to me as an individual are not relevant, but only those concerning me in my communal capacity. Within the categories characterized by those factors, everybody should equally contribute and equally pull his weight. It is only in virtue of everybody's being, according to the relevant principle, equally liable, that anyone can reasonably be held to be liable at all. The shirker is to be despised not only because by evading his share of the burden he increases everybody else's, but because his principle of action is one that cuts at the root of the communal enterprise altogether. It is in everyone's interest to be a fare-dodger, just as it is in each prisoner's interest to confess. It is only if we resolutely set our face against preferring our own individual interests to the common interest that we shall be able to achieve a state of affairs which is better, not only from a communal point of view, but even from the individual's. Hence the need to stress togetherness, and play down individuality. And so we have as a canon of contributive justice the strong principle of universalisability rather than the weak, the principle of equality rather than equity. And in this sense it is true that there is no equity in taxation.

Contributive justice requires that there should be some sort of equality in shouldering the burden, so that each man can be sure that others are doing their share. What sort of equality serves this purpose varies from case to case. Often it is a strict arithmetical equality, as in a voluntary society where everybody pays the same subscription. But a poll-tax is not necessarily the fairest tax. Even in a voluntary society there may be special rates for married couples or families, and in the State many other bases of apportionment are

[7] Ch. 9, pp. 177–8.

felt to be appropriate. What contributive justice requires is that the categories should not be individuated indefinitely finely, as the principle of equity allows, but should be, and should be seen to be, relatively crude and simple, so that each contributor, looking over his shoulder at other contributors can assure himself that they are indeed pulling their weight. From this it follows that a tax system needs to be simple, so that the ordinary citizen can more or less see what is being demanded of him and of others, and to conform to what Mr Taverne, using the word 'equity' in a different sense from that elucidated in Chapter Three, calls horizontal equity;[8] and that is that people within the same simple general categories should be assessed the same. There is great merit in simple broad-based taxes, like the sales tax in some American States; and so long as the rate is kept low, it can be defended as being not even a tax but merely a service charge by the State for the use of money. But when the rate is raised to increase the yield of revenue, the tax becomes regressive, bearing more heavily on the poor than the rich, and therefore, in default of other provision for the poor, objectionable. Often we meet this objection by taxing luxuries but not necessities. The difficulty is to draw the line. Is cake a necessity? or ginger beer? or real beer? A system with many different rates—like the old purchase tax—is complicated, full of anomalies and open to abuse. Even the former VAT, with three rates of 0 per cent, 8 per cent and $12\frac{1}{2}$ per cent imposed great administrative burdens on shopkeepers, though it could not be said to be inherently unfair. So far as justice is concerned, there may be differences in what different people are called upon to contribute, but there should not be very many differences, and such as there are should be generally acceptable, so that taxpayers can know that they are all in the same boat.

What differences are, or should be, generally acceptable is a difficult question. Once we abandon strict arithmetical equality in which everybody pays the the same, different arguments can be adduced, some based on principles of contributive justice, some on other principles of justice, some on other social purposes or values, for adopting different grounds of apportionment. Expected subsequent benefit is a ground for differentiating between contributors, itself based on contributive justice. If a common goal will benefit me more than you, it is only fair that I should contribute more than you to securing it. In time past property owners were required to

[8] D. Taverne, "How to Reform Tax", *Management Today*, August 1976, p. 54.

pay more than landless labourers, because they had a bigger stake in the country and stood to gain more from the maintenance of law and order and defence against foreign enemies; and greater burdens may be placed on the broad shoulders of the rich simply because they are better able to bear them. Other principles of justice may be applied, as when veterans who have served their country well are exempted from further demands. Or we may be guided by con- siderations of need, or temper strict contributive justice with mercy, as the Mosaic law did in its provision that "when a man is newly married he shall not be liable for military service or any other public duty. He shall remain at home exempt from service for one year and enjoy the wife he has taken."[9] So, too, the authorities have often forborne to call up the widow's only son. Often in voluntary associations we excuse old age pensioners from paying full contri- butions, and sometimes anyone who feels he cannot afford the subscription is allowed to join free. In the medieval world there was a considerable element of bargaining between government and people in levying taxes, and some modern taxes, too, especially licence fees and levies for government services, are raised on a basis of mutual agreement. Visitors and aliens are often taxed less or more heavily than citizens, and universities vary their charges according to status. Fiscal policy is often guided also by social considerations. Mortgage relief and the wife's earned income allow- ance are not particularly fair, but are intended to encourage home- ownership and sending wives out to work. Indirect taxes are of necessity guided largely by social considerations extraneous to those of pure contributive justice. We tax alcohol, tobacco and petrol, and not milk, potatoes and electricity, because we regard the former as unmeritorious luxuries, whose consumption may properly be discouraged, whereas we regard the latter as necessities in the modern world, which people ought not to be discouraged from consuming. Opinion on these matters can change. Tea was once taxed and is now regarded with fiscal favour. We may come to regard electricity as an extravagant form of fuel, and might even come to think milk-drinking bad for health, and tax them accord- ingly. But although the incidence of indirect taxation is guided by extraneous social considerations, issues of justice still arise. Those on whom the burden falls may complain, even though there is, as we have noted,[10] some element of voluntariness which should

---

[9] Deuteronomy 24:5.   [10] See above, pp. 238–9.

deflect most complaints of injustice. We can say to smokers, drinkers and drivers that they do not have to smoke, or drink, or drive, and if they choose to, knowing what the price level in Britain is, they have only themselves to blame; but we do not succeed in silencing them altogether. Smokers, drinkers and drivers do complain. Why are their activities picked upon for revenue-raising, and not singing, tea-drinking or rowing? It is a reasonable question, and the answers we normally give, that smoking ought to be discouraged for the sake of the individual's health, the drinking of alcohol for the sake of both the individual's and the community's well-being, and that driving uses up scarce resources, damages the environment and endangers other people—in short, that these are unmeritorious activities which deserve to be taxed—although cogent, are not conclusive. In the first place, there are arguments on the other side. Country dwellers can hardly avoid using cars, whereas for many town dwellers it is an easily dispensed with option, so that an adequate petrol tax would bear harder on one section of the community than another. In the second place, and more fundamentally, there is an objection on the score of contributive justice to any section of the community being landed with a disproportionate part of a communal burden. Suppose the tax on tobacco were enormously increased—by a factor of twenty, say—and that demand proved relatively inelastic, so that this single import raised enough to finance all public expenditure, and we were free of all other taxes. Desirable as this might seem to me, a non-smoker, I should nevertheless be impelled to protest on the part of smokers that they should not be saddled with the whole burden of taxation, which benefits us all and should be borne by us all. To land on any one section the whole load is to do them down. They can be asked to carry part of the burden, and it is in the nature of contributive justice that the apportionment should be somewhat crude and that there can be individualised reasons for calling for greater contributions from some than from others, but they are entitled to be assured that others should bear their share. Although we can select different sections of the community to bear different burdens, and can justify our selection on grounds extraneous to considerations of pure contributive justice, the selection and the imposition of burdens is still subject to criticism from the standpoint of justice. We consider the levy from the taxpayer's point of view, and ask what the rationale of the tax is, and whether it justifies this particular man being picked on to bear the burden imposed on him. The standard of justification required and the weight of burden that can be justified depend on the rationale of the tax. In so far as a tax is prohibitive, intended to discourage use rather than to yield revenue, it raises the same issues as are raised by other legislative enactments which impose a burden of law-observance on citizens. If we were to put a prohibitive tax on tea, it would be difficult to defend the impost. Why should not a person drink tea? Unless good reason can be given, it would be oppressive to seek to deny tea-drinkers solace. Where taxes are intended primarily to raise revenue, a less stringent standard of justification is required of the choice of what is to be taxed, but equally contributive justice sets a lesser limit to what is a proper level of taxation. Such taxes may be high, but not prohibitive. In so far as they are high, there should be proper consideration of those so situated that they are in danger of being done down by them. And even though taxes may fairly be substantial, and raise a substantial proportion of the total revenue raised, those who pay them should know that they are not being called upon to carry the whole load, and that other members of the community are in other ways contributing their share.

Direct taxes are those imposed on individuals rather than on commodities or activities. The purest case is a poll-tax. In the modern world income tax is the most important. Local rates and wealth tax are likewise counted as direct taxes, as also—though the case is not so clear—capital gains tax, death duties and capital transfer tax. Modern thinking about the bearing of justice on direct taxation is deeply confused. There is some recognition that contributive justice requires some sort of sameness in treatment, but once a poll-tax is rejected, it is assumed that the equality to be sought must be an equality of after-tax income, that the point of imposing taxes is not so much to raise revenue as to redistribute wealth, and that "vertical equity"[11] requires the rich to pay very much more than the poor. These assumptions seem more plausible if we take an entirely collectivist standpoint, and assume that the gross national product is entirely at the disposal of the civil authorities to distribute as they will. We often in this vein speak of the Chancellor of the Exchequer giving money, or handing out concessions, to the taxpayer. And if the money just happened, it is arguable that it should be distributed equally among all members of society equally. But the gross national product does not just happen. People have to

[11] D. Taverne, "How to Reform Tax", *Management Today*, August 1976, p. 54.

work, some of them quite hard, to produce it. And therefore it comes already structured, not an amorphous mass of goodies for the government to carve up and distribute as it pleases. In generating the national product we generate also claims on it, based on the principles of distributive justice. This is not to say that there are no other claims, either further ones of desert, or entirely different ones based on need, merit or status, that ought to be taken into consideration: we need not maintain, as some do, that the productive process is sacrosant, and that, with money, making is keeping. But we deny the simple assumption, on which much redistributive rhetoric is founded, that the national wealth is completely disposable as we, or the government, think fit. It is not. Money does not just accrue to the national exchequer but is taken from taxpayers who often are reluctant, and reasonably reluctant, to part with it. And if it is to be taken from them, it should be taken only in accordance with the principles of justice.

Even without adopting an entirely collectivist standpoint, politicians may be led to adopt egalitarian tax policies, either because they believe them to be required by contributive justice or because they accept equality as an ideal on extraneous grounds. Contributive justice does sanction greater burdens being placed on the rich than on the poor, partly because the rich are better able to bear them than the poor, partly because the rich stand to benefit more by the preservation of civil society than the poor. It is fair, in view of the diminishing marginal utility of money, to take more from a rich man than a poor man: £1 is worth less to him, and to exact contributions that were equal in monetary terms would be to impose sacrifices that were unequal as experienced by those called upon to make them. Again, if I have property, I should be willing to pay a premium to guard against losing it by foreign invasion or civil disorder, just as I pay to protect myself against loss by fire. Moreover, if I am rich, I am much better placed to enjoy all the facilities of civil society: Her Majesty's Consular service is available for all British subjects, but only those rich enough to travel in foreign parts actually avail themselves of it. For these reasons it is just to levy not the same tax on everyone, but one which increases with wealth, and not simply a tax proportional to wealth but one where the proportion increases with wealth. This much once conceded, it is easy to go to extremes. Once we admit the justice of progressive taxation, there will be a continual pressure to more and more progressive rates of tax, because at each moment on reflection it will seem fair that any further burden should be placed on the broad shoulders of the rich. So long as the marginal rate of tax does not reach 100 per cent, the rich will be better off after tax than will the poor. Even in Britain, a very rich man, paying until recently 98 per cent tax, was still left with 2 per cent; and 2 per cent of a lot of money was—to most of us—a lot of money still. And therefore it seemed only fair that next time more money was needed, the man enjoying that 2 per cent should be the first to be called upon to contribute. But that was to ignore the fact that he had already paid 98 per cent; and to ignore that fact is to show that we are not willing to look at things from his point of view at all, and not take into account the very great contributions already made. And that is to be unjust. Justice demands that we do not forget the past, and count for righteousness the contributions a man has already made. He is not likely to forget these. Nor should we, if we are concerned for him and anxious not to do him down.

From this it follows not only that the argument for ever more steeply progressive rates of taxation is invalid but that there is some counter-argument from justice against them. Enough is enough. In so far as our concern is to raise revenue fairly, there is a limit on how much we should dun any one man, no matter how rich he be. At some stage we should be prepared to say, "Thank you", and let him be. Where this stage comes, depends on many factors. All that we can say in general is that in determining further imposts we ought to have regard not merely to what people still have, but, equally importantly, to what they have already paid.

Other aspects of justice bear on the degree to which direct taxation may be progressive. The most obvious are distributive justice and the requirement that the authorities keep to their previous compacts and respect other men's freedom to dispose of their own wealth as they think fit. Even if we allow ourselves to think in terms of the gross national product and how it may be distributed, we have to acknowledge that some people have contributed more to its production than others; some have acquired legitimate expectations in virtue of agreements entered into and sacrifices made in time past. If the State pays no regard to these bases of distribution, it is being unjust. This is not to say that these are the only bases. The State may also have regard to need, or even generosity, in raising or spending revenue, but not so as to render the canons of distributive justice of negligible importance. It must be clearly honouring those whose efforts contribute to the common good, and must be clearly honouring existing commitments, or else it is making out that their efforts and choices mean nothing to it. It is, therefore, unjust to have, as some thinkers have suggested,[12] a non-Archimedean, or lexicographical, ordering as between needs on the one hand and deserts or entitlements on the other. Although some needs may be given priority over some deserts or entitlements, we cannot always give every need priority over every other claim without in effect discountenancing all other claims. If they are to be taken seriously, they must carry some significant weight even though there be some needs in the field. How much weight they should be given depends on circumstances, and cannot be laid down precisely. But a government which taxes the interest on government securities at a marginal rate of 98 per cent cannot be thought to be seriously honouring its commitments.[13]

Economic justice imposes its restraints. If we give people money, we give them the freedom to dispose of it as they please, for that, as we saw in Chapter Thirteen, is what money essentially is. And people's preferences cannot be guaranteed to be egalitarian. They may prefer pop-stars or footballers to civil servants or pensioners. If people choose to dispose of their money in such a way that inequality results, the State cannot set aside their choice, and ensure that the final outcome shall be equal none the less, without thereby denying the liberty of choice that money encapsulates. This is not to say that the State cannot impose any tax at all on monetary transfers. It can, and is entitled to. Money is a great convenience, provided by the State, and it is eminently fair that the State should tax its use. But it cannot tax it out of existence, nor ought it to try and render nugatory the combined individual choices of its citizens. Excessive rates of taxation lead to a barter economy, the development of "perks" invisible to the Inspector's eye, and ultimately to the breakdown of the economy: and the liberty of individuals ought to be respected, even if it leads to some people being rich. Excessive taxation is unfair, not only to those taxed, but to other members of

---

[12] e.g. A. M. Honoré, "Social Justice", *McGill Law Journal*, 1968, pp. 92–3; reprinted in R. S. Summers (ed.), *Essays in Legal Philosophy*, Oxford, 1968, p. 80.

[13] And it might be more. Mr Brian Sedgemore, MP for Luton West, seems to be looking forward to the time when "the principle of taxing unearned income at more than 100% can be established as a fair one". (*The Times*, 8 Aug. 1977, p. 19.)

society who have been given money, and thus, in effect, thwarted in spending it as they would like.

As we have already seen with regard to indirect taxation, contributive justice is itself offended if the contribution laid upon some is disproportionately heavier than what others are willing to assume. The sacrifices demanded are resented if they appear to be selective in their imposition, and if others are letting themselves off lightly. The logic of contributive justice is that everyone should contribute his share; and just as tax-avoidance seems in the eyes of most men much the same as tax-evasion, so tax legislation that imposes much greater burdens on some than on others loses its contributive air, and becomes a cause of dissension. Many modern taxes are felt to be penal or confiscatory because they appear to be levied as exercises in social engineering rather than in order to raise revenue. Death duties and capital transfer tax yield relatively little, and seem to be intended, rather, to weaken the effect of inheritance. Inherited wealth is felt to be wrong, and rather than confiscate it all at once, the State seeks to take it over piecemeal. It is difficult to see the rationale for hostility to inherited wealth. Once it is recognised that money carries with it the choice of how it is to be disposed, it follows that men will often dispose of it in accordance with the ties of family affection; and, since we believe that the family is a good thing, it is surprising that we do not follow the principle through. Many people will approve of the right of fathers to leave their money to their families, but feel uneasy about the right of sons to succeed to their fathers' wealth. "What have the sons done", they ask, "to deserve such wealth?" The answer is "Nothing". The recipients of other people's generosity do not deserve their good fortune, nor have any right to it, save as the correlative to their benefactors' liberty of choice. The injustice of confiscating, in whole or in large part, gifts or inheritances, is due not to the recipients being done out of their deserts but to its denying the donors their right to choose. Although a State *can* discriminate against some of its citizens, imposing a tax to mark its disapprobation, much as the Muslims did upon Christians and Jews, such a tax is an expression of prejudice rather than justice. It is a matter of great regret that the British system should contain discriminatory provisions. When the eighth Duke of Northumberland was killed at Dunkirk in 1940, his estate was liable for a higher rate of death duties simply because he was a commissioned officer. For other ranks there was an exemption—quite properly: if a man has given his life for King and Country, that is reason enough for not helping oneself to his property too. But for commissioned officers there was during the Second World War no remission. Such a discrimination can be defended only on the grounds that officers are undesirable creatures who ought, as a matter of public policy, to be suppressed. But once such a principle is acknowledged as informing public policy, the whole aspect of taxation is altered. It loses its justification under the head of contributive justice, and appears with a retributive aspect, inviting the question "What have these people done to deserve such treatment?" Although a legislature can enact a law imposing a levy on Jews or officers or people whose surnames begin with M, it will be seen no longer as a contribution, subject only to the rough and ready standard of contributive justice, but as a fine or forfeiture, requiring justification to a more exacting standard; and inviting, in default of an adequate justification, the classic responses of avoidance and evasion.

Exact limits on progressiveness cannot be laid down. Too much depends on circumstances—in a war for survival everything would be at the disposal of the State. But we need to lay down general rules, even though they cannot be hard and fast ones, or we are too vague to be helpful. Hayek's suggestion is a good one—that the maximum admissible (marginal) rate of direct taxation should be that percentage of the total national income which the government takes in taxation.[14] Such a principle is flexible, and conforms with the first canon of contributive justice. If a State adopts collectivist policies, as public expenditure increases so will the permissible top rate of tax: and the majority cannot impose taxes on any minority out of proportion with what they, by indirect as well as direct, taxation are prepared to impose on themselves.

Many tax systems have been worse than the British system. Tax officials have often been corrupt and cruel. Those in Britain are for the most part courteous, honest and competent, and often lean over backwards not to exact more than the minimum that is legally due. But their discretion is dangerously large, their procedures secretive and dilatory, their reasoning obscure, arbitrary and often inconsistent, treating quite differently cases apparently alike without any attempt to justify the difference. Punitive to the taxpayers' mistakes, they treat their own with extreme indulgence, requiring the tax-

[14] F. A. Hayek, *The Constitution of Liberty*, Ch. 20, §8, p. 323.

payer to make good to the Revenue errors of assessment of six years' standing. Half the cases of maladministration referred to the Parliamentary Commissioner concern the Inland Revenue, and many of them make scarifying reading when translated into human terms of worry, deprivation and misery. We need to bring the administration of the tax system under the rule of law in much the same way and for the same reasons as the administration of law and order, and especially to insist on the procedural virtues of openness, timeliness and definitiveness. We need also to rethink the actual taxes levied. Income tax and VAT are immensely complicated. It is partly because they are a hotchpotch. Finance bills are introduced annually and amended piecemeal, and finally passed by a tired and sleepy House of Commons which has neither the time nor the energy nor the expertise to think coherently about what it is doing. It is largely also because the marginal rates have been set too high. Because the tax burden is very heavy, people seek to lighten it, by having exemptions legislated into the Finance Bill: and it is difficult to resist such pleas, which often seem more than justified by the circumstances. But the more closely we attempt to tailor the burden to individual circumstances, the more complicated it becomes, and the more irksome to those whose shoulders do not quite fit. Contributive justice is rough justice. It cannot, for the reasons given earlier, fit the individual case exactly or be entirely governed by equity. Provided the burden is not too great, rough justice can be justified, and people will be prepared to pay up with a good grace. But once the burden is felt to be intolerable, or the tax perceived as being penal rather than contributive, the pressure for adjustment according to the principles of equity will build up: and each adjustment will create further anomalies, each exemption or concession further borderline disputes, with the result that the whole system becomes enormously complicated and highly inequitable. Not only does it lack "horizontal equity" in Taverne's terminology, it lacks "vertical equity" too in that it lays greater burdens on the poor, who are a minority of the voters, than on the not-so-poor, who constitute a majority.[15] Even from an egalitarian standpoint it is a failure. It redistributes not so much from the rich to the poor, as from the poor to the not-so-poor, from the politically weak to the politically strong, and from the stupid to those who read *Which?*. Because it is very complicated, it invites tax-avoidance, and because

[15] F. A. Hayek, ibid., Ch. 20, §4, pp. 312–13, 518.

it is heavy, and often avowedly penal or confiscatory in intent, it has generated—one of the most regrettable features of the modern social scene—a climate of opinion in which evasion flourishes. And once this begins to be the case, the injustice is multiplied: for then the skilful and the unscrupulous avoid or evade their taxes, and only the naïve and the honest get clobbered. And even egalitarians find this consequence of their policies hard to stomach.[16]

If we are to remedy matters, we need to reform the system of taxation. We need to distinguish the basic legal structure from year-to-year variations, and entrench in the permanent law the procedural requirements of natural justice and certain substantive limitations on the actual amounts that can be raised, while leaving different Chancellors to respond to different circumstances in the light of their differing political commitments. We should forswear oppresive taxes. We should think of what the taxpayer has paid, not of what he has not, and be grateful for contributions received rather than repine at what he has still got left. We should prefer taxes that are simple and broadly based to those that are complicated and fall heavily on small sections of the public. Where it is necessary to differentiate between one class of taxpayer and another, the difference should be based on distinctions that are clear and indisputable, and where lines have to be drawn, there should be marginal adjustment between the treatment accorded to those who fall on the one side or the other, so that not too much depends on which side a particular case actually falls. These general principles leave a lot of latitude in actually making fiscal decisions. We should not seek to tie down the government too much: but can reasonably set some limits, in order to prevent the great fiscal powers vested in the State from being abused, and to prevent anybody being unreasonably done down by them.

Fiscal justice differs from other species of justice, but is justice none the less, because important rights and interests of the individual are in issue. Taxes ought to be different from penalties; they can be seen as burdens to be apportioned, but better as contributions each man is called upon to make. Contributive justice has its own logic, and in particular requires the strong, rather than the weak, principle of universalisability, and to that extent there is, as we have seen, no equity in taxation. Nevertheless, there are important canons of distributive justice and economic justice as well as of

[16] D. Taverne, "How to Reform Tax", *Management Today*, August 1976, p. 54.

contributive justice for determining whether a system of taxation is fair, and also principles of natural justice which should govern the actual procedures employed. These need to be respected, or taxation will not be felt to be fair, and the system will lose public support, and will break down; as it is showing signs of doing in Britain now, and will surely do, unless we undertake radical reforms to bring our fiscal policies in line with fiscal justice.

15

JUSTICE BETWEEN STATES

International relations lie outside the scope of this book. The nation-state is a recent concept, and a confused one. Some thinkers in the Anglo-Saxon tradition deny its validity as a moral entity, and conclude that the relations between States should be governed by power politics and nothing else. Thinkers following after Hegel accord supreme moral status to the nation-state, and conclude that no nation should be shackled by the fetters of some seeming international morality. Other people take it for granted that States are strictly analogous to individuals, so that exactly the same rules govern the conduct of States in their dealings with one another as hold between individuals. Others again appeal to some higher entity, the brotherhood of man or the General Assembly of the United Nations, in whose breast alone true justice resides, and which alone should by rights be accorded sovereign sway.

These contentions lack cogency. The sceptical argument of the international amoralist is in the same case as that of the ordinary amoralist.[1] Nobody doubts that men can turn a deaf ear to the reasonings of morality: but there is no more reason why a statesman acting on behalf of many men should than there is for an individual to. True, the statesman has a duty to look after the interests of his people, and would be failing in his duty if he sacrificed those interests on the altar of some quixotic ideal. But the whole argument of this book is that justice should not be construed as some simple unconcern with one's own interests, but as a lively recognition of the validity of other men's interests alongside one's own; and in much the same way as the just father, without always putting his children last, will on certain occasions acknowledge his neighbours' rights to privacy as overriding his own children's interest in throwing stones, so the statesman should on occasion forbear to press the national interest to the uttermost out of respect for the rights of others. Even if we had metaphysical doubts about the ontological status of the nation-state, we should still condemn

[1] See further below, Ch. 16, pp. 259–61.

as unjust an authority which executed innocent aliens without just cause or any trial. We have duties of just dealing not only to fellow citizens but to fellow human beings. And if we condemn piracy and the slave trade as unjust, there can be no conceptual incongruity in condemning also as unjust acts of State which do down not merely particular individual persons but whole peoples together.

Nor should mystical notions of the State lead us to suppose that every action undertaken in order to further the national interest is therefore right. It is all too possible for the State to act unjustly towards its own citizens. If it is to observe the canons of justice, it must on occasion within its own borders abridge the public interest for the sake of the private interest of some particular individual. And the public interest is no more sacrosanct outside its borders than inside. It always is important, and often legitimately overrides private interests; and there may well be fewer private interests outside its borders which should weigh heavily with it than there are among its own citizens. But once we see that the public interest is not all-important, we have to acknowledge that there could be occasions in international as well as national affairs where it ought to be abridged, and it would be unjust if it were not.

It does not follow that international relations are strictly analogous to relations between individuals. National interests are different from individual interests, and public decisions are taken in ways often far removed from the ways private decisions are made. Many of the problems of international affairs have no analogue in individual life. Although claims to territory are—often misleadingly—construed as being like individual claims to landed property, the more fundamental question of what constitutes a nation has no parallel at all. In the American Civil War the claim of the Confederate States to secede from the Union was based on a doctrine of State rights, and contested on the grounds of the inviolability of treaties and the manifest destiny of the American people. When Biafra sought to secede from Nigeria, the arguments were murkier still. Since any system of domestic law carries with it the possibility of coercing recalcitrant individuals, every nation-state that is established or maintained is pregnant with the potentiality of injustice. Roman Catholics in Ulster are done down by the maintenance of the Union, since that precludes their being able to fulfil their national aspirations of being citizens of an Irish Republic, or being able even to have a decisive say in the political decision-making of Ulster: but if in the name of national unity Ulster were incorporated in Eire, the majority of Ulstermen would be done down by being deprived of their links with the British Crown, and by being reduced to an ineffective minority in a Roman Catholic Republic. Again and again territorial units fail to correspond to ethnic, cultural, linguistic, religious and emotional groupings. Sometimes within a territory there arises over the course of years a national sentiment which transcends some religious, linguistic or cultural difference, as has happened in Holland, Switzerland and, to a lesser extent, Belgium: but unless and until this has happened, the claim of any regime to exercise coercive power within its borders may be disputed, and may be upheld only at the cost of consider-able injustice. Although sometimes an analogy with individuals may guide us in discerning the outlines of justice between States, we must always be ready to look behind the façade of the nation-state, and determine the real balance of right and wrong that underlies its claims.

There has been much talk in recent years about distributive justice between nations, and the claim of the Third World for a fairer share of the earth's resources. Such talk should be treated with caution. Distributive justice is much more difficult to establish than some other forms of justice. That treaties should be kept, that territorial integrity should not be violated, and that war should not be an instrument of policy, can be grounded in a fairly basic understanding of the role of the State and the nature of in-ternational law: but before questions of distribution arise, there has to be an association which produces the goods to be distributed, whose values justify some suitable basis for distribution. No such association exists. The United Nations Organization produces very few distributable goods, and although it is intelligible to talk of the comity of nations in some more general sense, the values actually held in common are too few and too fragile to support any edifice of distributive justice. Although some distributive issues will have to be faced—the exploitation of Antarctica and the ocean beds—there is a danger of weakening the all-too-weak fabric of international justice if every claim one country may advance to assets located within the territory of another can be put forward under the aegis of distributive justice. Egypt may well envy Libya's oil, and reckon that arbitrary lines drawn across the Sahara desert should be realigned to give a more equitable disposition of mineral wealth: but if every envious wish can be represented as a claim of justice, justice will soon be emptied of serious content, and the claim of a country suffering aggression from a powerful neighbour will fall on ears deafened by the specious rhetoric of the greedy who covet other men's wealth or—more to the point in modern Britain—the idle who believe passionately that the world owes them a living.

We need, therefore, to be cautious but not sceptical about international justice. We need to think clearly before speaking grandiloquently. We need to be clear to what extent there is a national interest apart from the individual interests of particular people. Often the national interest is interpreted as requiring actions that appear to bring little benefit and impose considerable costs on most of the inhabitants of the territories concerned. Although there are undoubtedly arguments, usually of humanity rather than justice, for aiding the poorer peoples of the world, the actual policies pursued by the national authorities in, say, India, Pakistan or Uganda seem to be so much at variance with the interests of their peoples that any aid ought to be channelled away from the national authorities altogether. Justice does not require that rich nations provide poor nations with the wherewithal to buy arms or to subsidise national airlines which only a small minority of their peoples could ever afford to use.

But caution is not scepticism. We should not eschew the language of justice altogether. Great wrongs can be, and have been, done by one nation to another, and we should not hesitate to brand injustice as such. Although the concept of the nation-state is not well understood, it is sufficiently familiar for us to be able to discern the lineaments of what justice requires in international relations. Our perceptions have been sharpened in the agony of total war and under the shadow of nuclear holocaust. With a deepening understanding of the nature and limitations of the nation-state, we should not despair of international justice. But much more work and hard thinking is required before we shall even begin to understand it.[2]

---

[2] For a fuller, and rather different, account see Morris Ginsberg, *On Justice in Society*, London, 1965, Ch. XI, "Justice among States".

16

JUSTICE AND MORALITY

Our discussion of rationality in Chapter Three was left hanging in the air. We saw that it was reasonable to consider past facts as well as future possibilities, and the interest of others besides oneself, and that it was unreasonable to define rationality solely in terms of expediency and one's own self-interest. But these points, though valid, do not get us all the way. We still have to face the sceptic's question, originally posed by Glaucon and Adeimantus in the second book of Plato's *Republic*, "Why should I be just?", together with the further, subtler ones, of what the ways are in which justice and morality differ.

G. del Vecchio grounds the concept of justice in our consciousness of *alteritas*. He says:

For our task this principle above all must be firmly held: that there is a specific form of consciousness which we may call *trans*-subjective consciousness, through which the subject posits himself as an object in relation to others and recognizes himself as an element in a net of interrelations between selves; that there is, in short, an *objective consciousness of self, whereby the subjective self becomes co-ordinated with other selves.*[1]

We find his Idealist terminology difficult. We are more familiar with Strawson's formulation of the incoherence of solipsism, or some linguistic thesis that the first person singular would not be intelligible unless the second and third persons were intelligible too. We need not enter into such arguments in detail. They belong to a different branch of philosophy. Although philosophers may properly question whether other minds exist, and try to determine the logical status of our presupposition that they do, we must, before we can embark on moral or political philosophy, assume that other people do exist and that everyone knows it. Del Vecchio goes on to

---

[1] Giorgio del Vecchio, *Justice*, ed. A. H. Campbell, tr. Lady Guthrie, Edinburgh, 1952, Ch. VII, "Justice as a Necessary and Fundamental Attitude of Consciousness". The Idea of *Alteritas* (Consideration of the *Other* as a subject), p. 80.

argue that the awareness of others gives rise to an obligation on one's own part. He says:

This mode of consciousness corresponds to our deepest nature, to a true and necessary *vocation* of our being; it has not only a theoretical value as a form of the intellect but also a practical value, since it expresses an absolute requirement which lies at the base of one of the essential aspects of Ethics. Psychologically, it proclaims itself not only as an *idea* but as an imperious and irrepressible *sentiment,* but the idea and the sentiment both have the same root and they may with equal propriety be termed the idea and the sentiment "of justice", for justice is the true and proper name of that fundamental mode of consciousness which we have been describing.[2]

Ginsberg, although sympathetic to del Vecchio's conclusions, is critical of his argument and thinks "that his metaphysical deduction of justice from the concept of self-consciousness is delusive".[3] His difficulties are the traditional sceptical ones about deriving an 'ought' from an 'is'. "From the proposition that self-consciousness depends upon or implies intersubjective intercourse, nothing whatever follows as to the moral quality of such intercourse. The cognition of others does not necessarily imply respect for them as persons." He clinches his argument by pointing out that individuals can enter into relations with each other in societies full of inequalities, and says "We are aware of others when we hate, fear, or are suspicious of them, just as much as when we love them, sympathize with them or respect them." But del Vecchio would hardly deny this. He does not deny the facts of injustice, nor is he trying to *deduce* moral imperatives from epistemological facts (in the logicians' sense of 'deduce', viz. that a deductive argument is one where to affirm the premiss and deny the conclusion is self-contradictory). I do not contradict myself, I do not break any rule of language, or make myself unintelligible by some strange use of words, if I acknowledge that somebody exists and yet maintain that I ought to hate him. But although the locution is intelligible, the reasoning is obscure. I do not see why someone's existing is a reason for hating him, whereas to cite someone's existence as a human being is an immediately intelligible reason for treating him with forbearance and respect. The argument for hate needs amplification if it is to be accepted as even barely intelligible. Amplification

[2] pp. 80–1.
[3] Morris Ginsberg, "The Concept of Justice", *Philosophy*, XXXVIII, 1963, p. 100; reprinted in Morris Ginsberg, *On Justice in Society*, London, 1965, p. 51.

might, conceivably be forthcoming. Perhaps a Nietzschean could explain why the fact that other men existed was an adequate reason for hating them. We cannot rule out the possibility *a priori*. But the presumption of argument is very much against the Nietzschean. The burden of proof is on those who do *not* acknowledge the fact of another man's existence as a reason for treating him well. The recognition that the other chap is a chap like oneself is normally taken as a reason for treating him with consideration. Del Vecchio's elucidation of the reasoning may not entirely satisfy us: but Ginsberg's criticisms fail to fault it, because they assume that it must be a deductive argument and that it sets out to do what no moral argument could ever hope to achieve.

Plato offers three arguments in the *Republic*. He suggests, first, that justice is integrity, and that the unjust man will suffer disintegration of his personality. The dissolute life is bad for one's psychological health, and therefore contrary to one's own best interests. The peace and harmony enjoyed by the well-integrated man are the intrinsic concomitants of justice and show how blessed are those who lead an uncorrupt life. Plato follows this argument with an appeal to our *esprit de corps*. His readers are invited to identify with the Guardians to such an extent that they no longer have any use for words like 'I', 'me', 'mine', 'you', or 'yours'. The alternatives appear as unbridled self-aggrandisement on the one hard and absolute selflessness on the other, and faced with such alternatives we naturally feel impelled to choose self-abnegation, although with some qualms. Plato reinforces this feeling with his third argument where he attributes the decline of the constitution, both social and psychological, to the reassertion of self, culminating in the tyrant or autocrat, who is so much obsessed with himself that he imposes on himself the loneliness of emotional isolation from everybody else, so much so that he makes himself autistic. The life of the tyrant, however much surrounded by riches, is essentially solitary, and therefore poor, in addition to being nasty, brutish, and at least in his fears, as well as often in fact, short.

Of these three arguments the second need detain us no further. It is totally collectivist, and establishes not a principle of justice but the principle of utility or some other collectivist good. The first and the third say something to our purpose, although it is difficult to determine exactly what. The first is something like del Vecchio's, but clearly is arguing not only that we should be aware of other people, but that, if only for the sake of our peace of mind, we should seek to do them good. If I am to be a well-integrated personality, the different facets of my personality—the various motives, inclinations and principles of action on which I base my conduct—must be organized to form a coherent whole. Much of this has no bearing on my conduct towards other people, but some has. If I am unfair, I cannot but know that I am, and therefore cannot stand well in my own eyes. And I am concerned to stand well. If I am aware of other people, I cannot but be aware that other people are aware of me, and I shall find it difficult to disregard altogether their opinion of me. I value the good opinion of others, and I am concerned about the image I present to the world. Glaucon acknowledged this, and in his comparison of the just and unjust lives was careful to take away from the just man his reputation for justice and give it to the unjust man.[4] This is possible, as every public relations man knows. But it is not possible to fool all the people all the time. Not only will the victim of injustice know that he has been done down, but the perpetrator too will know, and will be unable to believe in his own image. There will be an inevitable dissonance between the line he shoots to the world and the truth he hears in his own heart, and this will destroy the harmony of his soul. He will not be able to see himself as others see him, and cannot but see through the face he presents to the world, and recognise that it is only a hypocritical mask, concealing an ugly visage underneath. The man who is scrupulously just in all his dealings, not only has no fear that the truth will out, but has no problem with the truth within. He has no lie in his soul, and so can live with himself happily and whole-heartedly.

This reconstruction of Plato's argument is still psychological, and could be attacked on psychological grounds. A man's image of himself may be less important than is here made out, and his resources of self-deception greater. Some people seem unworried by their many misdeeds and appear not to care what other people think of them. Still, they seem to be deviations from the norm. Most people's psychological well-being depends on their own self-esteem, and is connected with what they can accept as the well-grounded estimation of others; and the connection itself is based on each agent's necessary knowledge of his own actions.

Plato's third argument is based not on a man's knowledge of

----

[4] *Republic* II, 361.

himself, but his knowledge of others. The tyrant is a moral solipsist, and therefore an emotional one. He will brook no gainsaying of his will, and therefore surrounds himself, both in fact and in his own perceptions, with yes-men, who for that very reason are not really men at all. To be a man is to have a mind of one's own, and to have a mind of one's own is to be able to make it up differently from what other people had predicted or would like. If I know that I will not accept No for an answer from anybody around me, then I know that there is nobody around me with a mind of his own, that is nobody at all. I may have slaves and concubines to do my bidding and gratify my passions, but I cannot have any social intercourse or moral or intellectual companionship, because I cannot regard them as people since I know I am not prepared to treat them as such. If I am not to live in the self-imposed isolation of a solipsistic world, I must acknowledge the existence of others by acknowledging their autonomy, and recognising that each of them has his own view of things, and that view should have some validity for me. That is, I must give some weight to the principle of justice.

These arguments for justice establish only a limited identification between myself and others. I *read* their opinions into my own view of myself, and my views into their appreciation of the consequences of my actions. I recognise them as persons, but only somewhat impersonally. One might start by saying that I considered them as third persons rather than addressed them as second persons; but clearly this is an exaggeration, because often we do have face-to-face negotiations, and so it is better to use the distinction in Chapter One,[5] and say that it is not so much an I–thou relation as an I–you one. For the arguments of justice are essentially coercive arguments, not merely persuasive ones. They are arguments I can press on you, whoever you are, and on anyone; and if you fail to be convinced, they are compelling none the less, and can be insisted on, against your better judgement, and even against you wishes. They are very different from the first-personal arguments I may find persuasive and seek to share with somebody else in an I–thou relationship. In such a relationship there may be many persuasions, but can be no insistence. The mere fact that you are not convinced vitiates my argument, and makes me desist from pressing my point. It would violate the relationship if I were to go on and seek to force your compliance by appeal to other motives, or even by invoking the

[5] pp. 14–16.

coercive power of the State. It is conceptually inappropriate to attempt to enforce first-personal persuasions, whereas it is always appropriate conceptually and sometimes legitimate morally to enforce the deliverances of justice. But since I am entitled to be insensitive to your lack of conviction, when questions of justice are in issue, I am somewhat at a distance from you, and the relationship is not the intimate I–thou one, but only an I–you one. And, conversely, the obligations of justice, demand a less than total identification between the parties. In order to act justly by you, I do not need to marry you, or take all your interests to heart. Indeed, it would be presumption on my part, and an invasion of your privacy, were I even to attempt to do so without your leave or special invitation. I need to keep my distance and leave you free to make up your mind for yourself, unless you want it otherwise. Often, of course, you do. Often people like to talk about their affairs with others, and seek their advice. But although people want their interests to be considered by others, they do not welcome their advice unasked. "Mind your own business", although inadequate as a definition of justice, is still an important corrective to over-much solicitude for others. There is, as we have seen, thus a conceptual link between justice and liberty, inasmuch as it is part of the requirement of justice that everyone should be able to do his own thing.

The distance that should separate the parties depends on the circumstances. Traditionally, the law has laid down spheres of freedom within which each person has absolute discretion. That is far too crude. The degree of mutual identification required in negotiating the sale of a car is much less than in a partnership or a family. All we need to say for the present purpose is that justice requires only some but not complete identification between the various parties, and that therefore justice is set in a somewhat low moral key. It is sometimes slightly grudging. "To do him justice", I say, "I must admit that he is not out to gain advantage for himself—his spite is entirely disinterested"; or "To be fair to him, he did give notice that he would raise the question at the Annual General Meeting; but it was a crazy thing to do." It is an 'even though' concept in which a rational reluctance to do down has to override an emotional reluctance to do well by the man in question. Moreover, there are many moral ideals which are not demands of justice, and there may be morally relevant features of the case which ought not, in justice, to be taken into account. Justice has often been criticized for this. It lacks the warmth of complete identification, the authenticity of first-personal reasoning, and the integrity of total devotion, and cannot address a whole message to me immediately in the intimacy of my soul. I can be just, and yet lack many moral virtues. I may be fair-minded and yet lack love. Justice by itself is not enough. It does not make a man happy or fulfilled, and is no guarantee of salvation in this world or the next. There is no justification by justice alone. Nevertheless, it is not to be despised. It may not be everything, but it is something. It is a virtue, an important virtue, one of the cardinal virtues; for it is the bond of peace, which enables the individual to identify with society, and brethren to dwell together in unity.

INDEX

Main entries are given in bold type